For Terry,
I wish this w...
as good a book as
you are a friend and
fellow gym rat.

Best Wishes,

William James Nichols

LUDWIG WITTGENSTEIN
– A CULTURAL POINT OF VIEW

In the preface to his *Philosophical Investigations* Ludwig Wittgenstein expresses pessimism about the culture of his time and doubts as to whether his ideas would be understood in such a time: "I make them public with doubtful feelings. It is not impossible that it should fall to the lot of this work, in its poverty and in the darkness of this time, to bring light into one brain or another – but, of course, it is not likely."

In this book William James DeAngelis develops a deeper understanding of Wittgenstein's remark and argues that it is an expression of a significant cultural component in Wittgenstein's later thought which, while latent, is very much intended. DeAngelis focuses on the fascinating connection between Wittgenstein and Oswald Spengler and in particular the acknowledged influence of Spengler's *Decline of the West*. His book shows in meticulous detail how Spengler's dark conception of an ongoing cultural decline resonated deeply for Wittgenstein and influenced his later work. In so doing, the work takes into account discussions of these matters by major commentators such as Malcolm, Von Wright, Cavell, Winch, and Clack among others. A noteworthy feature of this book is its attempt to link Wittgenstein's cultural concerns with his views on religion and religious language. DeAngelis offers a fresh and original interpretation of the latter.

ASHGATE WITTGENSTEINIAN STUDIES

Series editor: Mario von der Ruhr, University of Wales, Swansea, UK

Ludwig Wittgenstein was one of the greatest philosophers of the twentieth century, his work leading to a variety of differing readings which in turn have had a diverse influence on contemporary philosophy. As well as exploring the more familiar Wittgensteinian themes in the philosophy of language, this series will be a centre of excellence for Wittgensteinian studies in mathematics, aesthetics, religion and philosophy of the mind. Wittgenstein's philosophy has proved extremely fruitful in many contexts and this series will publish not only a variety of readings of Wittgenstein's work, but also work on philosophers and philosophical topics inspired by Wittgensteinian perspectives.

Ludwig Wittgenstein
– A Cultural Point of View

Philosophy in the Darkness of this Time

WILLIAM JAMES DeANGELIS
Northeastern University, Boston, USA

ASHGATE

Published by
Ashgate Publishing Limited
Gower House
Croft Road
Aldershot
Hampshire GU11 3HR
England

Ashgate Publishing Company
Suite 420
101 Cherry Street
Burlington, VT 05401-4405
USA

Ashgate website: http://www.ashgate.com

British Library Cataloguing in Publication Data
DeAngelis, William James
    Ludwig Wittgenstein - a cultural point of view : philosophy
    in the darkness of this time. - (Ashgate Wittgensteinian
    studies)
    1. Wittgenstein, Ludwig, 1889-1951 2. Spengler, Oswald,
    1880-1936 - Influence 3. Regression (Civilization)
    I. Title
    192

Library of Congress Cataloging-in-Publication Data
DeAngelis, William James, 1943-
    Ludwig Wittgenstein-- a cultural point of view : philosophy in the darkness of this time
/ William James DeAngelis.
        p. cm. -- (Ashgate Wittgensteinian studies)
    Includes bibliographical references and index.
    ISBN-13: 978-0-7546-6000-2 (hardcover : alk. paper) 1. Wittgenstein, Ludwig, 1889-
1951. I. Title.

    B3376.W564D435 2007
    192--dc22

ISBN-13: 978-0-7546-6000-2

2006026854

Printed and bound in Great Britain by TJ International Ltd, Padstow, Cornwall.

Dedicated to the memory of Norman Malcolm,
inspirational teacher and philosophical role model

Contents

Preface

It is both my hope and belief that this book constitutes a modest breakthrough. It contains the fullest treatment of its daunting subject to date. It is, I think, correct in most of its conclusions, if not in every detail of their elaboration. At the least, I believe it can be said to be a book that points its reader in the right direction regarding the interconnected subjects of Wittgenstein's cultural concerns, Spengler's influence on Wittgenstein's view of culture and philosophy, and the manner in which Wittgenstein's lifelong qualms about the expressibility of religion emerge in his later philosophy.

I began the work that has led to the completion of this book more than a decade ago. The first tangible result of that work was the publication in *Dialogue* of "Wittgenstein and Spengler" in 1994.[1] That article presented some of the ideas that receive much fuller articulation and, more important, far more careful support in the earlier chapters of this book. The hard thinking that went into the extended critical discussion of Norman Malcolm's last philosophical work, *Wittgenstein – A Religious Point of View?*, published in the same journal three years later, helped clarify for me some of the connections between Wittgenstein's cultural and religious concerns.[2] Perhaps equally important, the very fact that a philosopher of Malcolm's stature and seriousness of purpose was motivated enough by the possibility of an unstated point of view in Wittgenstein's later philosophical work to devote an entire book to the subject encouraged me to pursue a book-length project of my own. Ideas expressed in my original discussion of his book are more fully and carefully expressed and defended in this book – in part owing to further thoughts inspired by discussions and criticisms, both published and unpublished, of my original work by others. In this connection, I should offer thanks to the editor of *Dialogue* for allowing me to use some of the material from those writings – albeit reworked and, I hope, much improved – in this book.

I have received a great deal of help in the slow process that has resulted in the completion of this book. My Northeastern University colleagues, Steve Nathanson, Mike Meyer and Ronald Sandler read early drafts of its chapters, asked good questions and made helpful criticisms. Equally important, they have offered encouragement whenever my spirits or resolve have flagged. The same can be said for my friend, and one of the most acute and profound of Wittgenstein's interpreters, John V. Canfield of the University of Toronto. Jack and I have spent countless hours discussing and corresponding in our attempts to improve our understanding of this

---

1   William James DeAngelis, "Wittgenstein and Spengler", *Dialogue*, vol. xxxiii, 1994.

2   William James DeAngelis, "Ludwig Wittgenstein – A Religious Point of View?: Thoughts On Norman Malcolm's Last Philosophical Project", *Dialogue*, vol. xxxvi, 1997.

or that aspect of Wittgenstein's thought. We regularly read and comment on one another's works-in-progress, and Jack has read carefully and commented helpfully on at least one draft of every chapter of this book. He has taught me more about Wittgenstein than anyone. More important, he is a steadfast friend. Mikael Karlsson, a former Northeastern colleague who now does his philosophizing at the University of Iceland, has remained a good friend. An ocean lies between us, but has not come between us in any important way. Mike is an excellent philosophical critic. He has commented helpfully on much of what I have previously written about the subjects taken up in this book and on earlier drafts of some of its chapters. Finally, I must acknowledge the interest and encouragement offered by Stanley Cavell during a stimulating conversation about some of the ideas I express in this book. His seminal work dealing with the very difficult task of finding, in his words, a "Spenglerian valence" in Wittgenstein's later work has been both helpful and even inspirational to me. One of my aims in this book is to explain, defend and expand upon the views he expresses there. Some of my own ideas were stimulated by the substance and approach of Cavell's work.

Northeastern University, my long-time academic home, has provided me, over the last few years, an increasingly hospitable environment in which to pursue my philosophical interests and work. More specifically, and very important, it has made possible the completion of this project by providing me with a sabbatical leave for the fall 2004 semester. For all of this I am grateful.

My wife, Susan, and my children, Gabriel and Abby, have made their own unique contributions. Their shining presence from the very beginning has anchored me personally and afforded me distractions when needed. Without them in my life, I suspect this book may well have been completed sooner – although I doubt it would have been any better. Wittgenstein has emphasized that philosophy's progress is necessarily slow, that philosophers should take their time. On the other hand, he sought an unencumbered life that would not distract him from his philosophical tasks. I can say at least that my commitments to my family and to other concerns, my many encumbrances, have resulted in my not publishing too soon.

One of those concerns led me to take on the Academic Directorship of the W. E. B. DuBois Program in the Humanities, a worthy experiment in adult education for deserving people in Boston who would not otherwise have experienced college-level instruction in the humanities. Committed to the goals of this program, I helped steer it through its initiation during the 2002–2003 academic year. I greatly underestimated the requirements on my time of directing such a program and, in consequence, nearly all work on this book ceased during that period and the months preceding it. Still, I do not regret having taken on that task. Indeed, the people I met while directing the DuBois Program – especially the many bright, energetic, determined, and personally delightful students who willingly endured hardships and complications in order to take advantage of a useful educational opportunity – renewed me both personally and as a philosopher. They helped teach me something about commitment to a task.

I have dedicated this book to my late teacher and philosophical role model, Norman Malcolm. He was, without either of us realizing it at the time, my most influential teacher during my graduate education at Cornell University. His influence endures. He has taught me more about philosophical determination and honesty than anyone. His relentless pursuit of truth, his determination to give the best and clearest possible expression to his good ideas, and his admirable willingness to abandon the others stands for me as an ideal.

Introduction

Wittgenstein and "The Darkness of this Time"

Readers of Wittgenstein are familiar with a remark from the preface to the *Philosophical Investigations* which expresses a remarkable attitude toward the publication of his ideas:

> I make them public with doubtful feelings. It is not impossible that it should fall to the lot of this work, in its poverty and in the darkness of this time, to bring light into one brain or another – but, of course, it is not likely.[1]

What is one to make of such an assertion? It explicitly expresses the author's doubts that his work will be understood and, significantly, cites "the darkness of this time" as one of the impediments to understanding. This is an extraordinary and puzzling remark. One might be inclined to read it as an expression of a passing mood or, perhaps, of a more general and enduring pessimistic predisposition. In fact, I will argue, it is much more. In a sense, my book is an attempt to come to a deeper understanding of Wittgenstein's remark. It seeks to establish that Wittgenstein, in writing these words, was giving partial expression to a viewpoint on the civilization of his time that had occupied his thoughts for decades – a viewpoint that Wittgenstein, for the most part, decided on principle to keep to himself. Still, clear and compelling evidence of its existence and nature and can be gleaned from a careful, attentive investigation of the more esoteric expressions of his thought.

As it turns out, the book I have written is only occasionally concerned with the directly expressed content of Wittgenstein's later philosophy. Instead, it seeks to make sense out of a number of indications Wittgenstein gave, starting in the 1930s and continuing unabated until his death, about some of his unstated philosophical purposes – what he sometimes referred to as the *spirit* of his philosophical writings. First, he insisted that his philosophy was written in a spirit that was opposed to the tendencies of its time. Second, he suggested on a number of occasions that an appreciation of this opposition was needed in order to understand his work. Finally, the remark cited above from the preface of the *Investigations* is only one of Wittgenstein's characteristic expressions of persistent doubts that his work would be understood. Other such expressions, like that one, indicate that the character of the time would militate against an understanding of his work. This book is an extended attempt to understand the viewpoint from which Wittgenstein made these remarks. In putting the pieces together, one can establish that there is a body of

---

1   Ludwig Wittgenstein, *Philosophical Investigations*, Macmillan, 1953, p. ixe.

Wittgensteinian expression – a series of more or less consistent remarks – into which his remark about "the darkness of this time" from the *Investigations* has a natural place. Thus, the project undertaken by this book is the attempt to come to terms with Wittgenstein's assessment of his time, some of the unexpressed, underlying purposes of his philosophical writings, and the connections between them.

There are a number of keys to understanding these matters. The most important is the undeniable influence of Oswald Spengler's *The Decline of the West* on Wittgenstein. Wittgenstein explicitly acknowledged Spengler as an important influence on his view of his time. Some of his esoteric writings very explicitly and dramatically show the extent of that influence. This influence was at its peak in the early thirties, but Wittgenstein's assessment of his time continued to bear the stamp of Spengler's dark conception of an ongoing cultural decline for the rest of his life.

Spengler's influence did not end there. While his conception of cultural decline resonated deeply for Wittgenstein, it is equally important that his explicit notions of what limitations such a time imposes on what a philosopher can and ought to do can be shown to have had a striking influence upon the overall character of Wittgenstein's work. Spengler's prescriptions for philosophy in a time of cultural decline jibe remarkably well with Wittgenstein's later philosophical practices. Indeed, the most idiosyncratic and unique features of Wittgenstein's later philosophy are deeply Spenglerian features.

The Spenglerian influence is mostly a matter of Wittgenstein's unstated purposes, but this is not exclusively so. The shape and character of his overall conclusions, his rejection of philosophy as usually practiced, aspects of his unique approach to philosophical problems, and even, in some instances, the explicit philosophical content of the later work are strikingly Spenglerian. I seek, in what follows, to show this in a manner that is both clear and complete. One of the most difficult undertakings of the project of this book is to make some sense of Wittgenstein's claim that his philosophy is opposed to "the darkness" of his time, to cultural decline. After all, Wittgenstein, in the *Investigations*, never so much as mentions the nature of his civilization or cultural decline. How then is this opposition manifested in the work?

These concerns, it will be shown, lead naturally to the subject of religion, Wittgenstein's attitudes toward religion and religious expression, and the question of whether Wittgenstein, in some way or other, employed a religious viewpoint in his later philosophy. Wittgenstein's early work was preoccupied with the religious, the mystical, and "that which is higher", but his early doctrines notoriously denied the expressibility of such things. It was not, of course, that Wittgenstein thought that religious concerns were empty; rather, while taking them seriously, he was committed to doing so "wordlessly". The *Tractatus* certainly may be said to have had a religious viewpoint – but one which, by its own tenets, could not be expressed in words; at least not in a direct manner. The inexpressibility of the religious was a centerpiece of Wittgenstein's early philosophy. The later philosophical work, in contrast, has virtually nothing whatsoever to say on this subject. This is certainly true of the *Investigations*. It offers no direct assertions, no suggestive "elucidations", of a religious nature. Why? Was Wittgenstein no longer interested in religion? Or, does a religious viewpoint emerge again, as it were, wordlessly? Norman Malcolm, in his last published philosophical work, *Wittgenstein – A Religious Point of View?*, pondered these and related questions and concluded that something like a religious viewpoint can be attributed to the *Investigations*.

As it turns out, Spengler's views on cultural decline were internally connected to his views on religious decline. Could Spengler's attitude toward religion, as Brian R. Clack has suggested, have influenced that of the later Wittgenstein? If so, how? Understanding the nature of Spengler's influence on Wittgenstein does, I think, clarify the question of Wittgenstein's mature attitude toward religion. I have endeavored in this book to illuminate this central point of interpretation in an original way. I seek to show the source of Wittgenstein's later doubts about religious expression. I argue that it is very different from that of the *Tractatus* and connect it with Spenglerian influences.

The plan of this book is straightforward. In Chapter 1, I discuss Wittgenstein's frank indication that Spengler had been an influence on him and, beyond this, that many of his own ideas had been re-workings of some of Spengler's seminal insights. Toward this end I offer a preliminary overview of Spengler's main theses. I discuss a number of conjectures that have been made by prominent philosophers as to what aspects of Wittgenstein's explicit later philosophical thought were influenced by Spengler. Finally, I offer an original conjecture of my own.

In Chapter 2, I discuss Spengler's overall view of culture and cultural decline. I show that, during the early thirties, Wittgenstein was clearly and very strongly influenced by these views and that he incorporated them into prefatory remarks intended for his transitional philosophical work, *Philosophical Remarks*. There, Wittgenstein not only accepts many specific aspects of Spengler's vision, but explicitly expresses that the spirit of *Remarks* was intended to oppose a cultural decline that he believed to be pervasive in Western Civilization. The similarities between passages from Spengler's *Decline* and Wittgenstein's prefatory remarks for *Philosophical Remarks* are striking, even astonishing, in their basic themes, their tone of dark negativism, and even, most pointedly, in their vocabulary. There is not the slightest doubt that Wittgenstein took on a Spenglerian outlook and saw his own philosophical efforts to be an expression of that outlook, at least in the early 1930s.

Wittgenstein, however, even when most influenced by Spengler, was never uncritical of his work. He sought to identify significant conceptual confusions in *Decline*. These significant caveats are discussed at some length in Chapter 1, as are some other early criticisms of aspects of Spengler's work. Could these critical insights, and perhaps later ones, have eventually weakened the esteem in which he held Spengler's work to the point where it was no longer much of an influence? The best evidence suggests that this is not so. On the contrary, I try to show, in Chapter 2, that, in the decades subsequent to Wittgenstein's initial acceptance of basic Spenglerian conclusions, very similar thoughts continued to occupy and shape his view of his time, and the relationship between his work and that time. There are many indications that this is so, and I try to both identify and interpret a large number of esoteric sources which show that to be the case. In doing so, I believe, I have remedied one of the weaknesses of my 1994 article, "Wittgenstein and Spengler" – an article which painstakingly documents the original influence, but does not sufficiently deal with the questions of whether, or for how long, that influence continued.

In Chapter 3, I take up the all-important subject of Spengler's prescription for philosophy in a time of cultural decline. Spengler's remarks are striking and describe a philosophical program so antithetical to traditional philosophy that it seems scarcely to amount to philosophy at all. Yet, it is remarkably clear that Wittgenstein's later philosophical practice seems, quite uniquely, to fit Spengler's blueprint. The details of this are fascinating. I strive to bring them out as clearly and persuasively as I can. Although this is the book's shortest chapter, it is, in one respect, the most complete. The case I make is, I think, unassailable and correct. As we shall see in Chapter 7, Brian R. Clack says in his recent *Introduction to Wittgenstein's Philosophy of Religion* (roughly five years after I made virtually the same claim), "Wittgenstein's philosophical project meets the restrictions laid down by Spengler concerning what is and is not possible in an age of decline." Chapter 3 not only makes this claim, but also presents in detail the overwhelmingly strong reasons for thinking that it is so.

Chapter 4, the book's longest, engages perhaps the most daunting aspect of its project. Having shown both that Wittgenstein embraced Spengler's view of cultural decline and also that he intended for his philosophy to oppose that decline, I take up the question of *how* Wittgenstein's later work can be interpreted as doing so. How can Wittgenstein's various remarks on language, reference, thought, intention, family resemblances, the privacy of experience, and the rest – *devoid as it is of any explicit mention of Spengler, culture, civilization, or cultural decline* – be a work that in any way engages these subjects? I discuss in careful detail, and, for the most part, accept Stanley Cavell's attempt to begin to answer this question and to find what he calls the "Spenglerian valence" of the *Investigations*. I hope, for some readers, my account of Cavell might serve as a demystification of his elegant, insightful, but sometimes daunting expression of seminal insights. In addition, I offer a number of original thoughts of my own on this difficult subject.

Chapter 5 takes up Wittgenstein's view of religious expression. I attempt to outline and contrast Wittgenstein's early and later views on the subject. The former are, by now, reasonably well understood. The latter, I argue, show both interesting similarities and even more interesting differences with the former. I seek to show that, while Wittgenstein always had doubts about religious expression, his later doubts were grounded in a very different conception of expressibility itself than the earlier. Further, the later view is, in important respects, Spenglerian in some of its basic conceptions – not only about religion, but about the connection between cultural surroundings and meaning.

Chapter 6 goes on to ponder the question of whether Wittgenstein's later philosophy may have been pursued from not only a cultural, but a religious perspective. In it I examine in detail the views of Norman Malcolm in his posthumously published *Wittgenstein – A Religious Point of View?* It is noteworthy that Malcolm takes very seriously Wittgenstein's various indications – many of them central to positions I argue for in this book – that he did not expect his philosophy to be understood. Malcolm took these as evidence that Wittgenstein's philosophy presupposes a religious point of view that was incommensurate with the underlying assumptions of his time. I take up in detail both Malcolm's views and the criticisms of them offered by Peter Winch, and conclude that Malcolm does indeed succeed in highlighting at least one aspect of Wittgenstein's later philosophy which, by Wittgenstein's own lights, qualifies as religious.

In this book's final chapter, I discuss the view of one of the few philosophers writing today who has argued that Spengler's influence on Wittgenstein is both pervasive and influenced his view of religion. Brian R. Clack, in his fine book, *An Introduction to Wittgenstein's Philosophy of Religion*, argues that the later Wittgenstein, influenced by Spengler's pessimism about religion in a time of cultural decline, became a kind of "atheist". While heartened that another writer has taken the Spenglerian influence on Wittgenstein as seriously as I have, I must, with some regret, reject Clack's conclusion. His view, I will argue, incorrectly assesses Spengler's view of religion in his time and overestimates its influence on Wittgenstein's view. Clack's interesting claim does not stand up to close scrutiny.

Many of my friends and colleagues who have read all or part of the writings that have slowly evolved into this book have asked me my own view of Wittgenstein's extreme cultural pessimism. What do I make of Wittgenstein's apparent belief that the twentieth century was a time of cultural decline in which art, religion, and philosophy were, if not dead, then at least seriously endangered and on the verge of extinction? What of his oft-stated sense that the human spirit and the dominant forms of human interaction in his time had deteriorated? The sobering truth is that, having spent a decade coming to understand a good deal about Wittgenstein's views on these subjects, I find it difficult to sympathize with many of them. Indeed, I must confess that I am sometimes amazed that Wittgenstein, a great critical thinker, would find so many of the more extravagant views of a thinker such as Spengler so congenial and could so enthusiastically have endorsed them, his caveats notwithstanding. Significantly, I find that Wittgenstein's cultural observations are most penetrating when they explicitly depart from those of Spengler.

I am inclined to think that many of the views shared by Wittgenstein and Spengler on these subjects amount to not much more than an intellectualized historical pessimism that each of them supported in his own informed, but idiosyncratic and selective manner. Each expresses, I think, the attitude of a man so taken with the great works and triumphs of past times that he became impatient, even disgusted, with what he saw as unworthy, even obscene, departures from them in his own time. One can certainly tolerate and even respect such concerns. Indeed, some of their shared criticisms of twentieth-century artistic, religious, and social forms are, for all their vitriol, interesting and insightful. They express concerns about the misuses of technology, the politics of globalization, the corruption of religion, social fragmentation, and personal alienation, which, at least in outline, seem even to have been prophetic. However, their shared vision encompassed much more – applied, as it was, virtually without restriction, to their entire civilization. Spengler and Wittgenstein believed that the Renaissance in Western Europe was the zenith of Western culture. In contrast, they viewed their own time as the sorry result of centuries of decline from that high point. They appear to have simply overlooked that the Renaissance was a time of rich, meaningful fulfillment for, at most, only a fragment of the most privileged people of that time and one of relative misery for almost everyone else. It seems a mistake to idealize any such social form. Further, their belief that such times of "high culture" are characterized by a genuine and widely shared religious sensibility seems to ignore the blatant religious hypocrisies, the political nastiness, and the systematically cruel class structure that characterized that time – hardly less, and perhaps more, than subsequent times, including our own. It is one thing to admire Michelangelo's Sistine art or Mozart's musical compositions and even to believe that nothing in contemporary art approaches them. It is quite another to imagine that a whole population was suffused with the same sort of spirit that inspired those works. As such, I find it nearly impossible to sympathize with Spengler's idealized view of that time. His dark view of the twentieth century is sometimes penetrating and incorporates important insights. Nonetheless, it seems perversely selective in its negativity.

A further source of perplexity for me is Wittgenstein's reluctance to express in any direct way the Spenglerian valence in his philosophy and his connected belief that such direct expressions would not be understood in his time. While I try to explain and come to terms with his reasons for thinking as he did, I remain perplexed. I am inclined to think that this is an extravagant and ultimately unsupported stance.

Having said all this, I cannot rest easily. I do not feel that I understand these matters sufficiently well to offer a definitive rejection of his stance. It must always be remembered that in confronting Wittgenstein's thoughts – perhaps more than those of any other philosopher – there are always new interpretations that reveal fresh and unexpected insights. His work encompasses an extraordinary volume of valuable, latent content. As such, I am disinclined to entirely reject Wittgenstein's various expressions of Spenglerian pessimism, nor to offer any more in the way of criticism of them than I have here. Instead, I remain content to lay them out clearly, accurately, and in detail for my reader.

I cannot help pondering what the ultimate value of this book might be. I have concluded that whatever value it has is twofold. First, it identifies some features of Wittgenstein's philosophy that have been scarcely noticed. It offers a fairly clear and complete account of those features, one that is the result of a good deal of painstaking attention. Second, it raises some difficult problems of interpretation of Wittgenstein's later writings. Some of these, I think, I have resolved more or less correctly. Others are posed and remain unresolved. It is my hope that someone else, perhaps aided by what I have written here, might one day come to understand and further illuminate them.

Chapter 1

Spengler's Influence on Wittgenstein: A First Approximation

I. Introduction

In 1931, writing in a personal journal, Wittgenstein enumerated the names of those thinkers whom he deemed to have been his most important intellectual influences. He makes the strong claim that these are thinkers whose seminal ideas he has taken over, further elaborated, and incorporated into his own work. Here are the names he lists in their order of appearance: Boltzmann, Hertz, Schopenhauer, Frege, Russell, Kraus, Loos, Weininger, Spengler, and Sraffa.[1]

At the time of the first publication of this list in *Culture and Value*, those familiar primarily with the most widely read and influential writings on Wittgenstein and his philosophical influences – probably, Norman Malcolm's *Memoir* (including Von Wright's introduction) and Janik and Toulmin's *Wittgenstein's Vienna* – would most likely have been surprised by the inclusion of Spengler's name. His is the only one on the list that does not appear in either book. Every other thinker named is mentioned as an influence on Wittgenstein in one or the other work. For each, some of the purported details of that influence are offered. Further, the appearance of Spengler's name is surprising, given the relatively low esteem in which his work is generally held. The other listed individuals, with the exception of Weininger, are well-respected figures.

Oswald Spengler was an extremely unorthodox historian and the author of *The Decline of the West* – a ponderous, two-volume work that is not well regarded by most professional historians. The work is avowedly opposed to the scientific method in history, makes repeated and vitriolic criticisms of history as it is usually practiced. It is unashamedly bold in claiming a major success for itself. It is often badly written, rambling, and repetitive. The work frequently makes pronouncements with little or no argumentation or documentation. These shortcomings are characteristic of the work. They stand out. Dray has described Spengler's style abusively as "oracular" and he, Toynbee, and Gardiner all question both Spengler's methods and his knowledge of some of the cultures he analyzes.[2]

---

1   Ludwig Wittgenstein, *Culture and Value*, ed. G. H. Von Wright in collaboration with Heikki Nymnan (Oxford, 1980), p. 19e.

2   Patrick Gardiner (ed.), *Theories of History* (London, 1959), especially pp. 188–9 and 200–201, in which the editor discusses, compares, and criticizes the methodologies of Spengler and Toynbee; and pp. 207–8, in which Toynbee discusses and criticizes Spengler. In addition, Dray's entry on Spengler in *The Encyclopedia of Philosophy* (cited in detail below) offers similar criticisms and a few of his own.

Some of Spengler's central claims appear to be contradictory. His writing is as unlike Wittgenstein's precise, elegant, economical prose as writing can be. Still, for all its faults, *Decline* offers an engaging viewpoint, makes interesting distinctions, and poses striking observations that appeal to the imagination. It created considerable interest both when it was published in 1918 and again when the English historian, Arnold Toynbee, re-examined some of its themes in the 1940s.

II. Spengler in Overview

i. The Comparative Morphology of Cultures

As a first step toward understanding Spengler's influence on Wittgenstein, I offer a brief outline of Spengler's main theses in *Decline*. Despite his ponderous writing and the extreme unconventionality of *Decline* in both form and substance, the main tenets of Spenglerian thought are fairly clear. I will enumerate the three that are most significant and characteristic and will elaborate and comment on each briefly. I seek to introduce some basic elements of Spenglerian thought and to offer needed background for further discussions. As I discuss the nature of Spengler's actual influence on Wittgenstein, I shall focus more upon the details of these three features.

Spengler held that history, properly practiced, is concerned primarily with *cultures*. It reveals that cultures all develop, mature, decline, and die out in discernibly similar stages. The unfolding of cultures, on his view, constitutes the entire content of history. He is intent to show that all known cultures have developed, flourished, and exhausted themselves in accordance with similar principles, passing through similar sequences of stages. His own efforts focus primarily upon the Classical (which he calls "Apollonian"), the Egyptian, the Arabian, and the modern (which he names "Faustian") cultures. He attempts to identify patterns of cultural development and document them in some detail. He purports to describe the stages that known cultures, and presumably every culture, have passed through. This is the major task of *Decline*. He summarizes his purported findings in elaborate, graphic fold-out sheets in appendices to the work. These foldouts outline, in the left-hand column, the supposed *prototypical* sequences of cultural development and, in parallel, columns to the right outline the developmental sequences of *actual* cultures. The resulting graphic purports to show how world cultures have actually developed along the lines of the Spenglerian prototype. He sees the shared patterns and stages in the development of different cultures as manifestations of a powerful internal principle of development (he refers to it as "spiritual") that is embodied in every known culture. Spengler saw this internal principle to be one of historical necessity – every culture *must* pass through the stages delineated in his stereotype.

This essential task of history Spengler calls the "comparative morphology of cultures". That expression suggests an analogy that he emphatically endorses – namely, one between the development of a culture and that of an organic entity or process. Spengler writes frequently of "youth", "maturity", "decline", "aging", and "death" with reference to cultures. This, he insists, is more of an aid than a detriment to real historical understanding. As a seed develops into a plant, or an infant into an adult, in a predictable sequence of stages, cultures too so develop. He also writes of the development of cultures in terms of the succession of the seasons – indeed many of his major conclusions are couched in these terms. Here is Dray's incisive account of Spengler's main morphological contentions about cultures, expressed in these terms:

> They have their spring in an early heroic period when life is rural, agricultural, and feudal. In the Apollonian culture this was the Homeric period; in the Faustian it was the high Middle Ages. This is a time of seminal myths, of inspiring epic and saga, and of powerful mystical religion. With summer comes the rise of towns not yet alienated from the countryside, an aristocracy of manners growing up beside an older, lustier leadership, and great individual artists succeeding their anonymous predecessors. In the Apollonian culture this was the period of the early city-states; in the Faustian it was the time of the Renaissance, of Shakespeare and Michelangelo, and of the Galilean triumphs of the uncorrupted intellect. Autumn witnesses the full ripening of the culture's spiritual resources and the first hints of possible exhaustion; it is a time of growing cities, spreading commerce, and centralizing monarchies, with religion being challenged by philosophy and tradition undermined by "enlightenment". In the classical world, this was the age of the Sophists, of Socrates and Plato; in the west it was the eighteenth century, which reached the apogee of creative maturity in the music of Mozart, the poetry of Goethe, and the philosophy of Kant. Transition to winter is characterized by the appearance of the megalopolis, the world city, with its rootless proletariat, plutocracy, esoteric art, and growing skepticism and materialism. It is an age, furthermore, of imperialism, of increasing political tyranny, and of almost constant warfare, as political adventurers skirmish for world empire. In general, culture loses its soul and hardens into mere "civilization", the highest works of which are feats of administration and the application of science to industry… [Modern] culture is, according to Spengler, well into its autumn period, at a point roughly equivalent to 200 B.C. in the Apollonian culture. An early sign of our advanced cultural age is the career of Napoleon, who is morphologically contemporary with Alexander the Great; our Julius Caesar is yet to come.[3]

Actually, Spengler is not consistent in his characterizations of twentieth-century European and North American civilization in terms of seasons. The inconsistency is not a serious one, but it should be noted that while he does, as Dray states, sometimes write of late autumn in this regard, he also, as we shall see, characterizes his time as one of early winter.

ii. A Principle of Cultural Insularity

While emphasizing the morphological similarities he saw between vastly different cultures, Spengler also insisted upon their insularity from one another. Spengler held most radical views along these lines: that earlier cultures do not in any important way influence later ones; that the widespread belief that they do is a delusion of prejudice; that standing within one culture, one cannot adequately grasp the perspective of

---

3   Stephen Dray, s.v. "Spengler, Oswald", *The Encyclopedia of Philosophy*, vol. 7, ed. Paul Edwards (New York, 1967), p. 529.

another culture. For example, he insists repeatedly that the Modern Mind has not been influenced by and cannot even understand the Classical Mind.

The notion of the "prime symbol" of a culture is basic in Spengler.[4] For him a culture is a "spiritual" orientation shared by a people which includes a conception of their world which influences all their activities – their art, religion, philosophy, politics, economics, and even their modes of warfare – and which expresses itself in a distinctive concept of "the space" in which they live. This space-concept functions as the culture's "prime symbol" and is the main key to the understanding of its history. Most significant, he insists that different cultures cannot grasp one another's prime symbols. Nonetheless, Spengler writes at great length about the space-concepts of the classical, the Egyptian, and the modern culture. The details need not concern us here: what is important is that Spengler thinks that each culture is characterized by its *unique* conception of human life and of all its enterprises. This uniqueness is such that one culture's mode of conception is by its nature alien and impenetrable from "inside" that of another.

This view, while stimulating, nevertheless raises obvious questions. For example, how can Spengler – who presumably thinks from "inside" the unique and limiting perspective of the modern culture – come to understand the perspectives of other cultures given what he says about cultural insularity? His answer is both *ad hoc* and immodest. In effect, he held that there are rare, intuitively talented individuals who, with effort, can overcome the obstacles of cultural insulation. (He never explains what such an intuitive talent might hope to accomplish by writing a book that makes his thoughts available to an intuitively untalented readership.) Oddly, he never offers what would appear to be the more reasonable suggestion that an intelligent person might, by making a considerable effort to immerse himself fully in the particulars of past cultures, come to an adequate understanding of them. Spengler never seems quite comfortable with the tension between what he says about cultural insularity and his willingness to expound upon the prime symbols of other cultures. In commending his own historical scheme in comparison with others, he says:

> In opposition to all these arbitrary and narrow schemes…into which history is forced, I put forward the "Copernican" form of the historical process which lies deep in the essence of that process and reveals itself only to an eye perfectly free from prepossessions.[5]

This last description is remarkable, suggesting, as it does, that one could transcend one's own rootedness in a culture and view history, as it were, from outside that particular viewpoint. There are other such passages. One states a need to view things,

> not with the eyes of the partisan, the idealogue, the up-to-date novelist, not from this or that "standpoint", but in a high, time-free perspective…if we are really to comprehend the great crises of the present.[6]

---

4   Oswald Spengler, *The Decline of the West*, vol. I, (New York: Modern Library, 1965), see especially pp. 174–80.

5   Ibid., p. 25.

6   Ibid., p. 34.

Could anyone be so "perfectly free from prepossessions" so as to view things from what amounts to a perspective-free perspective? Evidently, in some moods Spengler thought so.

There are, however, passages that suggest another tendency. For example, Spengler describes the hoped-for result of the implementation of his historical scheme: "at last will unfold…the picture of world-history that is natural to us, men of the West, and to us alone."[7] The latter qualification seems mysterious and unnecessary given Spengler's previous remarks about being "perfectly free from prepossessions" and his suggestions that an individual's cultural boundedness can be overcome. Dray sees this as a hopeless muddle.[8] My sense is that this conflict is embedded deeply in Spengler's thought and that he never resolved the tension.

Still, I believe that the idea of cultural insularity is one that probably always held some appeal for Wittgenstein. When he encountered this idea in Spengler's *Decline*, he was, himself, in transit between the early philosophical conceptions of the *Tractatus* and those of the later *Investigations* views. Given this, I think, Spengler's version of cultural insularity took on special significance for him. I address this, and related matters in section V of this chapter and again in Chapter 5.

iii. An Assessment of Contemporary Civilization

Spengler was intent to assess, with the aid of morphological analysis, the Western Civilization of the twentieth century. The picture he offers is depressingly bleak. He writes:

> every Culture has its own Civilization. In this work, for the first time, *the two words, hitherto used to express an indefinite, more or less ethical distinction, are used in a periodic sense, to express a strict and necessary organic succession.* The Civilization is the inevitable *destiny* of the Culture …Civilizations are the most external and artificial states of which a species of developed humanity is capable. They are a conclusion,…death following life, rigidity following expansion…They are an end.[9]

> Pure Civilization, as a historical process, consists in a taking-down of forms that have become inorganic or dead.[10]

> We are civilized, not Gothic or Rococo, people; we have to reckon with the hard cold facts of *late* life, to which the parallel is to be found not in Pericles' Athens but in Caesar's Rome. Of great painting or great music there can no longer be, for Western people, any question. Their architectural possibilities have been exhausted these hundred years… . [W]e have not chosen this time. We cannot help it if we are born as men of the early winter of full Civilization, instead of on the golden summit of a ripe Culture in a Phidias or Mozart time.[11]

---

7   Ibid., p. 40.
8   Stephen Dray, "Spengler Oswald", p. 528.
9   Oswald Spengler, *Decline of the West*, vol. I, p. 31.
10 Ibid., p. 32.
11 Ibid., p. 40.

This is a radical view. It insists that its time is one of stark cultural decline, one in which great cultural works are no longer possible. Equally important, it sees this state of affairs as a natural unfolding, as an inevitable consequence of the ways in which all cultures, including our own, develop, mature, and decline.

Spengler represents the decline of a culture into a civilization, both as an exhaustion of the culture's artistic forms and possibilities and, further, as the development of new tendencies. The latter include the ascendancy of science, technology, industry, and a new all-consuming focus on economic and political power on the global scale. It must also be emphasized that the most important feature of the transition from culture to civilization, for Spengler, is *the diminution of religion* as an active force, a movement toward *irreligiousness*. The waning of religion is not just a concomitant to those other changes that characterize cultural decline. It plays a central role in bringing them about. In a time of high culture, Spengler writes:

> Every soul has religion, which is only another word for its existence. All living forms in which it expresses itself – all arts, doctrines, customs, all metaphysical and mathematical form-worlds, all ornament, every column and verse and idea – are ultimately religious, and *must* be so.[12]

So, cultures are *essentially religious*. Civilizations, in dramatic contrast, are not. In fact, civilizations, for Spengler, are, by their very nature, irreligious. Immediately following the above passage, he writes this:

> But from the setting in of Civilization, they *cannot* be so any longer. As the essence of every Culture is religion, so – and *consequently* – the essence of every Civilization is irreligion, the two words are synonymous.[13]

and, he adds:

> It is this extinction of living inner religiousness…at the turn from the Culture to the Civilization…in which a mankind loses its spiritual fruitfulness forever.[14]

For Spengler, the diminution of religion as an effective social force *underlies* the other manifestations of cultural decline that he enumerates. It stands as the most basic of those manifestations.

III. The Nature of the Influence: Examining Some Suggestions

There has been speculation, but much less in the way of careful documentation, concerning the nature or extent of Spengler's influence on Wittgenstein. There is very little hard evidence – a few passages from Wittgenstein's various writings published in *Culture and Value* and Drury's accounts of some conversations in which he and Wittgenstein discussed Spengler. These provide the only clues about

---

12 Ibid., p. 358.
13 Oswald Spengler, *Decline of the West*, vol. II, pp. 50–1.
14 Oswald Spengler, *Decline of the West*, vol. I, p. 359.

what Wittgenstein did and did not like in Spengler's work (his regard for Spengler was far from unreserved) and almost nothing about which of Spengler's ideas might have influenced him. Any attempt to uncover the nature of Spengler's influence on Wittgenstein would require going beyond this direct evidence to the writings of the two thinkers. Are there ideas in Wittgenstein's work that resemble any to be found in Spengler's *Decline*? Which of these might plausibly have been influenced by Spengler?

Some first-rate thinkers have offered thoughts on the subject over the years. Von Wright,[15] Cavell,[16] Monk,[17] and others have made suggestions about the nature of Spengler's influence on Wittgenstein. These do not claim to be definitive – or even more than impressionistic. Some of these are helpful; I have doubts about many of them. My overall goal in this book is to elucidate, both in some detail and also more broadly, the nature of Spengler's influence upon Wittgenstein. I attempt to break some new ground and, perhaps, give others a foundation upon which to build. In a first step toward this end, I will explain some of the suggestions about the nature of this influence that have been made by a number of important contemporary writers.

i. Von Wright and Family Resemblances

As we shall see, there are some striking similarities between some of Wittgenstein's remarks on Spengler and others made in well-known passages in *Philosophical Investigations*. For example, in the former, he employs the term "family resemblance" – the first instance of which I am aware in Wittgenstein's writings. Later, in the *Investigations*, Wittgenstein offers his well-known rejection of an essentialist conception of "game" and, in so doing, uses the term "family resemblances" to explain his alternative conception.

G. H. Von Wright has noted and commented upon this. In his interesting article "Wittgenstein in Relation to His Times", he briefly discusses Spenglerian aspects of Wittgenstein's later thought. Drawing upon the above-mentioned similarities he writes: "The actual influence pertains, it seems, to an idea in Wittgenstein's later philosophy, indeed to one of its most characteristic thought manoeuvres. This is the idea of 'family resemblance'".[18] He goes on to say that the "family resemblance"

---

15 G. H. Von Wright, "Wittgenstein in Relation to His Times", in Brian McGuiness (ed.), *Wittgenstein in His Times* (Chicago, 1982).

16 Stanley Cavell, "Declining Decline: Wittgenstein as a Philosopher of Culture", *Inquiry*, vol. 31, no. 3, September 1988, pp. 253–64 [hereafter referred to as "Declining Decline 1"]. There exists also an article by Cavell with the title "Declining Decline", which is an expanded version of the former. It appears as follows: Stanley Cavell, "Declining Decline", *This New Yet Unapproachable America: Lectures After Emerson After Wittgenstein* (Albuquerque, NM, 1989). This article is conveniently republished in a readily available collection of Cavell's work: *The Cavell Reader*, edited by Stephen Mulhall (Oxford, 1996), Stanley Cavell, "Declining Decline", pp. 331–52 [hereafter referred to as "Declining Decline 2"].

17 Ray Monk, *Ludwig Wittgenstein: The Duty of Genius* (New York, 1990). See especially pp. 302–3 and 315–16.

18 G. H. Von Wright, "Wittgenstein in Relation to His Times", p. 116.

idea in Wittgenstein "appears to have its origin" in Spengler's work.[19] This suggests that Wittgenstein's anti-essentialist views and his related focus upon family resemblances can be found, perhaps in a less developed form, in Spengler's work. The impression is that Wittgenstein's views on family resemblances may have been a reworking of ideas he encountered in Spengler's writings. It is not perfectly clear that Von Wright meant to suggest this – though it is a natural reading of the passage. Nevertheless, careful analysis, I think, does not support the suggestion of such a strong and direct influence. Von Wright is correct to claim a connection here. I will try to show, in subchapter IV–*ii* below, that it is misleading to characterize it as a case of Wittgenstein's "thought manoeuvre" regarding family resemblances "having its origin in" Spengler's work. Such a claim must be qualified and the needed qualification would require that certain relevant distinctions be drawn. I will attempt to offer that qualification and those distinctions.

ii. Von Wright: A Disease of Culture

In that same article, Von Wright offers a different thought about Spengler's influence on Wittgenstein – one that is more striking and more sweeping in its importance and consequences. It concerns Wittgenstein's relation to his times and his expression of that relation in his later philosophy. Von Wright's thought is, I think, both important and, at least in bold outline, correct. He writes:

> Wittgenstein…thought that the problems with which he was struggling were somehow connected with "the way people live", that is, with features of our culture or civilization to which he and his pupils belonged. His attitude toward this culture was…one of censure and disgust. Wittgenstein is much more "history-conscious" than is commonly recognized and understood. His way of doing philosophy was not an attempt to tell us what philosophy, once and for all, *is* but expressed what for him, in the setting of the times, it had to be.[20]

Later, in Chapters 2 and 3, I shall support and elaborate upon the primary contentions of this passage. For now, it will be helpful to cite one of Von Wright's own elaborations upon them. He writes:

> Because of the interlocking of language and ways of life, a disorder in the former reflects disorder in the latter. If philosophical problems are symptomatic of language producing malignant outgrowths which obscure our thinking, then there must be a cancer in the *Lebensweise*, in the way of life itself. His conception of philosophy is intimately allied to a way of viewing contemporary civilization. This much we must concede. But whether this had to be a Spenglerian form of seeing our times as a dissolution of those traditions in art, religion, science, and philosophy which had constituted the relative unity of Western culture is, of course, another matter.[21]

These passages are interesting. They presuppose two major themes of Wittgenstein's later philosophy – first, that philosophy, as it is usually practiced, employs serious

---

19 Ibid.
20 Ibid., p. 118.
21 Ibid., pp. 118–19.

misuses of language, and second, that language is best viewed in connection with the notion of a *language game*. Language games, for Wittgenstein, are rule-governed human practices in which words play a role. They are importantly connected with wider social practices and with a complicated form of life. The second passage imputes to Wittgenstein the view that philosophers' misuses of language – violations of the rules governing language games – may be thought of, metaphorically, as "malignant outgrowths" which in turn are symptomatic of a systemic condition, an underlying cancer, in the forms of life underlying those misuses.

In the first passage, Von Wright claims that Wittgenstein's late philosophy is Spenglerian in at least one important respect. Like Spengler's work, he thinks, Wittgenstein's philosophy expresses a sense of and a concern for its time – a concern that takes the form of censure, disapproval, even disgust. Von Wright, however, leaves open the question of whether the details of Wittgenstein's negative take on his own time are the same as those that Spengler enumerates in *Decline*. The second passage explicitly withholds judgment as to whether the "malignant outgrowths" it addresses should themselves be viewed as features of a Spenglerian cultural decline. Von Wright's caution on this last point is understandable. Nonetheless, I shall argue – especially in Chapters 2 and 3 – that there is good reason to think that Wittgenstein's negative sense of his time did in fact incorporate many Spenglerian details.

iii. Cavell and the Natural Decline of Culture

In two distinct papers, both titled "Declining Decline: Wittgenstein as a Philosopher of Culture", Stanley Cavell explicitly agrees with Von Wright that the *Investigations* expresses a sense of its own time and that this is connected to a Spenglerian influence. More boldly, he explicitly describes the *Investigations* as "a depiction of our times" and Wittgenstein as a "philosopher – even a critic – of culture".[22] He attributes to Wittgenstein's *Investigations*, "a Spenglerian valence".[23] Beyond this, and in contrast to Von Wright's cautious stance on the matter, Cavell emphatically endorses the notion that the *Investigations* incorporates a view of its time which is, in many of its important particulars, Spenglerian in nature. I will examine Cavell's views in detail in Chapter 4. For the present, I want to focus upon a point upon which Cavell explicitly criticizes Von Wright.

As we have just seen, Von Wright, employing a disturbing metaphor, imputes to Wittgenstein a viewpoint that likens our philosophical misuses of language to malignancies. On that viewpoint, these linguistic malignancies are seen as manifestations of a cancerous condition in the way of life underlying our language or, at least, our temptations to so misuse it. Von Wright says this in the context of a discussion of a possible connection between Wittgenstein's thought and Spengler's. Thus, he may mean to suggest that the notion of a cultural malignancy that he imputes to Wittgenstein is also Spenglerian. Cavell reads Von Wright in this way and expresses serious doubts about such a suggestion. He writes:

---

22 Stanley Cavell, "Declining Decline 2", p. 336.
23 Ibid., p. 337.

the idea of a cancer in a culture's way of life does not strike me as a Spenglerian thought. "Cancer" says that a way of life is threatened with an invasive, abnormal death, but Spengler's "decline" is about the normal, say the internal, death and life of cultures.[24]

Citing a number of passages from Spengler's *Decline* (including the first of those cited in subchapter II–*ii* above), Cavell explains correctly that, for Spengler, the decline of cultures – and, more specifically, the decline represented by his own times – are natural processes which take place in a regular sequence of stages. So, he concludes, Von Wright's view that Wittgenstein's central thought about his own time expressed itself as a concern with something like a cancerous condition in our way of life is not, at bottom, Spenglerian. Cavell rejects the view – both as an account of the Spenglerian component in Wittgenstein's thought and, more importantly, as an accurate representation of Wittgenstein's understanding of his own time.

Cavell sees in the *Investigations* a preoccupation with the very features of civilization that Spengler thought of as typical of cultural decline. He is quite clear that Wittgenstein is focused upon "Spengler's vision of the destiny toward exhausted [cultural] forms,…toward loss of culture, or of home, or of community".[25] More specifically, he sees the *Investigations* as a carrying out of Wittgenstein's intention to *combat* the conditions of cultural decline as they manifest themselves in the misuses of language that characterize the errant thoughts of philosophers. I believe that Cavell's thoughts on this are insightful. I will try in Chapter 4 to address them far more fully.

Still, Cavell's account of Wittgenstein's intentions leaves open a formidable question: How could it be that the *Investigations* – which, after all, neither mentions cultures, civilizations, cultural forms, or cultural decline, nor discusses them in anything resembling a direct manner – constitutes a "philosophy of culture"? The direct focus of the *Investigations* is on language, the nature of its referring function and its relationship to human action and thought. As such, the *Investigations* directly addresses reference, meaning, sensation, thought, intention, human action and practice, the dismantling of the *Tractatus* picture of language, and directly related subjects. Again: in what way could such a work address cultural concerns when these are never mentioned? Cavell's answer is ingenious and, I believe, very plausible in many of its important details. We shall return to it.

IV. The Nature of Spengler's Influence on Wittgenstein: Possibilities and Caveats

I will, in subsequent chapters, move on to a fuller account of my positive conclusions about the Spenglerian components of Wittgenstein's late philosophy. First, I want to establish some preliminary conclusions.

---

24 Ibid., p. 338.
25 Ibid.

i. Wittgenstein's Rejection of "The Comparative Morphology of Cultures"

There is no doubt whatsoever that Wittgenstein did not accept Spengler's overall theses regarding the comparative morphology of cultures, Spengler's methods, or Spengler's ambitious overall plan. Whatever he valued in Spengler and explicitly characterized as a major influence, it was not, ironically, those themes which Spengler was most intent upon establishing. There is clear and incontrovertible evidence that Wittgenstein rejected them

Drury relates that in 1930 – significantly, about the time of Wittgenstein's original citation of Spengler as an important influence – he was urged by his teacher to read Spengler. He describes his own reaction to the work and Wittgenstein's response:

> Wittgenstein advised me to read Spengler's *The Decline of the West*. It was a book, he said, that might teach me something about the age we were now living in. It might be an antidote for my "incurable romanticism". After I read the book I said to him,
>
> DRURY: "Spengler wants to put history into moulds, and that you can't do."
>
> WITTGENSTEIN: "Yes you are right; you can't put history into moulds. But Spengler does point out certain very interesting comparisons. I don't trust Spengler with details. He is too often inaccurate. I once wrote that if Spengler had the courage to write a very short book, it could have been a great one."
>
> DRURY: "I conceived the idea that I might write a book to try and bring out just what is important in Spengler."
>
> WITTGENSTEIN: "Well, perhaps some day you might do just that."[26]

This conversation makes clear both Drury's and Wittgenstein's strong reservations about Spengler's main thesis. They liken it abusively to putting history into moulds. The strong suggestion is that Spengler's procedures *distort* history by forcing its evident facts to fit his conceptions of cultural development, thus undermining objectivity. This, in turn, seems connected to Wittgenstein's explicitly expressed mistrust of Spengler on details. His idea seems to be that someone inclined to force historical facts to fit a theory cannot be trusted with details.

There is further corroboration and elaboration of this in *Culture and Value*. In a passage written about a year after Wittgenstein's discussions of Spengler with Drury he writes:

> Spengler could better be understood if he said: I am *comparing* different cultural epochs with the lives of families; within a family there is a family resemblance, though you will also find a resemblance between members of different families; family resemblance differs from the other sort of resemblance in such and such ways, etc. What I mean is: we have to be told the object of comparison, the object from which this way of viewing things is derived, otherwise the discussion will constantly be affected by distortions. Because willy-nilly we shall ascribe the properties of the prototype to the object we are viewing in its light; and claim "*it must always be…*".

---

26 M. O'C. Drury, "Conversations with Wittgenstein", in Rush Rhees (ed.), *Ludwig Wittgenstein – Personal Recollections* (Totowa, NJ, 1981), p. 128.

This is because we want to give the prototype's characteristics a purchase on our way of representing things. But since we confuse prototype and object we find ourselves dogmatically conferring on the object properties which only the prototype necessarily possesses.[27]

While this passage will receive more careful analysis in what follows; for now, two points may be noted. First, Wittgenstein again criticizes Spengler for employing an historical prototype in such a way as to lead to "distortions" and "dogmatism". By "prototype" he seems to mean Spengler's system of historical concepts. This, presumably, would include the categories or "moulds" indicated in his discussion with Drury. His idea seems to be that Spengler fails to keep in mind that his prototype is a conceptual construct and, so, has a very different status than the concrete, historical phenomena that it is framed to elucidate. Further, it should change to fit them and they should not be altered to fit it. The prototype has a structure, a conceptual structure, which should not be confused with the structure of historical reality. His suggestion seems to be that the prototype itself be either dispensed with or employed very differently.

On this reading, the passage suggests a confusion in Spengler between his "prototype" and the historical facts which are his "objects" of scrutiny. Beyond this, it suggests that *conceptual* relations within his prototype, which are, as such, *necessary* relations, are somehow confused with *historical* necessities. This appears to be his point when he writes, "willy nilly we…ascribe the properties of the prototype to the object we are viewing in its light; and claim *'it must always be…'*". It is hard to know exactly what Wittgenstein had in mind here, or what he might have offered by way of an example of this mistake. I shall offer a suggestion in IV–*iii*, below.

ii. An Indirect Influence: More on Family Resemblance

As noted in IV–*i* above, there is a striking similarity – one noted by Von Wright – between the passage from *Culture and Value* cited above and some well-known passages in the *Philosophical Investigations*. The former contains a very early employment of the term "family resemblances" – the first that I am aware of in his writings. That term is, of course, also employed in the *Investigations*, in those passages in which Wittgenstein rejects an essentialist conception of the term "games" and denies that a there exists a prototype for games – a set of necessary and sufficient conditions for something's being a game.[28] He argues that the essentialist assumption is made *a priori* and is destructive to understanding the workings of the term. He explicitly likens the actual patterns of similarities among the things we call "games" to "family resemblances".[29] At a well-known point in those familiar passages Wittgenstein exhorts his reader not to assume an essence or prototype for games, but rather to "look and see" whether there is any such thing.[30] Having noted this, I will comment upon the suggestion that Von Wright appears to make (already

---

27 Ludwig Wittgenstein, *Culture and Value*, p. 14.

28 Ludwig Wittgenstein, *Philosophical Investigations* (New York, 1953), Pt I, paragraphs 65–71.

29 Ibid., paragraph 67.

30 Ibid., paragraph 66.

cited in subchapter III–*i* above) that Wittgenstein's views on family resemblances "have their origin in" Spengler's work.

That suggestion contains a measure of truth, but is misleading in an important way. It is true that the passage in which Wittgenstein first mentions family resemblances does occur in a discussion of Spengler. Still, it is important to recognize that, far from imputing any such conception to Spengler, Wittgenstein suggests it as *a preferable alternative to* Spengler's historical "essentialism", *a needed correction to* a mistake in Spengler's presentation, and a palliative for the historical distortions to which it leads. He is taking Spengler to task here. Far from adopting an idea of Spengler's as his own, he is, rather, suggesting his own idea – that of family resemblances – as a way of eradicating a confusion in Spengler. Given this, it is natural to conclude that Wittgenstein, far from embracing Spengler's notion of cultural prototypes, instead, would have asked Spengler to "look and see" whether the historical facts really fit those prototypes.

Of course, one must concede that thinking about Spengler spurred Wittgenstein to begin thinking in ways that would develop into this major theme in his later work. Nonetheless, this is far different from Wittgenstein taking over an idea already present in Spengler. No such thing occurred. Wittgenstein's later remarks on family resemblances may well "have their origin" in *his reading of Spengler*; but then Kant's ideas on causality, in a similar way, "had their origin in" his reading of Hume without thereby being Humean. In summary, Von Wright's claim that Wittgenstein's remarks about family resemblances in the *Investigations* have their origin in Spengler should be accepted – but with the significant proviso just explained.

iii. Another Indirect Influence: Metaphysics as Misconstrued Grammar

This same passage from *Culture and Value* in which Wittgenstein first uses the term "family resemblances" has another noteworthy connection with the *Investigations*. As noted and discussed in the previous section, the passage addresses a confusion between "prototype" and "object" and a need to be mindful of a ramification of that confusion in which "we find ourselves dogmatically conferring on the object properties which only the prototype necessarily possesses". Let us return to that passage, examining it more fully:

> we have to be told the object of comparison, the object from which this way of viewing things is derived, otherwise the discussion will constantly be affected by distortions. Because willy-nilly we shall ascribe the properties of the prototype to the object we are viewing in its light; and claim "*it must always be…*".
>
> This is because we want to give the prototype's characteristics a purchase on our way of representing things. But since we confuse prototype and object we find ourselves dogmatically conferring on the object properties which only the prototype necessarily possesses. But the prototype ought to be clearly presented for what it is; so that characterizes the whole discussion and determines its form. This makes it the focal point, so that its general validity will depend on the fact that it determines the form of discussion rather than on the claim that everything which is true of it holds too for all the things that are being discussed.[31]

---

31 Ludwig Wittgenstein, *Culture and Value*, p. 14.

This warning and the very words in which it is couched, seem to anticipate a related concern later expressed in an important passage in the *Investigations*:

> We predicate of the thing what lies in the method of representing it. Impressed by the possibility of a comparison, we think we are perceiving a state of affairs of the highest generality.[32]

I want first to discuss what may be the nature of the connection between these two passages. Both describe a confusion that wrongly ascribes to reality – to objects, to the world – characteristics that apply instead to "the method of representing it". The problem is that a system of terms or concepts, that constitutes a "method of representation" or a "prototype", has properties which do not apply to reality itself, but which philosophers confusedly do so apply. Later in the *Investigations* this idea is expressed more elaborately in the form of well-known observations about *grammatical remarks* and metaphysics. As is well known, Wittgenstein explicitly characterized the *Investigations* as a grammatical investigation and his own remarks as grammatical remarks. Wittgenstein believed that grammatical truths are, at bottom, truths about the rules that govern the use of words in language and, more specifically, the uses of words in the language games employed by language users. Grammatical truths are intrinsically connected with those rules and often take the form of statements of those rules. As such, they have the status of *necessary* truths.[33]

Beyond this, Wittgenstein saw complications and difficulties. For one thing, he believed that grammatical truths are often expressed in forms that obscure their true nature. Connected to this, he also believed that there is a *natural tendency* to mistake grammatical truths – truths, in effect, about language use – for truths about the world. This tendency leads to a further confusion – one between the structure of language and the structure of reality. The result is that grammatical truths, necessary truths about language use, may be mistaken for necessary truths about the structure of reality.

Wittgenstein's best-known illustrative example may be found in his writings in the *Investigations* about the "privacy of experience". Traditional philosophers have long insisted that experience is "private"; that experiences, as a matter of metaphysical necessity, are accessible only to those who have them. A simple expression of this conviction might be: "Only I can have my experiences, you cannot; only you can have your experiences, I cannot." Against this philosophical tendency, Wittgenstein held that such expressions, masquerading as metaphysical truths about the nature of experience itself, are, at bottom, grammatical remarks about sensation talk. Grammatical truths, he thinks, sometimes present themselves to us as metaphysical pictures of the essential structure of the world. Failing to see these pictures for what they are, we take them for pictures of reality. Compounding the confusion, we confidently ascribe the necessity that applies to the underlying grammatical truth

---

32 Ludwig Wittgenstein, *Philosophical Investigations*, Pt I, paragraph 104.
33 See Newton Garver, *This Complicated Form of Life* (Chicago, 1994), Chapter 11 and John V. Canfield, *Wittgenstein, Language and World* (Amherst, MA, November, 1981), Part I, Chapter 3.

to reality itself. He writes: "The proposition 'Sensations are private' is comparable to: 'One plays patience [solitaire] by oneself'".[34] Here, Wittgenstein compares the propositions 1) Sensations are private and 2) One plays solitaire by oneself. 1) appears to be a metaphysical statement about the deep metaphysical nature of experience; 2), however, is clearly grammatical in Wittgenstein's sense. It is connected to a rule governing solitaire (one that specifies that solitaire is a game for a single player) and can even, in the right setting, be used to express that rule. The passage, then, urges its reader to view 1), like 2), as a grammatical proposition – one whose truth depends, at bottom, on the rules governing our language games. This was, in fact, Wittgenstein's view. Consider this passage: "I know…only from my *own* case" – What kind of proposition is this meant to be at all? An experiential one? No. – A grammatical one?[35]

Here again, Wittgenstein directs attention to an expression that is often used to express the traditional doctrine of the privacy of experience. He inquires into the nature of the expression. He considers the traditional view that it serves to articulate a claim about reality with "experiential" content, but rejects it with a single word. His alternative suggestion is that the expression is grammatical. The clear suggestion is that what looks like a deep truth about the nature of the world is, at bottom, a truth about grammar. More generally, he says "When we look into ourselves as we do in philosophy, we often get to see…[a] full-blown pictorial representation of our grammar. Not facts; but as it were illustrated turns of speech."[36] Grammatical truths, Wittgenstein thinks, often represent themselves to us as pictures. These, he thinks, are mistakenly taken to be pictures of reality, of facts – but he insists that they are not. Instead, they are, on his view, *pictorial representations of our grammar* or *illustrated turns of speech* that we mistake for pictorial representations of fact or illustrations of fact.

We might say of Wittgenstein's diagnosis of metaphysics as misconstrued grammar, as Von Wright does of his remarks on family resemblances, that it constitutes a "thought manoeuvre" that "has its origin in Spengler". This is fine so long as we realize that Wittgenstein's fully articulated ideas were neither expressed nor even contemplated by Spengler. Rather, such ideas took shape in Wittgenstein as he identified and spelled out fully some of his own objections to Spengler's ideas and procedures.

Recognizing such connections are helpful, so long as one realizes that the Wittgensteinian "thought manoeuvres" in question are not to be found in Spengler's work. The main focus of this book, especially the early chapters, is upon more direct influences that Spengler had upon Wittgenstein. These more direct influences take the form of Wittgenstein incorporating, in one way or another, genuinely Spenglerian ideas – that is, ideas that Spengler himself formulated and expressed – into his own philosophical work. It is such influences, influences whose presence in Wittgenstein is characteristically expressed subtly, implicitly, or indirectly, that I seek to identify and explicate in subsequent chapters.

---

34 Ludwig Wittgenstein, *Philosophical Investigations*, Pt I, paragraph 104.
35 Ibid., paragraph 295.
36 Ibid.

Before ending the present discussion, I want to raise the issue of why Wittgenstein thought that Spengler was guilty of a confusion between prototype and object. I would like to explore his suggestion in some depth. The passage cited above specifies a confusion in Spengler between his "prototype" and the historical facts which are his objects of scrutiny. It suggests that the structure of the conceptual relations within his historical prototype – relations which can be expressed as grammatical or conceptual necessities – are somehow confused with historical necessities. This appears to be his point when he writes, "willy nilly we…ascribe the properties of the prototype to the object we are viewing in its light; and claim '*it must always be…*'". It is hard to know exactly what Wittgenstein had in mind here, or what he might have offered by way of an example of this mistake.

I will now offer a modest conjecture. To begin, let us focus on Spengler's use of the terms "culture" and "civilization". As he uses them, the correct application of the term "culture" to a society requires, at least, the presence of certain *intrinsic* observable features. These include the prominence of art and religion as social forces, and a shared sense of religious, aesthetic, and ethical values. The correct use of the term "civilization" similarly requires certain intrinsic observable features. These include irreligiousness, prominent technological and scientific accomplishments, politics on the global scale, and a paucity of influential artistic activity. It is worth noting that the two terms specify features that are not compatible. No society to which the term "culture" applies will, at that time, be one to which the term "civilization" applies. This should be obvious on a moment's reflection: a society in which religion and art dominate cannot also be artless and irreligious.

In some passages, Spengler seems to use the terms "culture" and "civilization" straightforwardly and simply to refer to societies that display these intrinsic characteristics. On such a use, the terms "culture" and "civilization" simply refer to two different, distinguishable types of social organization by means of these intrinsic features. Using these terms in this way, Spengler's historical claim that cultures develop into civilizations counts as an empirically significant historical claim. It would state that societies with certain sorts of intrinsic features (cultures) develop into societies with very different sorts of intrinsic features (civilizations). I will call this straightforwardly descriptive use of the terms "culture" and "civilization", *the minimal descriptive use.*

Other passages in Spengler suggest a different tendency and a more complicated usage. I will refer to it as the *ramified periodic use.* On this use, the term "culture" is meant to pick out societies that meet the descriptive requirement of the minimal descriptive use of "culture" *and that also subsequently decline in certain specified ways into societies that have the intrinsic features associated with the term "civilization".* Similarly, on the ramified periodic use, the term "civilization" is meant to pick out societies which meet the descriptive requirement of the minimal descriptive use of "civilization" *and also have evolved from prior stages that displayed the intrinsic features associated with the term "culture".* The requirement of these further historical or periodic features as part of their meaning would link the terms *conceptually.* On this use, it is *conceptually true, necessarily true,* both that cultures develop into civilizations and that civilizations develop from cultures. This is important. If I am right, on this use of Spengler's terms, his statement that cultures develop into civilizations would count, not as an historical claim, but merely as a definitional truth and, so, devoid of empirical content.

On what I have called Spengler's minimal descriptive use of "culture" and "civilization" the statement "Cultures develop into civilizations" is an empirical claim that is historically true or historically false depending upon the historical facts. On what I have called Spengler's ramified periodic use of "culture" and "civilization" the statement "cultures develop into civilizations" is an empty conceptual truth that has no empirical significance. Was Spengler reflectively aware that his usage of the terms "culture" and "civilization" might have shifted between the minimal descriptive and the ramified periodic uses? How did *he* think he was using these terms?

He appears to have been confused. He states that "the two words ... are used in a periodic sense, to express *a strict and necessary organic succession*".[37] What does *he* mean by "a periodic sense" and by a "necessary organic succession"? By the former, Spengler probably did not have anything *exactly* in mind. Wittgenstein's main complaint with Spengler is that he did not have a sufficient reflective understanding of the concepts he employed. Spengler seems to think that his terminology *both* illuminates the succession from culture to civilization as a natural historical process, an "organic succession", *and also* shows that succession to be necessary. If I am right, Spengler is entitled either to the claim that this succession is historical or to the claim that it is necessary – but not both. The former would emerge on the minimal descriptive use of his terms; the latter, on the ramified periodic use. It is worth considering that Spengler was able to claim both with an air of triumph because he failed to notice any distinction between the two uses. Unconsciously conflating them, he was able to claim to have discovered both an historical truth and a necessary one. On his minimal descriptive use of these terms, his claim that cultures develop into civilizations is historically significant and, if true, very interesting. It would however be no more necessary than any other empirical truth. On his ramified periodic use, he can claim a "necessary succession" from cultures into civilizations, but one that is merely conceptual or grammatical – not one that operates in the world as an organic historical necessity. I am suggesting that Wittgenstein's stated difficulties with Spengler may be explained in the terms I have introduced here. First, Wittgenstein was, in effect, frustrated with Spengler's inattention to the fact that he sometimes employed something like the ramified periodic use of "culture" and "civilization". Second, and more important, Wittgenstein recognized something along these lines: Spengler's ramified periodic uses of the terms bestowed a *conceptual* necessary connection between "culture" and "civilization" which Spengler confused with an actual *historical* necessity between cultures and civilizations.

The following might serve as a plausible account of Spengler's mistake: First, when Spengler claimed that he had *discovered* the significant historical truths that cultures develop into civilizations and that civilizations evolve from cultures, he had a minimal descriptive use of his terms dimly in mind. Second, when he asserted that his claims express a *necessity*, he was thinking – neither consciously nor clearly – along the lines of the ramified periodic use. He failed to notice that the latter robbed

---

37 Oswald Spengler, *Decline of the West*, vol. 1, pp. 23–4.

his claim of any empirical content. Third, failing to recognize clearly any distinction between a minimally descriptive and a ramified periodic use of his terms, he was able to believe that his claims were *both historically significant and also necessary.* Finally, his belief that his claims expressed an *historical necessity* was a blatant confusion. He failed to appreciate that the necessity of his claims was merely the conceptual necessity bestowed upon them by a ramified periodic use of "culture" and "civilization". Instead, he misapplied this necessity to a historical process. On this reconstruction, Wittgenstein's negative comments about Spengler's procedures mean that they allow necessities that hold only at the level of his prototype – necessities which emerge from his system of interdefined terms on the ramified periodic use – to be confusedly misapplied to historical phenomena.

I offer this conjecture only as a first attempt to interpret some of Wittgenstein's critical remarks about Spengler that were cited above, to supply some detail where the passages themselves suggest only a direction. I offer it with less than full confidence. In contrast, I am quite sure of the following: 1) Wittgenstein's remarks offer a basic criticism of Spengler's methodology. 2) There are clear and obvious indications that Wittgenstein thought that Spenglerian methodology embodied conceptual confusions. 3) Wittgenstein believed both that these confusions are connected to historical distortion and dogmatism in Spengler and, perhaps most important, that they obscured his real insights.

V. A Direct Spenglerian Influence?: Meaning and Context

My attempts, in the chapters that follow, will be, almost exclusively, to locate and identify features of Wittgenstein's later writings that were influenced by Spengler, which present themselves in ways that are neither directly nor explicitly found in the content of those writings. In so doing, I deal more with the spirit of those writings – with content that is latent and not directly expressed. My tendency will be to focus on influences that show themselves not so much in what Wittgenstein states, but, rather, in his intimations, evocations, and hints. I am not, however, persuaded that there is no more direct Spenglerian influence on Wittgenstein's later writings. That is one reason why I have taken seriously the attempts of others to do this.

Wittgenstein's reading of Spengler may well have led to his observations about family resemblances and his view of metaphysics as misconstrued grammar. I have argued that neither were Spenglerian ideas. On the contrary, Wittgenstein proposed these ideas in connection with his criticisms of Spengler. Monk, Peterman, and Haller have suggested that Wittgenstein's emphasis in the *Investigations* on "seeing connections" – and the connected notion of a "perspicuous representation" – derives from Spengler.[38] I do not reject this, but I will not discuss it in any detail. The evidence presented for it is respectable. My major misgiving with respect to this suggestion is that it identifies tendencies that are very general. It is true that both Spengler and Wittgenstein were concerned with seeing connections. What important thinker

---

38 See the following: Ray Monk, *The Duty of Genius*, pp. 302–3, 315–16; James F. Peterman, *Philosophy as Therapy* (New York, 1992), pp. 71–74; Rudolf Haller, *Questions on Wittgenstein* (Lincoln, NB, 1988), pp. 79–83.

is not? What needs to be shown with specificity is that they were both concerned with seeing connections in discernibly similar ways for discernibly similar purposes. Monk, Peterman, and Haller, I think, do not quite succeed in this. None of them gives any very specific account of the importance of seeing connections in Spengler and its connection to a similar specific tendency in Wittgenstein's grammatical approach to philosophy. What they offer, I think, is a fertile but uncompleted thought – a suggestion that might, at some future time, be spelled out in sufficient detail to provide significant illumination [39]

One noteworthy suggestion has been made by Cavell. In both versions of "Declining Decline", after a brief discussion of some parallels between Spengler's conception of a culture as a natural or organic entity and Wittgenstein's notion of a form of life, he writes:

> I am not in a position to claim that Wittgenstein derived his … idea of forms of life from Spengler's idea of cultures as organic forms … but Spengler's vision of Culture as a kind of Nature … seems to me shared, if modified, in the *Investigations*.[40]

Here, Cavell is straightforward in admitting that he is offering a suggestion that he is not prepared to support – that the central Wittgensteinian notion of a *form of life* was derived from "Spengler's vision of Culture as a kind of Nature". He knows that his suggestion, if correct, is important. Perhaps after further investigation, Cavell or someone else might be "in a position to" offer it as a claim and elaborate upon it. Straightforwardness of this form is laudable. About this suggestion, I will have nothing further to say. In what follows, however, I seek to emulate this sort of straightforwardness. Like Cavell, I would like to suggest a *direct* Spenglerian influence on Wittgenstein's later philosophy. Also, like Cavell, I want to make it clear that, my attempts to support my own suggestion notwithstanding, I am not yet in a position to offer it as more than an intriguing possibility. I will, however, say this much: if the conjecture I am about to offer is correct, it is a very important contribution to the understanding of the development of Wittgenstein's later thought. Indeed, it may well uncover the inspiration for one of the most important shifts in Wittgenstein's thought – that between one of the most central features of the Tractarian view of language and the very different conception that replaces it in the *Investigations*.

Is there any idea in Wittgenstein's later philosophy, a "thought manoeuvre" that plays a direct role in the grammatical program of the *Investigations*, which is itself a Spenglerian idea? There is, I think, an intriguing possibility. My main suggestion in this section is that there is a link between Spengler's thought and a very significant feature of Wittgenstein's later philosophy. The latter is both prominent and pervasive in the *Investigations*. The feature I have in mind is important for reasons other than its prominence in the *Investigations* and elsewhere in the later writing, but, also,

---

39 In fairness, Monk has recently offered a more extended account of the importance of seeing connections in the *Investigations* than he does in *The Duty of Genius*. This account, however, does not elaborate specifically on any connection of the notion of seeing connections in Spengler. See Chapter 4 of his recent short work, *Reading Wittgenstein* (London, 2005).

40 Stanley Cavell, "Declining Decline 2", p. 341.

because it runs contrary to one of the central features of the *Tractatus*. For now, I will simply outline this tendency, some of its components and similarities to striking tendencies in Spengler's thought. I will return to this suggestion, offering a bit more in the way of specificity, in Chapter 5.

The tendency of thought in the *Investigations* that I have in mind is one that connects the *meaning* of an utterance, an action, a gesture, a mental occurrence, a facial expression, or an interpersonal interaction to its *context*. Context may be thought to include immediate surroundings, wider social or cultural settings, and, finally, the human form of life, which, for the later Wittgenstein, underlies all meaningful expression. Later, when I return to this idea, I will do so with special attention to its connections to Spengler's notion of cultural insularity and Wittgenstein's lifelong qualms about religious expressiblility as they manifest themselves in his later work. For now, it will be helpful to discuss a feature of Wittgenstein's early philosophy, specifically, the idea that a proposition "shows its sense" and to show how Wittgenstein's later insistence upon context and human surroundings as determinants of meaning constitutes a dramatic rejection of that early view.

The change in Wittgenstein's *Tractatus* conception of language to that of his *Investigations* may be viewed as a striking change in his conception of meaning. In the *Tractatus*, Wittgenstein writes of propositions and their sense. The sense of a proposition is, in effect, the Tractarian notion of meaning. It is a univocal notion. Sense, or meaning, in the *Tractatus* is of a singular type. The *Investigations* rejects the *Tractatus'* highly technical conception of a basic or elementary proposition and further rejects the connected notion of the sense of such as proposition. These, he came to think, were deeply misguided, illusory notions. Instead, in the later works, he emphasizes famously the many, disparate sorts of human expression. The meanings of words, sentences, utterances, gestures, natural expressions, and social interactions were, for the Wittgenstein of the *Investigations*, bewilderingly various.

The early work saw sense or meaning as essentially *representational*. Any bearer of meaning, any proposition capable of conveying a sense, did so in virtue of being a *picture*. Word sentences and other representational forms had sense because they functioned as *pictures*. Every basic proposition shared a structure or form, "logical form" was Wittgenstein's term in the *Tractatus*, in common with the possible fact that it depicted. Wittgenstein believed that every proposition, linguistic or otherwise, was a picture of some possible fact. He insisted too that a proposition *showed its sense*. So long as one grasps details of vocabulary, syntax, projection conventions, and logical form, one may, when presented with a proposition, grasp its sense – that is, grasp what the proposition represents pictorially by its form. Finally, Wittgenstein insisted, with a flourish, that the logical form of a proposition, the structural requirement for picturing, could not itself be pictured, and, so, could not be stated, but only shown.

Thoughts played a unique role in his early conception. For one thing, Wittgenstein insisted that thoughts *are* propositions. On a dominant interpretation of the *Tractatus*, shared by many Wittgenstein scholars, thoughts are propositions of a singular type.[41]

---

41 For an incisive explication of Wittgenstein's picture theory and a defense of the more controversial claim that thoughts are *intrinsically* pictures, see Norman Malcolm, *Nothing is Hidden* (London, 1989), Chapter 2.

Unlike other propositions, which convey their senses given common conventions, a thought, in the *Tractatus*, functioned as a purer sort of proposition *par excellence*. Wittgenstein appeared to think that thoughts, unlike other propositions, were *intrinsically* pictures – that is, anyone with a certain thought, *ipso facto*, grasped its sense without further ado. No conventions or other externals are necessary for a thought to convey its representational meaning. Thoughts, for Wittgenstein, were *intrinsically* pictures, and so, thoughts conveyed meaning in a manner that required neither interpretation nor other forms of mediation. To have a thought is, in the *Tractatus* scheme, to be presented with a mental representation of a possible reality and, so, with a sense, a meaning. The connection between thoughts and meaning was *internal* and unmediated. A thought is intrinsically a picture.

In the *Investigations*, a completely different conception emerges. It is not just that Wittgenstein rejected the highly formal *Tractatus* conceptions of proposition and sense. All meaningful expressions acquire their meaning against a background without which meaning is impossible. In the *Investigations*, Wittgenstein stresses repeatedly several themes that are characteristic of the work. First, one and the same word, sentence, gesture, or mental occurrence may, in different circumstances, convey different meanings.[42] Second, what may be meaningful in one set of circumstances may not be meaningful in another.[43] Finally, he rejects the *Tractatus* conception that thoughts, mental particulars, are any different in this respect.[44] Many of the *gedanke* experiments in the *Investigations* seek to convince the reader of these contentions and seek to draw philosophical conclusions from them.

Wittgenstein came to reject the *Tractatus* conception of a proposition, of thoughts that show their sense, in favor of his more contextualized view of meaning. This is highly characteristic of the *Investigations*. Perhaps significant, the notion that there is a relationship between meaning and surroundings, between meaning and cultural conditions, is a deeply Spenglerian notion. It is Spengler, after all, whose *Decline* presented to Wittgenstein the striking idea that the prime symbol of a given culture can be understood only by someone who is immersed in that culture. For Spengler, cultures are organic and one cannot understand the important expressive forms of a culture unless one is a functioning part of that organism. One can only understand a culture's expressive forms from inside the practices and interactive forms characteristic of that culture. Far from seeing the meaning of an expression, *Tractatus* style, as something intrinsic to an expression itself, an underlying thought or picture that shows its sense *in any setting*, Spengler emphasized that whatever meaning an expression has is internally connected to its cultural surroundings.

This may well have had a radicalizing effect on Wittgenstein at a time when he was getting ready to rethink seriously his early view. In 1931, Wittgenstein wrote a striking sentence; one that was reminiscent of the *Tractatus* view of propositions as pictures with an inexpressible logical form, but which also looked forward to what can be seen as a (possibly Spenglerian) theme in the *Investigations* views: "Perhaps

---

42 For example, *Philosophical Investigations*, Pt I, paragraphs 141–3, 151–6, 181, 432.

43 Ibid., paragraphs 27, 583. Also see my discussion in Chapter 5, section III–*iii*.

44 *Philosophical Investigations*, Pt I, paragraphs 141–2, 181.

what is inexpressible (what I find mysterious and am not able to express) is the background against which whatever I could express has its meaning."[45]

The idea here is that the surroundings – perhaps, the immediate situation, the cultural setting, or the form of human life within which an expression is made – play a very large role in bestowing its meaning upon it. They are "the background against which" it has its meaning. These, he suggests, are "inexpressible". Wittgenstein does not say whether this background is inexpressible *in principle*. He may have thought this. More likely, he thought that the background of which he writes is so complicated and pervasive, so deeply embedded in the surroundings of any given expression, that its role is largely unconscious and unstated. If so, a natural consequence would be that an individual unfamiliar with the background against which certain expressions have their meaning – an individual from a wholly alien culture, for example – could find little or no meaning in those expressions and, hence, could not understand them. This, of course, is a deeply Spenglerian notion.

VI. Final Remarks and a Glimpse Ahead

Some of the conjectures considered above about Spenglerian ideas incorporated into the content of Wittgenstein's later philosophy, including the one I have just outlined, may well have merit. Nonetheless, I believe that Spengler's most important influence on Wittgenstein manifests itself not in the explicit content of the later work, but, rather, in its overall intentions, its approach, and what Wittgenstein has referred to as its *spirit*. The "Spenglerian valence" of Wittgenstein's later work is, for the most part, not directly expressed but, rather, latent and implicit. I will, in the next two chapters, move on to stating and defending my own conclusions about that influence in detail. I offer three main conclusions.

First, Wittgenstein's prefatory comments to his *Philosophical Remarks*, both in their final published version and in earlier drafts, incorporate strikingly Spenglerian ideas. The content, tone, and, most pointedly, the vocabulary of these remarks are deeply Spenglerian. There are dramatic, point-for-point similarities between their assessment of modern civilization and that found in Spengler's *Decline*. They are, I think, the clearest reflection of Spenglerian ideas to be found in Wittgenstein's writings. I will both show this in detail and argue that the perspective expressed in these remarks, to a significant extent, remained with Wittgenstein for the rest of his life. This perspective influenced his late philosophical work, his assessment of its relation to his time, and his persistent pessimism that it would not be understood by the people of his or closely subsequent times. I take these subjects up in the next chapter.

Second, there is a remarkable affinity between Spengler's prescription for a twentieth-century philosophy of modern civilization and the final expression of Wittgenstein's mature philosophy in the *Investigations*. I can think of no other philosopher whose work so closely conforms to Spengler's prescriptions, nor can I write this off as mere coincidence. This affinity, to my knowledge, has never

---

45 Ludwig Wittgenstein, *Culture and Value,* p. 14e.

been explored in detail and provides another key to understanding the nature of Spengler's influence upon Wittgenstein. I identify and analyze Spengler's desiderata for a philosophy of civilization and Wittgenstein's remarkable adherence to them in Chapter 3.

Third, and finally, I will try to show that some of the most prominent features of Wittgenstein's mature philosophy can be seen as a more detailed working out of powerfully stated but underdeveloped ideas of Spengler that held great appeal for Wittgenstein as he returned to philosophy in the late twenties and early thirties

Chapter 2

Wittgenstein's Spenglerian Assessment of his Time

I. Introduction

In this chapter, I shall argue that Spengler influenced Wittgenstein's attitude toward his own time. Beyond this, and far more important, I want to show that this influence, in turn, helped shape Wittgenstein's attitude toward his philosophical work. This attitude reflects itself both in Wittgenstein's view of the relation of his work to his time and his gloomy expectation that his work would not be understood in its time. Finally, I believe that some of the most characteristic features of Wittgenstein's late philosophy can be shown, with near certainty, to have been influenced by Spengler. In this chapter, I will begin to make my case for this. The most important details of the case, however, will emerge in subsequent chapters.

There are very clear indications that, as Wittgenstein worked on the *Philosophical Remarks* around 1930, he explicitly held a view of his time that was pointedly Spenglerian in many of its particulars. Even more interesting, there is scattered but compelling evidence that many of the particulars of this Spenglerian attitude toward the time remained with him until the time he was completing the *Philosophical Investigations* in the late 1940s. Such a view, he explicitly avowed, was somehow a constituent of both works. He believed both works to be opposed to the spirit of their time. He feared that neither work was likely to be understood. His concern – expressed at different times in different ways – was that works so opposed to the deepest tendencies of their time would be both misunderstood and resisted in that time.

There can be no doubt that Wittgenstein thought about the *Remarks* in this way. As I will show, Wittgenstein's own prefatory remarks for that work show this explicitly and in remarkable detail. Showing this is true of the *Investigations* as well requires more work, but a strong case can be made. A significant body of scattered remarks that Wittgenstein made over the years while he was engaged in the philosophical program that culminated in the *Investigations* provides compelling indications that he saw that work, as he had seen the *Remarks*, as one written in opposition to the spirit of its time. I turn now to the fascinating details.

II. Remarks on *Remarks*

i. The Prefatory Remarks for Philosophical Remarks

Wittgenstein's *Philosophical Remarks* is a work from what is sometimes called his "transitional" or "middle" period – a time when he had become deeply skeptical about the major themes of the *Tractatus* and had begun to develop the methods and observations that were to be endorsed in the *Investigations*. It concerns itself explicitly with the problems that Wittgenstein always took seriously: the meanings of words and sentences, the relationship between language and the world and between language and thought. There are also remarks on the foundations of mathematics. Against its content, the preface to the *Remarks* comes as a surprise. It announces intentions that, on the surface, would appear to have nothing to do with the content of the work. Indeed judging from the evidence of the preface alone, one would have virtually no indication that a work in philosophy was to follow. He does not mention propositions, meanings, words, thoughts, verification, pictures, metaphysics, behaviorism, solipsism, dualism, or even philosophy itself. What little he does say concerns the "European and American civilization in which all of us stand" – a civilization whose spirit, he explicitly states, is opposed to that of the work.

Wittgenstein's preface to *Remarks* is short – only two paragraphs (each shorter than some of the sentences in Spengler's *Decline*). It is helpful that a somewhat longer earlier draft for a preface (I'll call it the "proto-preface") survives and is included in *Culture and Value*. For convenience I will refer to the actual preface and the proto-preface together as "the prefatory remarks". It is worth noting that while Wittgenstein ultimately opted not to use much of the proto-preface in his actual preface, he did not do so because he was unhappy with the material itself. Rather, he wanted to avoid a long preface because he did not think that much of what he said there would be understood no matter how elaborately he expressed his intentions. He writes, "the danger of a long forward is that the spirit of the book has to be evident in the book itself and cannot be described."[1] He adds, "telling someone something he does not understand is pointless, even if you add that he will not be able to understand it."[2]

ii. The Prefatory Remarks: A Spenglerian Account of Cultural Decline

In the prefatory remarks Wittgenstein refers in astonishingly negative terms to the civilization of his time and claims that it is a time of cultural decline. Here are some excerpts:

> This book is written for those who are in sympathy with the spirit in which it is written. This is not, I believe, the spirit of the main current of European and American civilization. The spirit of this civilization makes itself manifest in the industry, architecture and music of our time, in its fascism and socialism, and it is alien and uncongenial to the author.

---

1 Ludwig Wittgenstein, *Culture and Value*, ed, G. H. Von Wright in collaboration with Heikki Nymnan (Oxford, 1980), p. 7e.
2 Ibid.

I have no sympathy for the current of European civilization and do not understand its goals if it has any.

... the spectacle which our age affords us is not the formation of a great cultural work, with the best men contributing to the same great end, so much as the unimpressive spectacle of a crowd whose best members work for purely private ends.

A culture is like a big organization which assigns each of its members a place where he can work in the spirit of the whole ... In an age without culture on the other hand forces become fragmented and the power of an individual ... is used up in overcoming opposing forces and frictional resistances.

It is not ... as though [I] accepted what nowadays passes for architecture as architecture or did not approach what is called modern music with the greatest suspicion.

... the disappearance of the arts does not justify judging disparagingly the human beings who make up this civilization. For in times like these, genuine strong characters simply leave the arts aside and turn to other things and somehow the worth of an individual man finds expression.[3]

I want to start with these excerpts. Specifically, I will show that each of the main ideas they express is strikingly Spenglerian in substance, tone, and vocabulary.

First we must emphasize Wittgenstein's disparaging attitude toward the "civilization" of his time and his clear sense that it is a time in which "culture" has declined if it has not died out. This, of course, is exactly Spengler's assessment. He believed that modern culture is approaching its winter – consequently, that it is in a process of sharp decline, degenerating into a civilization. As we have seen (Chapter 1, II–*iii* above), Spengler writes:

every Culture has its own Civilization. In this work, for the first time the two words, hitherto used to express an indefinite, more or less ethical, distinction, are used in a *periodic* sense, to express a strict and necessary *organic succession*. The Civilization is the inevitable *destiny* of the Culture ... Civilizations are the most external and artificial states of which a species of developed humanity is capable. They are a conclusion ...death following life, rigidity following expansion ... They are an end.[4]

Equally dramatic is this passage: "Pure Civilization, as a historical process, consists in a taking-down of forms that have become inorganic or dead."[5]

Thus we can see a striking affinity between Spengler's and Wittgenstein's negative sense of the civilization of their time. Far from giving the word "civilization" the positive connotation it usually has, both use it to denote the result of a deterioration of a living culture into something degenerate and lifeless. Wittgenstein, it seems, chose to use the term in a way that is very close to Spengler's use of it in order to express a very similar view of his time and its relation to its past. I have argued in Chapter 1 that Wittgenstein did not share Spengler's sense of the historical inevitability of the deterioration of cultures into civilizations and shall return to that point. Still, it

3   All of these excerpts may be found on pp. 6e–7e of *Culture and Value*.

4   Oswald Spengler, *The Decline of the West*, vol. I, (New York, 1965), p. 31.

5   Ibid., p. 32.

seems clear from the prefatory remarks quoted above that he saw in his own time the results of a prolonged deterioration of a once vital, living culture. That culture, which united people's efforts, feelings, and sensibilities, he thinks, has degenerated into a fragmented, alienated, artless civilization.

It is worth remembering that Wittgenstein, as we have seen, urged Drury to read Spengler in order to teach him "something about the times in which we live". Despite his misgivings about Spengler's grand "morphological" conclusions and convictions about historical necessities, Wittgenstein certainly shared the historian's sense of his own time as one of cultural decline. Evidently he hoped such a view might serve as a palliative for what he took to be Drury's naive "Romanticism". It seems that a certain attitude of resignation and loss in Spengler, an attitude connected to his sense that the best his culture had to offer lies in the past, is what appealed most strongly to Wittgenstein. It is, I think, this part of Spengler's perspective on the times that Wittgenstein meant Drury to take seriously. Consider this claim of Spengler:

> We are civilized, not Gothic or Rococo, people; we have to reckon with the hard cold facts of *late* life, to which the parallel is to be found not in Pericles' Athens but in Caesar's Rome. Of great painting or great music there can no longer be, for Western people, any question. Their architectural possibilities have been exhausted these hundred years … we have not chosen this time. We cannot help it if we are born as men of the early winter of full Civilization, instead of on the golden summit of a ripe Culture in a Phidias or Mozart time.[6]

By way of emphasis, he adds this:

> Everything depends on our seeing our own position, our *destiny*, clearly, on our realizing that though we may lie to ourselves about it we cannot evade it.[7]

Finally, as we shall see in II–*iii* below, Wittgenstein's conviction that strong characters, in such times, will leave the arts behind is anticipated by a strikingly similar remark of Spengler.

Wittgenstein, like Spengler, saw his time, in bleak terms, as one of cultural decline and sought to oppose the spirit of the time in his philosophical writings. Beyond this, his account of cultural decline is pointedly Spenglerian in nature. He employs Spengler's terminology (specifically his use of the terms "culture" and "civilization") and, like Spengler, writes of artistic decline, a loss of cultural orientation, and the exhaustion of cultural forms. The only significant point of departure to be observed thus far is Wittgenstein's skepticism about Spengler's conviction that the phenomena of cultural decline are historically necessary. I have argued in Chapter 1 that Wittgenstein regarded that conviction as the result of a confusion in Spengler.

There are two further questions relating to cultural decline that need, at some point, to be addressed. One is this: Did Wittgenstein hold, with Spengler, that the diminution of religion as a social force was a central component of that decline?

---

6   Ibid., p. 40.
7   Ibid., pp. 40–41.

Much depends upon the answer to this question. It is a difficult question, one that requires quite a bit more in the way of preliminaries and distinctions than can be gracefully incorporated into this chapter. As such I will postpone addressing it until Chapter 5. For now, I can say that I will try to show that Wittgenstein did believe that his time was an increasingly irreligious one and that, by the time he wrote the *Investigations*, he had adopted what he thought of as a religious approach to philosophical problems in his own philosophical writings. He believed this approach to be opposed to the tendencies of his time.

A second question, not yet addressed, concerns the role of philosophy in a time of cultural decline, in a time of civilization. I will address this question in the next chapter. For now, I will indicate that Spengler offered an explicit detailed prescription for a philosophy of civilization. Remarkably, Wittgenstein's *Investigations* agrees in virtually every detail with that prescription – I would certainly think, more than any other major work of twentieth-century philosophy. The details of this are fascinating and have not, to my knowledge, been explored in detail before.

iii. The Prefatory Remarks: Beyond Cultural Decline to Civilization

It should be emphasized that Spengler not only described those features of a high culture which he believed civilizations lacked, but sought also to describe the preoccupations that are characteristic of civilizations themselves. As we have seen, he focused upon increases in scientific knowledge and its technological applications, more specifically, upon industrial and military applications, and upon expansionist quests for global power. He saw war as the natural result of such preoccupations. Spengler's *Decline* correctly predicted a world war in the near future with more to follow. Let us recall Dray's compression of Spengler's vision of a civilization as "an age ... of imperialism, of increasing political tyranny, and of almost constant warfare, as political adventurers skirmish for world empire", and one in which "the highest works of which are feats of administration and the application of science to industry". Spengler believed that civilizations are characterized by dramatic scientific and technological breakthroughs, but by neither the motivation nor the restraint necessary to use these for truly constructive purposes. Instead, he saw runaway misuses of them, in industry and in imperialistic adventures designed to achieve global dominance. The latter tendencies, he thought, characteristically result in "feats of administration" which amount to "political tyranny".

Speaking for himself, Spengler, true to form, is even more dramatic and bleak:

> Imperialism is Civilization unadulterated. In this phenomenal form the destiny of the West is now irrevocably set. The energy of culture-man is directed inwards, that of civilization man outwards. ... He stands for the political style of a far-ranging, Western ... future, and his phrase "expansion is everything" is the ... reassertion of the indwelling tendency of *every* Civilization that has fully ripened. ... It is not a matter of choice – it is not the conscious will of individuals, or even that of whole classes or peoples that decides. The expansive tendency is a doom, something daemonic and immense, which grips, forces into service, and uses up the late mankind [of civilization]. ... Hard as the half-developed

Socialism of today is fighting against expansion, one day it will become arch-expansionist with all the vehemence of destiny.[8]

This passage makes clear Spengler's own attitude to these tendencies. It is manifest in his description of them as "dacmonic", as a "doom". The passage also shows that Spengler believes fully in their historical necessity, and that any attempt to influence them – by individuals or groups – is useless. In a noteworthy passage he writes:

And I can only hope that men of the new generation may be moved by this book to devote themselves to technics [technology] instead of lyrics, the sea instead of the paintbrush, and politics instead of epistemology. Better they could not do.[9]

Here Spengler goes so far as to *advise* the people of the next generation to abandon poetry, art, and philosophy in favor of technology, the control of nature, and even participation in the politics of civilized time. On its face, this is very strange. Why would Spengler advise the people of his time to participate in what he regarded as demonic tendencies toward doom? Why would he explicitly state that they could not do better?

There is, of course, a measure of irony in the advice Spengler offers in the passage above. It is not meant to indicate his *approval* of civilization and its tendencies. No doubt, Spengler *personally* preferred poetry, art, and philosophy to technology, aggressive expansionist politics, and conquest. Still, he believed that the time for poetry, art, and philosophy had passed, that efforts in these endeavors could no longer succeed. All this, he thought, was historically necessary. The key to understanding the above passage is, I think, the recognition that his take on his time convinced him that persons *determined to succeed* could do so only in those endeavors which best served the tendencies of the time, however much he disliked them. His advice to the "men of the new generation" expressed neither a moral nor personal preference for technology, expansionism, and global politics. It expressed only his grim conviction that, in a time of civilization, success could only be achieved in such endeavors.

Now, what of Wittgenstein? Did he share Spengler's bleak and pessimistic characterization of civilization? Was he influenced by it? Returning to the prefatory remarks, it may be seen that Wittgenstein's view of civilization is, in many respects, reminiscent of Spengler's. His most explicit remarks about the civilization of the time are these:

The spirit of this civilization makes itself manifest in the industry, architecture, and music of our time, in its fascism and socialism, and it is alien and uncongenial to the author.

… it's proper to say that I think this book has nothing to do with the progressive civilization of Europe and America.

And while its spirit may be possible only in the surroundings of this civilization, they have different objectives.

---

8   Ibid., pp. 36–7.
9   Ibid., p. 41.

I have no sympathy for the current of European civilization and do not understand its goals if it has any. So I am really writing for friends who are scattered throughout the corners of the globe.

It is all one to me whether the typical Western scientist understands or appreciates my work, since he will not, in any case understand the spirit in which I write. Our civilization is characterized by the word "progress". Progress is its form rather than making progress being one of its features. Typically it constructs. It is occupied with building an ever more complicated structure. And even clarity is sought only as a means to this end, not as an end in itself. For me on the contrary clarity, perspicuity are valuable in themselves.[10]

These remarks suggest a sketchy outline of civilization's tendencies. It is very clear that he, like Spengler, felt opposed in spirit to those tendencies. In many details, the tendencies he suggests remind us of those mentioned by Spengler. Wittgenstein cites the growth of industry, emerging forms of social organization such as fascism and socialism, and the spirit in which the scientific work of the day is carried out. Like Spengler, he thinks of the tendencies of civilization as runaway tendencies. He sees a perversion of genuine progress carried out in its name, a preoccupation with construction, with building, that is lacking in any clear overall vision of its goals – and so, from his standpoint, out of control. There is the suggestion that the uses of scientific and industrial innovation are caught up in these runaway tendencies. As we shall see, Wittgenstein never relinquished this particular aspect of suspicion and pessimism. Writing years later, Wittgenstein characterized the focus on scientific progress in his time as "a delusion and a trap".[11] Finally, he sees all of these trappings of civilization to be connected with fascism and socialism.

One last point of comparison: it concerns a striking notion expressed in the prefatory remarks that is reminiscent of an often expressed Spenglerian idea. Remember, Wittgenstein in detailing a particular problem posed to an individual by his age, says "in an age without culture, … forces become fragmented and the power of an individual … is used up in overcoming opposing forces and frictional resistances." This seems an echo an idea forcefully expressed by Spengler that civilizations, unlike cultures, are times of *tension*. More specifically, he emphasizes that the lot of individuals living in a cultured time is natural and hospitable in dramatic contrast to that of individuals living with the internal difficulties posed by the surroundings of a civilization:

Heat and tension, blood and intellect, Destiny and Causality are to one another as the country-side in bloom is to the city of stone, as something existing *per se* is to something existing dependently. Tension without cosmic pulsation to animate it is the transition to nothingness. But Civilization is nothing but tension. …

Tension … knows no form of recreation but that which is specific to the world-city – namely, *détente*, relaxation, distraction.[12]

---

10 All of these excerpts may be found on pp. 6e–8e of *Culture and Value*.

11 Ibid., p. 56e.

12 Oswald Spengler, *Decline of the West*, vol. II, pp. 102–3.

To say more would be to engage too much in speculation. Wittgenstein simply doesn't tell us *exactly* what "frictional forces" operate on a civilized individual or how, if at all, they relate to the tensions of civilization, as conceived by Spengler. More important, he does not tell us what specific forms of blind construction, what kind of unreflective building, he thinks typify a civilization. With respect to the latter: is he thinking of physical structures? Social, economic, or political structures? He simply doesn't say – nor does he say how socialism and fascism fit in. They are, he suggests, social phenomena that are connected to all this building, but he offers no further elaboration. Perhaps they themselves are seen as elaborate constructs, and, so, *instances* of it. In the absence of further textual evidence, it would, I think, be foolish to draw conclusions that are more specific.

It is sufficient for my purposes to note some of the obvious affinities between Wittgenstein's characterization of the tendencies and preoccupations of a civilization and Spengler's. It must be admitted that these do not take quite the form of the startling detail-for-detail similarities that characterize their views on cultural decline. A reasonable conclusion might be that Wittgenstein's conception of cultural decline is dramatically Spenglerian in many, even most, of its details. Beyond this, it is reasonable to conclude that this was directly influenced by Spengler. Wittgenstein's less detailed conception of the characteristics of a civilization are very much like Spengler's. Spengler's view was remarkably unique. Wittgenstein explicitly cites Spengler as a major influence. The conclusion that Spengler influenced Wittgenstein's view of civilization is unavoidable.

It is worth making some further observations regarding the stances Spengler and Wittgenstein took toward their time – especially insofar as these influenced their attitudes toward their own work. In one respect, Spengler was more pessimistic than Wittgenstein; in another, less so.

Of course, neither Spengler nor Wittgenstein personally regarded their civilized time to be congenial. As we have seen, Spengler believed its negative features were historical necessities, details of larger, unavoidable tendencies. In effect, he foresaw the carrying out of a death sentence for Western culture. Wittgenstein appears not to have concurred – at least regarding the inevitability, the historical necessity, of decline. As noted already, he explicitly criticized this feature of Spengler's work, citing it as the result of a deep confusion. This is not to say that Wittgenstein ever believed with much conviction that the tendencies of civilization would be reversed. He probably never had any such expectation. Unlike Spengler, however, he did not rule it out as an historical impossibility. As we shall see, Wittgenstein came to entertain, at least as a possibility, the notion that the civilization of his time might produce something better – perhaps even a culture. Apparently connected to this, we shall also see that he later spoke of the possibility of his work being understood in the next century by a very different sort of readership. Finally, in opposition to those who think in terms of historical necessities, Wittgenstein – about the time he was reading Spengler – cautioned:

When we think of the world's future, we always mean the destination it will reach if it keeps going in the direction we can see it going in now; it does not occur to us that its path is not a straight line but a curve, constantly changing direction.[13]

In a strange and ironic contrast, Wittgenstein was far less optimistic about the prospects for his own work than Spengler was about his. He did not hold much hope that the *Remarks* would be understood by more than a few people at best. In 1931, a year after writing his proto-preface, he wrote:

If I say that my book is meant only for a circle of people (if it can be called a circle), I do not mean that I believe this circle to be the elite of mankind; but it does comprise those to whom I turn ... because they form my cultural milieu, my fellow citizens as it were, in contrast to the rest who are *foreign* to me.[14]

Wittgenstein believed that only a few exceptional persons – those not caught up in but, rather, opposed to their time of civilization – would understand him. This attitude, we shall see, remained with him for the rest of his life. His prefatory remarks do not express a conviction that *nobody* of his time would understand his work. They do describe, somewhat hopefully, "friends who are scattered throughout the corners of the globe". The above passage mentions "a circle of people" who might understand him. Later, as we shall see, he expressed similar hopes. These hopes, however, were never vivid or optimistic. We shall also see that he later explicitly described it "very remarkable" that his kind of opposition to the spirit of civilization could even emerge. Wittgenstein was never far from feeling alone, from despairing that he would not be understood in his own or any subsequent time.

For his part, Spengler, convinced that it was historically impossible to successfully resist the civilized trends of his time, did not seek to oppose them. In *Decline*, he sought only to write a book that clarified the real nature of his civilization. It appears that he expected to be understood. He boldly asserted that he had found the key, a perspective, a "new language", which would enable his generation to understand their historical situation. In *Decline*, we find no grim warnings that its pronouncements will not be understood. As we have seen, Spengler – with characteristic bravado – likened his new perspective to that of the Copernican Revolution and it is fair to conclude that he thought of it in similar terms: a new mode of thought, radically opposed to prevailing modes, but one which could be understood by any literate person with intelligence and a determination to do so. The Copernican analogy and, at least at times, his tone suggest that he might even have looked forward to a widespread acceptance of his perspective.

Wittgenstein and Spengler shared a vision of cultural decline – still, in their writings, they sought to address cultural decline in different ways. Their works and their goals were different. Spengler's work sought to *describe* the civilization of the time utilizing "a new language" ideally suited to that task. He did not seek to oppose civilized tendencies, believing, as he did, that such opposition was pointless. Wittgenstein, in contrast, did not seek to describe the civilization of his time in the

---

13 Ludwig Wittgenstein, *Culture and Value*, p. 3e.
14 Ibid., p. 6e.

main body of his philosophical works. Instead, he sought, at most, to address cultural decline indirectly – in the form of hints, intimations, and other features of his work that suggested what he referred to at times as its spirit. In further contrast to Spengler, Wittgenstein did seek to oppose, to combat, cultural decline – again, not by means of direct expression, but in a manner of expression that was latent and indirect.

III. The *Investigations* and "The Darkness of this Time": A Continuation of Spenglerian Attitudes?

i. The Question of Continuity

Was Wittgenstein's acceptance of a Spenglerian view of the times, so evident in the prefatory remarks for *Philosophical Remarks*, a mere passing enthusiasm? Did he enthusiastically embrace Spengler's assessment of civilization in the early thirties only to give it up not long afterwards? I very much doubt it. The evidence clearly suggests otherwise.

To show this, I want to introduce some scattered remarks which Wittgenstein made much later than those just analyzed. Throughout the forties, when he was composing and, in the later years, completing *the Philosophical Investigations*, he occasionally mused – either to himself or to others – about the civilization of the time, its relation to his own work, and what reception his work might have in such a time. The best known such remark, of course, comes from the preface to the *Investigations* and cites "the darkness of this time" as an obstacle to the understanding of the book. That remark does not, however, stand alone. Wittgenstein offered quite a few others which can be used to help achieve a better understanding of the concerns it expresses.

I will begin with that remark from the preface to the *Investigations* and work backwards. My plan is to show that Wittgenstein's reference to "the darkness of this time" belongs to a family of interesting observations that he made in his writings and conversations over a very long period of time. They collectively express very similar attitudes toward his time as those that he had earlier offered in the Spenglerian prefatory remarks for *Philosophical Remarks*. Those later observations can be seen as evidence that Wittgenstein approached not only the *Remarks*, but also the *Investigations*, with a Spenglerian attitude toward his time. I will suggest in advance that it is illuminating to regard Wittgenstein's Spenglerian prefatory remarks for *Philosophical Remarks*, written in 1930, as a kind of original ancestor from which this family of later remarks is descended. In overview, I am gathering these later remarks together in such a way as to present what I would hope the Wittgenstein of the *Investigations* might have accepted as a "perspicuous representation" of his take on his own times – one that remained discernibly Spenglerian in nature.

ii. The Investigations *and the Darkness of this Time*

In the preface to the *Philosophical Investigations*, Wittgenstein writes:

> It is not impossible that it should fall to the lot of this work, in its poverty and in the darkness of this time, to bring light into one brain or another, – but of course it is not likely.[15]

Of course, this is a strange and puzzling remark. In the preface to what he intended to stand as his definitive philosophical work, Wittgenstein expresses his pessimistic expectation that the work will not be understood. It is noteworthy, but not surprising, that he cites the "poverty" of his own book in this regard. It is not unusual for a self-reflective and self-critical writer to preface his or her work with an expression of doubt regarding its value. Wittgenstein may well have felt a special need to do so. It is well known that he fretted over, disapproved of, and took pains to combat his own vanity – especially about his work in philosophy. One can imagine that he intended his remark about the "poverty" of the *Investigations* as a kind of counterbalance. It may be significant in this regard that Wittgenstein does explicitly mention his vanity earlier in the Preface.[16] Whatever Wittgenstein intended by that remark, I think it much more interesting that he also cites "the darkness of this time" as a notable impediment to the understanding of the *Investigations*. It is this feature of the passage that I seek to explore and elucidate.

There is certainly good reason to interpret the above passage, at least in part, as an expression of a deep dissatisfaction – one connected with the nearly impossibly demanding standards that Wittgenstein imposed both upon himself and others. An ultra-perfectionist, he would naturally see much to criticize, much to regard as unworthy, in his own work, and in the philosophical capabilities of his readers. But, beyond this, he surely saw much that he deemed unworthy in the human scene around him, the civilization of his time. The passage expresses, no doubt, widespread dissatisfactions. It is illuminating to probe more deeply, to ask questions about Wittgenstein's profound tendencies toward dissatisfaction – especially those that led him to write of "the darkness of this time". What was Wittgenstein's perspective on his time as he composed the *Investigations*? What features of his perspective led him to the remarkable conclusion that his philosophical writings would not be understood in his time? Was his perspective similar to the one with which wrote the *Philosophical Remarks*?

iii. Preserving the Investigations *for a Better Sort of Reader*

Culture and Value contains some remarks, written in 1948, which Wittgenstein considered putting into the Preface of the *Investigations*. While they do not appear in the final version of the Preface, they serve to illuminate the passage with which we began:

---

15 Ludwig Wittgenstein, *Philosophical Investigations* (New York, 1953), p. ixe.

16 Ibid., pp. ixe–x: "I was obliged to learn that my results (which I had communicated in lectures, typescripts and discussions), variously misunderstood, more or less mangled or watered down, were in circulation. This stung my vanity and I had difficulty quieting it."

It is not without reluctance that I deliver this book to the public. It will fall into the hands which are not for the most part those in which I would like to imagine it. May it soon – this is what I would wish for it – be completely forgotten by the philosophical journalists, and so be preserved for a better sort of reader.[17]

Leaving aside Wittgenstein's interesting, dismissive swipe at "philosophical journalists", I would focus upon what he calls his wish that his book might be "preserved for a better sort of reader". The word "preserved" is an interesting one. It suggests, in context, his sense that a passage of time might be necessary before his book could be properly appreciated, that the development of the right sort of readership for his book might require such a passage of time.

One might read the passage as an expression of doubt that the *Investigations* would be understood in its time and that, in consequence, it might not be appreciated until a later time. This certainly suggests that the work does not fit the tendencies of its time. The passage does not, however, explicitly state any of this. In the absence of some corroboration, such a reading might well be resisted. Corroboration, however, is not hard to find. It comes in the form of an interesting earlier remark made by Wittgenstein in a conversation with Drury and preserved by the latter for posterity. It is this earlier remark to which I now turn.

iv. The Investigations' *Opposition to its Time – Hope for the Next Century?*

Drury reports a remark made by Wittgenstein in a 1947 conversation that pre-dated the writing of the above-cited passage by about a year. This was a time when the latter was working on the last part of the *Investigations*: "My type of thinking is not wanted in this present age. I have to swim so strongly against the tide. Perhaps in a hundred years people will really want what I am writing."[18] In an interesting respect, his remark is more explicit than those cited so far. Wittgenstein does not merely intimate that his philosophical thinking is somehow opposed to the tendencies of his time. Far more specifically, he states bluntly that it "is not wanted in this present age". Beyond this, he muses – ruefully, it seems – that it might take a century before his thoughts might find a willing readership. This remark is evidently connected to, but goes well beyond, his expressed hope that his work might be "preserved" for "a better sort of reader". It serves to confirm that Wittgenstein believed the *Investigations* to be directly opposed to the thinking of his time – a situation which he evidently regarded not as a function of a temporary fashion of thought, but one which would not likely change, if at all, for a century. Such concerns frequently arose when Wittgenstein contemplated the reception of his later work. Clearer expressions of these concerns, as we shall see, are not hard to find.

Drury, in commenting upon the conversation in which Wittgenstein made this remark, proceeds to identify another – one made later in the same conversation – which, he thought, might suggest a *rationale* for Wittgenstein's pessimism about

---

17 Ludwig Wittgenstein, *Culture and Value*, p. 66e.

18 M. O'C. Drury, "Notes on Conversations with Wittgenstein", in Rush Rhees (ed.), *Ludwig Wittgenstein – Personal Recollections* (Totowa, NJ, 1981), p. 94.

the reception of his work: "I am not a religious man but I cannot help seeing every problem from a religious point of view."[19]

Drury plainly regarded this as amplification upon the earlier remark. Beyond this, he raises the question of whether "the problems discussed in the *Philosophical Investigations* are being seen from a religious point of view".[20] Fascinated by Wittgenstein's remark and by Drury's suggestion, Norman Malcolm, arguably Wittgenstein's most prominent interpreter and defender, spent the last days of his life writing a remarkable book which sought to identify and explain a religious point of view latent in the *Investigations*.[21] Later, in Chapter 6, I shall discuss features of that book and the issue of whether Wittgenstein's late philosophy was written from a religious point of view. In so doing, I will explore some of Malcolm's interesting conclusions on the subject. For now, however, it is best to defer such questions until other issues have been more completely discussed. Chief among these is this chapter's main subject, Wittgenstein's perception of his time and its relation to his work. These and other issues, I think, provide some of the background against which any discussion of Wittgenstein's religious intentions should proceed. What can be noted for now and then put aside is this: Wittgenstein's two remarks to Drury taken together suggested to the latter a way of thinking about the metaphorical tide against which he felt he had to struggle. Drury's inference, one that is reasonable, is that it connotes, in part, that *irreligious* point of view which Spengler and, as it turns out, Wittgenstein saw as a central constituent of their civilized time.

v. Civilization and Culture: Again

Culture and Value is replete with writings, gathered from scattered sources, which serve as indications of Wittgenstein's grave reservations about the civilization in which he lived and carried out his program of thinking and writing. Unlike the passages above, which specifically indicate that he believed his own work to be opposed in spirit to that of his time, many of these simply register one or another detail of his dissatisfaction with the tendencies – cultural and intellectual – of the time. It is useful to examine some of these.

In 1947 Wittgenstein wrote:

> Perhaps one day this civilization will produce a culture. When that happens there will be a real history of the discoveries of the 18th, 19th, and twentieth centuries which will be deeply interesting.[22]

This remark contains two noteworthy features. The first is the juxtaposition – by now familiar – of the notion of a culture and that of a civilization. The distinction between a culture and a civilization, we have seen, was important to Wittgenstein. It is reasonable to think that "culture" and "civilization" are still being used here in

---

19 Ibid., p. 95.

20 Ibid., p. 94.

21 Norman Malcolm, *Wittgenstein – A Religious Point of View?* (Ithaca, NY, 1992), edited with a response from Peter Winch.

22 Ludwig Wittgenstein, *Culture and Value*, p. 64e.

something like the Spenglerian sense that he had employed in the prefatory remarks for *Remarks*. There is, however, one interesting difference that is worthy of note.

As we have seen, Spengler thought of a civilization as the result of cultural decline. Civilizations, by their nature, come into being when cultures exhaust themselves and degenerate. As such, Spengler's theory-laden use of these terms dictates that civilizations proceed from cultures, and not vice versa. Cultures produce civilizations; civilizations do not produce cultures. In the passage quoted above, however, Wittgenstein, against this, entertains a contrary possibility – one in which "this civilization will produce a culture". This would tend to corroborate my earlier contentions that Wittgenstein did not accept Spengler's theory of the comparative morphology of cultures or its conclusion that cultures *inevitably* decline and whither away.

Wittgenstein makes clear his own sense that his time is one of civilization and not one of culture in the passage quoted above. Its first sentence, however, regards it as *a bare possibility* that this civilization might, one day, produce a culture. It is certain, of course, that he thinks it has not yet done so. We should also note his subsequent claim that the emergence of a culture from his civilization would produce, at least, one worthy result – namely, a "real history", a "deeply interesting" one, of both the discoveries of his own century and of those which immediately preceded it. This cryptically expressed conviction is anything but self-explanatory, and raises a number of questions. Nonetheless, it is clear, in context, that Wittgenstein believed that his own time of civilization had failed to produce an "interesting" historical understanding of itself or of its preceding times. This is a striking claim, suggesting as it does, that all intellectual histories of his time are deficient in some fundamental manner. Perhaps just as surprising is his mysterious claim that this is a deficiency that the production of a culture might correct. His thought here is both bold and striking. He holds that our civilization is somehow blind to itself and to its own tendencies. Further, it is stated that its evolution into a culture – were that possible – would provide the requisites for illuminating and understanding its real nature.

It is natural, here, to ask three questions: 1) Could Wittgenstein have thought that the *Investigations*, like the *Remarks*, was opposed not just to the spirit of his time but, more specifically, to its being a *civilized* time? 2) Could he have thought the evolution of our civilization into a *culture* might provide not only a more satisfactory historical understanding of the times, but also the "better sort of reader" for his own work of which he wrote elsewhere? 3) Might he have hoped that the *Investigations* might, at some time, play some role, however slight, in combating the civilized spirit of his time, and perhaps even help pave the way for the re-establishment of a culture? There are, I think, overwhelmingly good reasons to answer the first question in the affirmative. I shall try to show this in what follows. The second and third questions raise issues that are more difficult. They are harder to answer, but are, I think, worth reflecting upon. They may well provide further keys to a more adequate understanding of Wittgenstein's philosophy.

vi. A Negative Picture of Civilization

In 1946 Wittgenstein wrote a passage that is plainly related to the one cited above:

> It is very *remarkable* that we should be inclined to think of civilization – houses, trees, cars, etc. – as separating man from his origins, from what is lofty and eternal, etc. Our civilized environment, along with its trees and plants, strikes us then as though it were cheaply wrapped in cellophane and isolated, from God, as it were. That is a remarkable picture that intrudes on us.[23]

Again, we see a dramatic expression of Wittgenstein's dissatisfaction with his time and, more specifically, with its *civilized* nature. Here, he directly expresses – in more vivid terms – his negative "picture" of the civilization of the time in which he wrote and worked as one which does, in fact, cut people off from what is most important. There is the striking suggestion that civilization is "isolated from God". More generally, there is the intimation that civilization alienates humankind from what is most valuable. This fits in well with all of the previously cited passages in this section, with my comments upon them, and with a basic component of a Spenglerian assessment of the time.

I would call attention to an interesting feature of this 1946 quote. Wittgenstein states that it is "very remarkable" that the negative thoughts about civilization that he expresses in the passage should occur at all – that "we" should be inclined toward such thoughts. Why did he think this *remarkable*? One possibility – one which, as we have seen, fits in well with some of Wittgenstein's most striking pronouncements on such matters – has to do with one's relationship to one's own culture or civilization. It will be shown that Wittgenstein, in his later thought, recognized a pervasive tendency to accept unreflectively the underlying assumptions, values, aesthetics, and tendencies of thought that characterize one's own culture or civilization. In recognizing this tendency, he worried about one of its natural consequences. Specifically, he often remarked about the difficulty of "getting outside" the deep perspective of one's own time and place in a way that would allow for the understanding of another culture or for a perspicuous and even a critical assessment of one's own. It is as if one is so imbued with the deep assumptions of one's own culture or civilization, so rooted in that, that it is impossible to think in any other terms. From such a stance, of course, it would indeed appear "very remarkable" that anyone should be able to get outside of his or her own perspective in order to come to terms with it. This is a theme and a problem that we shall revisit.

There is another noteworthy and puzzling feature in this quote. Wittgenstein writes of a negative picture of civilization not just as *his own* picture, but, rather, one that "intrudes on us". It is presented as something that "we" are inclined toward – rather than, as one might expect, something *he alone* accepts. This is surprising. All of the preceding passages provide indications that Wittgenstein felt alienated from the dominant tendencies of his time, from its civilization, and that he directly opposed them both in attitude and, more importantly, in his philosophical writings. This sense appears to connect with his various gloomy assertions that virtually

---

23 Ibid., p. 50e.

nobody would understand his work – at least during his time. It would seem, then, from all of the previously cited remarks, that Wittgenstein felt isolated in this respect – at best, *nearly* alone; at worst, *hopelessly* alone. Certainly, in speaking to Drury of his need "to swim so strongly against the tide", he evokes a picture of one man swimming alone. Against all this, the use of the first-person plural – the "we" and the "us" in the above passage – seems out of place. What could it mean? I want to dwell on this question briefly. The underlying issue is important enough to reflect a bit upon Wittgenstein's use of first-person plural pronouns – not only in this passage but, more generally, in his later philosophical writings.

vii. A Tangent: Wittgenstein's Uses of First-person Plural Pronouns in the Investigations

Based upon the other passages we have examined, I would strongly doubt that Wittgenstein believed the 1946 passage's negative "picture" of his civilization to be one that he shared with most, or even with many people. Indeed, I would insist that he felt that very few people, if any, shared it. Why, then, his use of the first-person plural in the passage discussed above? I believe Wittgenstein's use of "we" and other first-person plural forms in that passage is similar to some characteristic uses of these terms in the *Investigations*. Here are some examples (one of which we have already examined in a different context):

> We feel as if we had to *penetrate* phenomena: our investigation, however, is directed not towards phenomena, but, as one might say, towards the '*possibilities*' of phenomena. We remind ourselves, that is to say, of the *kind of statement* that we make about phenomena. Our investigation is therefore a grammatical one.[24]

> We are under the illusion that what is peculiar, profound, essential, in our investigation, resides in its trying to grasp the incomparable essence of language.[25]

> We predicate of the thing what lies in the method of representing it. Impressed by the possibility of a comparison, we think we are perceiving a state of affairs of the highest generality.[26]

> Here it is difficult as it were to keep our heads up, – to see that we must stick to the subjects of our every-day thinking, and not go astray …[27]

> What *we* do is bring words back from their metaphysical to their everyday use.[28]

Wittgenstein uses the first-person plural in unusual and idiosyncratic ways in these and many other passages. When he writes about illusions that "we are under", or the nature of "our" philosophical misconceptions, it is reasonable to conclude that he is thereby referring to a large number of people – perhaps even to everyone who has tried seriously to do philosophy. Wittgenstein, after all, states repeatedly in

---

24 Ludwig Wittgenstein, *Philosophical Investigations*, Pt I, paragraph 90.
25 Ibid., paragraph 93.
26 Ibid., paragraph 104.
27 Ibid., paragraph 106.
28 Ibid., paragraph 116.

the *Investigations* that he is combating deeply entrenched preconceptions, shared mistakes that are pervasive in philosophy, and pathologies of thought that are extremely difficult to recognize and combat. James F. Peterman has argued in his interesting book, *Philosophy as Therapy*, that this is the *primary* use of the first-person plural in the *Investigations*.[29] It is a very important use, to be sure. Still, I want to focus upon others.

In these passages Wittgenstein also writes about how "we" go about doing philosophy, the nature of "our" investigations, the difficulties "we" face in keeping "our heads up" and thinking correctly. Here, his focus is not on mistaken tendencies of thought – rather, it is his own thoughts, new thoughts which are being expressed. They are thoughts that are designed to identify *and eliminate* the pervasive mistakes to which philosophers are prone. Something in this is puzzling. As we have seen, Wittgenstein often feared that his own thoughts would not be understood at all. Why then would he express his own thoughts by writing of what "we" do in philosophy, about the nature of "our" investigations? The evidence examined so far shows that he recognized all too well that there might be only one person – namely, himself – included in the "we". So, again, we must ask: why did he use these plural forms?

I would call attention to two functions that first-person plural pronouns often perform in the *Investigations*. The first is associated with a remarkable feature of his late philosophical writings – one that I will discuss in a different context, and at greater length, in Chapter 6. Specifically, Wittgenstein frequently bifurcates his philosophical presentation into a confrontational dialogue between two voices. One of these is a wayward voice, which labors under and expresses philosophical prejudices, misconceptions, and other pathologies of thought. The other is a wiser voice, one that represents a more positive direction in late Wittgensteinian thought, which attempts to combat these. The exchanges are sharp and dramatic. The effect is striking. These represent, perhaps even re-enact, Wittgenstein's philosophical conversations with himself. These self-dialogues lend themselves naturally to the use of first-person plural terms ("we", "us" and "our"). It can readily be verified that many uses of these terms in the *Investigations* occur in just such contexts. As such, his uses of "we" and the other first-person plural forms in these self-dialogues usually refer to the personifications of the wiser voice and that of its wayward disputant.

A second function – not always distinct from the first – is similar to, if not an instance of, that performed by the common *editorial* "we". In the *Investigations*, Wittgenstein uses words like "we", "us", and "our" in passages that are not obviously written as self-dialogues. This use of plural pronominal forms is used to pick out those who are capable of the kind of rigorous thinking which the *Investigations* demands – those who are engaged in the sort of grammatical analysis that Wittgenstein advocates. Used in this way, the plural pronouns are not used to refer to those who labor under the deep, shared mistakes to which philosophers are prone. On the contrary, most of them refer to those who have begun to master and employ Wittgenstein's own thoughts. So used, "we" refers to a select few. As we have seen, even in optimistic moods, Wittgenstein did not believe that the world included more

---

29 See James F. Peterman, *Philosophy as Therapy* (New York, 1992), pp. 42–5.

than a small, scattered band of such people. In less optimistic moods, he probably feared that he alone constituted this "we".

The passages cited above from the *Investigations* are interesting in that they can be read as serving either of these functions. All of them occur close enough to passages that are presented as self-dialogues that they can plausibly be read as continuous with them – and, so, as part of a conversation Wittgenstein is holding with himself. Yet, none of them, *need* be read in this way. When, for example, Wittgenstein says that "our" investigations are grammatical or that "we" must keep our heads up and avoid illusions, the surrounding passages do not make it altogether clear whether he is addressing his wayward alter ego or employing the specialized use of the editorial "we" I have just described. My purposes do not require deciding this issue because neither his self-dialogue use of "we" nor his quasi-editorial "we" implies the actual existence of even one other person who shares his thoughts.

I would think the same is true of Wittgenstein's use of the first-person plural in the 1946 quote. One might ask: just who are included in the "we" that are inclined to think of civilization as separating men from what is most important? Who constitutes the "us" upon whom this negative picture of the civilization of the time imposes itself? Unfortunately, this fragment from *Culture and Value* does not tell us. Still, I think it is both natural and reasonable to suppose that Wittgenstein – as he does so often in the *Investigations* – is using the "we" of that passage either in self-dialogue mode or as an editorial device to point to those individuals who are capable of the "very remarkable" task of overcoming their rootedness in their own civilization and realize the passage's perspective upon it. Certainly Wittgenstein didn't think that this "we" amounted to much of a crowd. If he was not merely conversing with himself, then the "we" of which he wrote picked out, at most, a small number of rare individuals capable of such a take on the times. I would offer the further suggestion that this particular use of the first-person plural – in addition to many used in the *Investigations* – may well have served the function of helping him feel a little less lonely.

viii. A Fragment on Art and Technology

During a 1949 wide-ranging discussion between Wittgenstein and Drury, the latter remarked about the great improvement in the quality of recorded music represented by the advent of long-playing records. He noted their superiority to older recordings. Wittgenstein, for his part, did not disagree and acknowledged that a technological improvement had taken place. He failed, however, to enter into the spirit of Drury's modest enthusiasm. Displaying a kind of dark humor, he said, "It is so characteristic, that just when the mechanics of reproduction are so vastly improved, there are fewer and fewer people who know how the music should be played."[30] This remark is, of course, not just notable for its mixture of humor and gloom. It appears to be a pointed remark about the time and about a direction that is "characteristic" of the time. More specifically, it regards a remarkable technological breakthrough – the sort of technological development typical of a civilized time as Spengler conceived it – as having come too late. Why? His strong suggestion is that an enhanced ability to

---

30 Rush Rhees (ed.), *Personal Recollections*, p. 96.

reproduce art is practically meaningless in a time when artists rarely produce anything worth reproducing. If the occasional artist does produce anything worthy, there are very few people who are able to appreciate it, and, so, the value of its reproduction is negligible. The remark, of course, is strongly reminiscent of Wittgenstein's earlier Spenglerian belief that the arts had all but disappeared during his time and also of a mistrust of its technological productions. It strongly suggests that such Spenglerian notions were still very much with Wittgenstein more than a decade after their initial impact on him. Elsewhere, in *Culture and Value*, writing more generally, but in the same vein, Wittgenstein likens the fascination with scientific progress as "a delusion and a trap".[31] So, this passage, while not as directly significant as some of the others we have examined, is an interesting one. It may be seen to express, by way of black-humored pessimism, something akin to a cartoon, a caricature, of the time – one whose mode of presentation is that of a synecdoche.

IV. Concluding Remarks

I have argued in this chapter that Wittgenstein 1) carried a Spenglerian view of his time to his later philosophical work, 2) viewed that work as opposed, at least in spirit, to its time, and 3) maintained deep doubts as to whether his work would ever be appreciated in that time. I am confident of these conclusions and I regard them as considerations that must enter into any adequate understanding of Wittgenstein's philosophical work.

Against this, it is important to recognize how little has thus far been achieved. I have established that Wittgenstein believed that his later philosophical work was written in opposition to the tendencies of the civilization of his time. This is no small matter. I have not, however, indicated *in what way* Wittgenstein's later philosophy may have so opposed his time. Addressing this, even making worthy suggestions about it, constitutes a more important component of this book's project than anything undertaken in this chapter. This extremely important and very difficult task will be taken up in Chapters 3 and 4, and – insofar as it relates to Wittgenstein's opposition to the irreligiousness of his time – in Chapters 6 and 7.

There is a related issue that has rarely, if ever, been fully addressed. It concerns Spengler's conception of the proper role of philosophy in a time of civilization. In the next chapter, I will examine Spengler's very specific pronouncements on this subject as they appear in *Decline*. Doing this, I think, will help support my contention that Wittgenstein's late philosophy was undertaken, in part, with a Spenglerian understanding of its nature. Specifically, I seek to show the *Investigations* to be in dramatic agreement with the detailed prescription for a philosophy of civilization that Spengler offers in *Decline*. It will, I am confident, emerge that no other major work of twentieth-century philosophy coheres as well with Spengler's *desiderata*. It is to this project that I now turn.

---

31 Ludwig Wittgenstein, *Culture and Value*, p. 56e.

Chapter 3

Philosophy for a Time of Civilization: Spengler's *Desiderata* and the *Investigations*

I. Introduction

In the preceding chapter, I have argued that Wittgenstein's reading of Spengler's *Decline* strongly influenced the prefatory remarks to *Philosophical Remarks*. At the time he wrote those prefatory remarks, Wittgenstein explicitly regarded Spengler as a thinker who had influenced his own ideas. I have also taken pains to show that Wittgenstein carried basic elements of a Spenglerian perspective to his later philosophical writings. I believe that all this is worth noting in itself. More important, however, it may help illuminate Wittgenstein's later writings. I am well aware that I have, so far, restricted my focus to almost entirely peripheral features, external features, of Wittgenstein's later writings. I have restricted myself mainly to his characterizations of the spirit of his work as one that opposes that of its time and to his many Spenglerian remarks about the civilized time in which he produced that work. I have not yet related these characterizations to Wittgenstein's distinctive approach to the problems of philosophy in the *Investigations* – much less, to its philosophical content. Can I show, or even suggest, how the methodology or the content of the *Investigations* might directly proceed from Spenglerian conceptions? I shall begin doing so in this chapter. I want, specifically, to show that the *Investigations* can plausibly be seen to represent a Spenglerian philosophy for a time of civilization. Roughly, in this chapter, I seek to show how some of the unique and characteristic *goals and methods* of the *Investigations* were influenced by Spengler. In the next chapter, I consider the far more difficult question of *which specifics of its content* might have been so influenced.

There is much in Wittgenstein's late philosophical writings – especially the *Investigations* – that is Spenglerian in an important way that has not yet emerged. I will explore some of Spengler's specific remarks in *Decline* about *philosophy itself*, and especially philosophy in an age of civilization. These remarks offer a quite specific prescription, a fairly clear list of *desiderata*, for such a philosophy – one that is both radical and distinctive. I will show that some of Wittgenstein's explicitly stated philosophical goals are in accordance with this Spenglerian prescription. Perhaps even more important, I will also show that the character of Wittgenstein's approach to philosophical problems, his ways of addressing them in the *Investigations*, is in *striking, unique accordance* with that prescription. I emphasize that no major philosopher of the twentieth century has produced a body of philosophical work that more closely fits Spengler's prescription than has Wittgenstein.

This has not been discussed in much detail in the philosophical literature. The discussion here meets a need – that of showing methodically that Spengler influenced both the goals and methods of Wittgenstein's later work. It may well be the most important indication so far to emerge. Beyond providing evidence of such an influence, it provides broad indications about the specific details of that influence. In that respect at least, this short chapter offers a modest breakthrough. It is a breakthrough in that it offers fresh evidence of one feature of Spengler's influence on Wittgenstein that is both significant and, at least in outline, correct. The breakthrough is modest, because it does not yet address the far more difficult questions that will not be addressed until the next chapter.

II. Spengler's Prescription for a Philosophy of Civilization

Just what did Spengler think of philosophy? More important, what did he think about the prospects, if any, for philosophy in an age of civilization? He does not offer a detailed answer to either question. His *Decline of the West*, however, contains a number of fascinating, pointed remarks on the subject of philosophy in a time of civilization. These remarks, taken collectively, suggest philosophical goals and approaches that are unconventional in the extreme. They call for a philosophy that will put an end to all philosophy employing a methodology that is radical in a number of ways. I shall turn now to these remarks. My plan has two parts. First, in this section, I want to examine Spengler's remarks in order to draw some conclusions about the directions he felt a philosophy of civilization should take. Then, in the next section, I want to show how well Wittgenstein's later philosophy coheres with Spengler's view.

This chapter is necessarily short. Brevity and simplicity are not characteristic of Spengler's *Decline*, which is, for the most part, a work that is repetitive in presenting its main themes – a work that eschews concision, much less understatement. Against this, Spengler's treatment of philosophy is surprisingly brief and even truncated. Still, what he writes is sufficient, especially when read in the context of his overall views and, more specifically, that of his treatments of art and religion, to suggest a view of philosophy that is clear and detailed enough to understand. One would like to have seen some of his striking remarks elaborated or further explained, but his views on philosophy – both in a time of high culture and in a time of civilized cultural decline – can be grasped reasonably well. His more specific comments on philosophy in a time of civilization, the limitations on philosophy that civilization imposes, and his hints about the form it must take in such a time are especially interesting. They prescribe a philosophical program that is idiosyncratic in the extreme. More important, the idiosyncrasies that characterize his recommendations jibe, to an astonishing degree, with those that are characteristic of Wittgenstein's later work. My considered view is that the striking parallels are too close to dismiss – especially given Wittgenstein's insistence that Spengler was indeed an important influence upon him. It is a near certainty that Spengler's view of philosophy was a major influence on Wittgenstein during the period in which he developed and formulated his later work.

In keeping with his dark characterization of his time as one that marks the end of both the arts and any shared sense of values, Spengler's remarks about philosophy's prospects are bleak. For the most part, they consist of warnings about what philosophers *cannot* do; there are only a few remarks about what legitimate job, if any, philosophy may serve.

Spengler believed that systematic philosophy, like the arts and religion, approaches extinction in a time of civilization. He says:

> Systematic philosophy closes with the end of the 18th Century. Kant put its utmost possibilities in forms both grand in themselves and – as a rule – final for the Western soul.[1]

Spengler's remarks are somewhat scattered and unsystematic. He does not make clear just what features of civilization make systematic philosophy impossible. Furthermore, despite his often-stated admiration for Kant, he does not seem to unreservedly regret the passing of systematic philosophy. Such an attitude is an interesting departure from his attitude toward the passing of the arts and religion. This, it seems, connects with a strong reservation he has about the goals of philosophers – even those writing in times when a culture is still manifest. About Kant he says:

> When, however, Kant philosophizes ... he maintains the validity of his theses for men of all times and places. He does not say this in so many words, for himself and his readers, it is something that goes without saying. In his aesthetics he formulates the principles, not of Phidias's art, or Rembrandt's art, but of Art generally.[2]

Ignoring his strange claim that this "goes without saying" for Kant, it is worth noting that Spengler attacks the philosophical tendency he imputes to Kant. His admiration for Kant and other philosophers whose work preceded the decline of Western culture notwithstanding, he sees in their work a deep failure. He does so – unsurprisingly, given certain tendencies of his overall thought – because he does not believe that it is possible for *any* philosopher to establish anything of substance for *all* men and for *all* times. The philosopher, for Spengler, must accept that even a work in philosophy must be rooted in – and its scope limited by – its historical setting. Spengler accepted this limitation as inescapable, unwelcome, and elusive.

Against this discouraging background, it comes as something of a surprise that Spengler sees in our own age of civilization a new, if limited, possibility for philosophy. Specifically, he suggests a philosophical program that *accepts* philosophy's necessary limitations and directs itself against philosophy itself – even those impressive works of systematic philosophy which appear when culture is still in its ascendancy. Here are some of the remarks that suggest such a program:

> Systematic philosophy, then, lies immensely far behind us, and the ethical has been wound up. But a third possibility ... still remains to the soul world of the present-day West

---

1   Oswald Spengler, *The Decline of the West*, vol I, (New York, 1965), p. 45.
2   Ibid., p. 23.

...[T]his unphilosophical philosophy ... [is] the last that West Europe will know ... With that, the claim of higher thought to posses general and eternal truths falls to the ground.[3]

Here it is asserted that philosophy cannot attain what it has traditionally aspired to. There is the clear suggestion that this can be shown by a philosophy – a final philosophy – that will, once and for all, end all traditional philosophizing. Spengler doesn't say exactly why, but it is clear enough that he believes a time of civilization provides the right setting for the realization of such an "unphilosophical" final philosophy. Given his view of cultural decline, it is possible that he thought that a time of civilization provides a setting in which it is easier to understand philosophy's limitations because civilizations, by their very nature, are times of limitation, times in which it is futile to engage in pursuits which can only succeed in a time of culture. Still, I suspect there is more to the matter than this.

In this regard, I would note with emphasis that Spengler's high regard for philosophy in a time of culture and his lesser regard for philosophy in a time of civilization has a puzzling element. As I have shown, Spengler emphasizes that it is not possible for *any* philosopher to establish anything of substance for *all* men and for *all* times. Thus, any philosophical system that attempts to do so is doomed to failure. It is natural, then, to ask why Spengler held Kant and other philosophers of pre-civilized times in a higher regard than he did the philosophers of his own time. What is puzzling in Spengler's remarks is the suggestion that past attempts at systematic philosophy succeeded in ways that philosophy in his time could not. Yet, Spengler, in a seemingly contrary spirit, offers a powerful criticism of *any* attempt to do systematic philosophy, namely that no philosophy can succeed in establishing truths for *all* men and for *all* times. By this standard, Spengler ought to have held that the systematic philosophical systems of the past were failures. It is fair to question why he regarded some of the systematic philosophical systems of the past as successes that cannot be achieved in his own civilized time.

It is not exactly clear how Spengler would respond to such a question. Presumably, he believed that the philosophical systems of the past, while failing to produce truths for *all* men and for *all* times, succeeded in doing *something else* that he valued as equally important. In a passage that I will soon investigate more fully, Spengler provides a hint. He says, "a philosophy may absorb the entire content of an epoch".[4] As we shall see, he thinks this is especially important in a time of culture – less so in a civilized time. Why? The answer would seem to connect with a very basic tendency of Spengler's thought, namely the conviction that cultural epochs are rich and vital, affording deep, shared expressive forms, while civilizations, in contrast, present the limitations that accompany the death throes of once living cultures. Simply put, philosophy in a time of culture might "embody" the rich content of its epoch, while philosophy in a civilized time has less in the way of content to "embody". Civilizations, after all, are, for Spengler, times of expressive limitation, profound loss and negativity.

---

3   Ibid., pp. 45–6.
4   Ibid., p. 45.

Thus, Spengler's remarks, while puzzling, appear to present a coherent view. First, he thought the philosophical systems of the past, while failing to produce timeless truths for all people and all times, succeeded at least in expressing, by way of "embodiment", something of value – the living spirit of the culture that gave rise to them. For Spengler, a philosophical system in a time of culture might function, independently of its philosophical content, in much the way that a work of art does – embodying a greatness of spirit, a shared sense of the world and its value that characterizes its time. In contrast, philosophy in a civilized time can neither produce universal truths, nor can it embody anything of cultural greatness. Simply put, there is nothing great in a civilization – no positive spirit of the times that a would-be philosopher might embody in a philosophical work. As such, Spengler's point appears to be that the best that a philosopher can do in a civilized time is to, in one way or another, illuminate limitations – presumably both those that apply to philosophy itself and those that characterize a time of civilization. Hence, the "unphilosophical" philosophy that Spengler recommends for his own time.

As such, Spengler may have thought, or hoped, that a sufficiently clear-headed individual might approach philosophy in such a time, with a reflective understanding of the time and its many built-in limitations. Such a thinker might then come to realize and articulate philosophy's limitations. Certainly, given the above passage, one would think that the differences between such an "unphilosophical" philosophy and philosophy-as-traditionally-practiced would need to be dramatic. As it turns out, this is so.

Spengler further characterizes the "unphilosophical" philosophy that he feels the times demand. It is noteworthy that he did not believe that such a philosophy had yet surfaced. He explains this failure of latter day philosophers as follows:

> I think, all the philosophers of the newest age are open to a serious criticism. What they do not possess is real standing in actual life.[5]

This is significant. Spengler chides the philosophers of his day for a failure to recognize their "standing in actual life". What exactly could this mean? It is reminiscent of Spengler's insistence that any philosophy must be rooted in its historical setting in ways that limit its scope – but the passage seems to express more. In context, it seems to be making a new point, especially given that it offers not just a generalized criticism of philosophers, but one directed at a specific oversight characteristic of the philosophers of his day. The passage is not self-explanatory. It does not say just how present-day philosophers fail to appreciate their standing in actual life, or even who those philosophers are. With regard to these last points, I can offer a set of modest suggestions. I do not insist upon their veracity, nor does much depend upon it. It is probable that Spengler, in writing of "the philosophers of this time" had neo-Hegelian idealist philosophers in mind. These philosophers – influential, even dominant, in the early part of the twentieth century both among German-speaking and English-speaking philosophers – typically held that physical objects, space, and

---

5   Ibid., p. 42.

time are unreal.[6] Given that, it is not hard to imagine why, and on what grounds, one might criticize such philosophers for failing to recognize their "standing in actual life". One need only remind oneself, say, of G. E. Moore's "Defence of Common Sense", its well-known criticisms of such philosophers, and the way in which those criticisms trade upon the degree to which such philosophers have distanced themselves from the most commonsensical certainties of "actual life".

This said, we may return to Spengler's characterization of a new philosophy for the times. For one thing, he states:

> Its solutions are got by treating everything as relative, as a historical phenomenon, and its procedure is psychological.[7]

The last part of this passage describes the "procedure" of a philosophy for a time of civilization as "psychological". The passage does not indicate in just what way a philosophical approach might qualify as "psychological", and there is no further elaboration. Still, the remark is suggestive and, at the least, points in a direction that is removed from the philosophical mainstream. It is clear that Wittgenstein's later writings are strikingly, and uniquely psychological in ways that any reflective reader would quickly recognize. (I shall elaborate on this both in this chapter and in Chapter 6.) The rest of the passage presents more difficulties. What exactly are we to say of Spengler's prescription that philosophy "treat everything as ... a historical phenomenon"? Or "everything as relative"? These remarks offer nothing in the way of detail. They are probably connected to Spengler's insistence that philosophers understand their place in actual life – but there appears to be more. Elsewhere Spengler says:

> At highest, the philosophy may absorb the entire content of an epoch, realize it within itself and then, embodying it in some grand form or personality, pass it on to be developed further and further.[8]

This passage is a bit more helpful. Although certainly overstated (how could *any* work absorb, realize, or embody *the entire content* of an epoch?), its suggestion is more or less understandable. Ignoring bombast, its point seems to be that such a philosophy must somehow address or come to terms with its historical epoch. Beyond this, the suggestion appears to be that this coming to terms be somehow indirect or implicit. The passage writes not of *a description* of the content of an epoch. Such a description, presumably, would be an exercise in history or anthropology, not philosophy. Rather, Spengler writes about an *absorption*, a *realization*, an *embodiment* of it. These terms

---

6   There is a short summary of the Philosophy of Absolute Idealism in my "Metaphysics I (1900–45)", in John V. Canfield (ed.), *Philosophy of Meaning, Knowledge and Value in the Twentieth Century* (London, 1997). This anthology is volume 10 of *The Routledge History of Philosophy*, the 12 volumes of which were published from 1994 to 1998 under the general editorship of G. H. R. Parkinson and S. G. Shanker. See especially pp. 77–81.

7   Oswald Spengler, *Decline of the West*, vol. I, p. 45.

8   Ibid., p. 41.

suggest something subtler, more elliptical, less direct than a description – perhaps, something more akin to art.

The remarks just cited collectively convey Spengler's characterization of a new possibility for philosophy in this time. They describe – and, in context, prescribe – a remarkable sort of philosophy. Let us sum up the *desiderata* offered for such a philosophy. First, he insists that such a philosophy should be *final*. It should seek both to facilitate the end of philosophy and philosophizing, and to show why philosophy, as it has been practiced, is not a viable enterprise. Second, this philosophy should be *radical* in the sense that it is, in fundamental ways, discontinuous in both method and doctrine with all past philosophies. Third, this final philosophy should be *connected with actual life*. It should avoid the mistakes of those philosophers who have lost that connection and, preferably, elucidate their mistakes. Fourth, it is explicitly recommended that the procedures of this final philosophy should be, in some discernible manner, *psychological*. Finally, fifth, this philosophy should be one that comes to terms with its time, its epoch. As such, it would come to terms with the limitations and negativity of its civilization. This coming to terms is characterized in a way that suggests that it does not involve a description of its time or epic, but as some sort of indirect manifestation of that time or epoch within the work.

III. Spengler's Prescription and Wittgenstein's Practice: A Striking Agreement

In this section, I want to show, point by point, that Wittgenstein's late philosophical writings – in particular, the *Investigations* – adhere to Spengler's prescription for a philosophy in a time of civilization. This agreement is striking, indeed remarkable. I can think of no other major twentieth-century philosopher whose work fits Spengler's prescription nearly as well. I will not dwell long on any single point of agreement in this section, as all of them will need to be discussed in greater detail elsewhere.

In writing the *Investigations*, Wittgenstein certainly sought to construct a work of philosophy that was both *final* and *radical* in the senses explained in the last section. Indeed, the *Investigations* shares these characteristics – though not the other notable features of Spengler's prescription – with the *Tractatus*. Both works sought, at the least, to put an end to the traditional problems of metaphysical philosophy by showing that the purported expressions of metaphysical problems and doctrines involve misuses of language. In the *Tractatus*, his view had been that the purported propositions of metaphysics (ethics, aesthetics, and theology too) are *pseudopropositions* that amount to *nonsense*. His views on language and his specific accounts of how philosophers, especially metaphysical philosophers, misuse language are very different in the *Investigations*. Still, the two works share the conviction that philosophers radically misunderstand and misuse language. In this sense at least, both works seek to be not just final, but radical. They not only reject the expressions of traditional philosophy, but each seeks, in its own way, to show that something intrinsic to the traditional philosophical enterprise is fundamentally misguided – more specifically, that its attempts to express itself violate fundamental canons of correct expression.

In a passage from the *Investigations* which directly concerns a primary goal of the work, Wittgenstein writes:

> the clarity that we are aiming at is indeed *complete* clarity. But that simply means that the philosophical problems should *completely* disappear.
>
> The real discovery is the one that makes me capable of stopping doing philosophy when I want to. – The one that gives philosophy peace... – Problems are solved (difficulties eliminated), not a *single* problem. ...There is not a single philosophical method, though there are indeed methods, like different therapies.[9]

This passage marks well both important continuities and important discontinuities between the *Tractatus* and the *Investigations*. Both works sought to put an end to philosophy – to see its "difficulties eliminated" so that its "problems are solved" and "completely disappear". The earlier work sought to bring this about by showing that the things philosophers write and say fail to conform to its own systematic account of the essential and proper function of language. (I shall examine this conception in more detail in Chapter 6.) The later work rejected the systematic account of language of the *Tractatus* in favor of a more mundane set of remarks about the ordinary functions of the words philosophers use – or, rather, misuse – in their attempt to say something extraordinary. Still, like the earlier work, it sought to gain an understanding of language and to show that a proper understanding of it eludes philosophers. In a well-known passage from the *Investigations*, Wittgenstein writes:

> The main source of our failure to understand is that we do not *command a clear view* of the use of words. A perspicuous representation produces just that understanding which consists in "seeing connections".
>
> ...The concept of a perspicuous representation is of fundamental significance for us.[10]

A "clear view", a "perspicuous representation" of the use of words was a central goal of the later work. It was not, however, to be achieved via "a single philosophical method", a unified conception of language (as in the *Tractatus*), but rather via many connected observations about this or that use of words. A related goal was to show that once such a perspicuous representation has been achieved the impetus toward philosophy would whither away. Why? Presumably, a person who had achieved Wittgenstein's perspicuous representation of the uses of words would come to see that the formulations of philosophical problems *mis*use words. Wittgenstein believed, as he did when he wrote the *Tractatus*, that the things philosophers said and wrote constituted departures from correct uses of language, that seeing this clearly could help eliminate such misuses and, so, philosophy itself.

One of the most important criticisms of philosophy in the *Investigations* connects with Wittgenstein's primary diagnosis of philosophical mistakes. On that view, philosophers characteristically use words in ways that fail to jibe with, fall "outside" of, the natural language games of actual life. He writes:

---

9 Ludwig Wittgenstein, *Philosophical Investigations*, Pt I, paragraph 133.
10 Ibid., paragraph 122.

When philosophers use a word – "knowledge", "being", "object", "I", "proposition", "name" – and try to grasp the *essence* of the thing, one must always ask oneself: is the word ever actually used in this way in the language-game which is its original home?

What *we* do is bring words back from their metaphysical to their everyday use.[11]

Wittgenstein sees in philosophers' uses of words illegitimate departures from the proper, "everyday", uses of words, from the "original", natural uses of words. For him, words are used correctly only "inside" the language games of everyday life that are their original homes. Philosophers, he thought, lose sight of this and persist in trying to use them "outside" those language games. Elsewhere in the *Investigations*, he famously chides any philosopher (including his former self, the author of the *Tractatus*) for "[a]sking 'Is this object composite?' outside a particular language game".[12] The result of this specific mistake, he thinks, is nonsense that takes the form of metaphysical confusion about absolute or simples.

So, Wittgenstein sought to combat illegitimate, metaphysical uses of words outside the language games that provide their natural settings. He sought to achieve this end by "bringing words back" from these misuses to their correct "everyday use", to their proper setting. In this he was, in effect, both 1) accusing philosophers of losing sight of their connection with everyday life and 2) seeking to re-establish that connection. In 1) we can discern an echo of Spengler's complaint, cited earlier, that "the philosophers of the newest age … do not possess … real standing in actual life"; in 2), a very clear indication that Wittgenstein's later philosophy satisfies Spengler's requirement that a philosophy for a time of civilization must be one that is connected to actual life.

Does the *Investigations* satisfy Spengler's further requirement that the methods of a philosophy for a time of civilization have a *psychological* character? Admittedly, this requirement is not clearly specified. Spengler does not tell us in advance just what would count as a "psychological" methodology in philosophy. Still, there are a number of ways in which Wittgenstein's late philosophy is strikingly, uniquely psychological in its approach to philosophical problems.

We have already noted some of the features in virtue of which it can be so characterized. First, as we saw in Chapter 2, much of Wittgenstein's late writings take the form of self-dialogues – conversations with himself in which a wiser self engages in confrontational exchanges with a wayward self whose thinking is clouded by misleading pictures, conceptual confusions, and nonsensical formulations. More to the point his method being *psychological*, in these exchanges, and elsewhere, Wittgenstein describes and confronts – I use his own terms here – the *prejudices*, *mental cramps*, *inclinations*, *seductions*, and *temptations* that cripple philosophical thought. In 1948, while occupied with the final phases of the *Investigations*, he wrote: "Nearly all my writings are private conversations with myself. Things that I say to myself tête-à-tête".[13]

Second, Wittgenstein explicitly likens his philosophical procedures to *therapies*. We have noted just above his insistence that there "is not a single philosophical

11 Ibid., paragraph 116.
12 Ibid., paragraph 47.
13 Ludwig Wittgenstein, *Culture and Value*, p. 77e.

method, though there are indeed methods, like different therapies". On its face, this is a surprising simile. Therapies typically are directed against conditions of illness, sickness, and disease. So, taking the simile seriously, one would suspect that Wittgenstein thought of philosophical problems in such terms. This is an unusual way of characterizing philosophical problems. Yet, it was undeniably Wittgenstein's way – a fact that, in many contexts, is not emphasized enough. Following through on this thought, Wittgenstein later writes, "[t]he philosopher's treatment of a question is like the treatment of an illness".[14] Still later, he writes of a "philosophical disease".[15] I will discuss this tendency in greater detail in Chapter 6. For now, we can see that Wittgenstein characterizes his own procedures in highly unusual and strikingly psychological terms.

Wittgenstein's procedures are psychological in another way. There are many passages in which he writes not just of combating this or that wayward inclination, this or that symptom of philosophical illness. In addition, he recommends a major change in one's whole orientation toward the problems one confronts. This too, must not be underestimated. Wittgenstein writes, in *Culture and Value*:

> Working in philosophy ... is really more a working on oneself. On one's own interpretation. On one's way of seeing things.[16]

In the *Investigations* he writes of philosophical problems which "can only be removed by turning our whole examination round", adding immediately that "the axis of reference of our examination must be rotated, but around the fixed point of our real need".[17] Like the passage above, this suggests that philosophical progress requires a dramatic change in a philosopher's personal perspective, one that entirely alters the terms of one's philosophical examination, one that accommodates the real needs that are obscured before such a change is affected.

Finally, we come to the last *desideratum* on Spengler's list. He stipulates that a philosophy for an age of civilization should come to terms with its time not by directly describing its time but, more indirectly, by somehow absorbing, realizing, or embodying the characteristics of the time. I have shown in the first two chapters that Wittgenstein, on many occasions, characterized his work as being, in fundamental ways, opposed to the civilization of its time. Certainly, a work that *opposes* the tendencies of its time, by doing so, addresses and comes to terms with them. In addition, he denied that this feature of his work is contained there explicitly – he indicates that it is manifested primarily *in the spirit* of his writings. We have seen, in a number of passages, that he is explicit on this last point. It has been established that Wittgenstein was predisposed, for decades, to characterize his work in such terms. So, it is clear – if we accept Wittgenstein's own accounts of his later work – that it satisfies the last of Spengler's *desiderata*.

In the next chapter, I will have more to say about this last *desideratum*. I will address a number of more specific ways in which the *Investigations* might be

---

14 Ludwig Wittgenstein, *Philosophical Investigations*, Pt I, paragraph 254.

15 Ibid., paragraph 593.

16 Ludwig Wittgenstein, *Culture and Value*, p. 16e.

17 Ludwig Wittgenstein, *Philosophical Investigations*, Pt I, paragraph 108.

thought to attempt a coming to terms with its time in ways that are indirect but still discernable. Some of these involve observations of Cavell; others are original suggestions of my own. What is clear, for now, is that Wittgenstein, on a number of occasions, avowed an intention to address and oppose the tendencies of his time, at least, in the *spirit* of his work, and, so, to that extent, his work can be seen as in keeping with this *desideratum*.

So, Wittgenstein's later philosophy, especially as expressed in the *Investigations*, jibes in every detail with Spengler's prescription for a philosophy in an age of civilization. It is a radical and seeks to put an end to the problems of philosophy as it is usually practiced. It criticizes philosophers for abandoning their standing in actual life and seeks to re-establish that standing. It both employs and explicitly advocates an approach to philosophy that is peculiarly psychological in nature. It explicitly likens the causes of philosophical confusion to a disease of thought – one that manifests itself in wayward temptations, prejudices, seductions, and wayward inclinations. It utilizes a method that explicitly likens itself to a therapy for the cure of that disease. Finally, as Wittgenstein often avowed, it seeks – indirectly, in spirit – to embody his own sense of his time and come to terms with that time. It is hard to imagine this congruence of Spenglerian *desiderata* and Wittgensteinian practice to be a mere coincidence.

Is there another twentieth-century philosopher whose work so perfectly fits Spengler's prescription for a philosophy of civilization? When one reflects on this remarkable congruence, it seems overwhelmingly likely that Wittgenstein's reading of Spengler played a role in shaping some of the more prominent features of his later philosophy. This likelihood only increases when one reflects upon Wittgenstein's explicit statement in *Culture and Value* that he was influenced by Spengler – more specifically, that some of his own ideas are elaborations upon more seminal ideas derived from Spengler.

I will offer one final observation. It has been noted that Spengler held the philosophical systems of the past in high regard, even though he believed that they sought something unattainable – namely truths for all people in all times. Apparently, Spengler valued those systems in spite of this failing. He valued those systems as embodiments of the rich, positive content of the cultures from which they sprang. A philosophy of civilization, of course, could never aspire to do this. What attitude, then, might a Spenglerian philosopher of civilization have toward the philosophical systems of the past? Clearly, Spengler thought it the job of such a philosopher to show that a systematic metaphysics is beyond the reach of *any* philosopher. Would Spengler want his "unphilosophical" philosopher to be contemptuous of the philosophical systems of the past?

Presumably, he would not. Spengler, while recognizing their failures, valued the great philosophical systems of the past as great works whose successes could not be repeated. What about Wittgenstein? There is no doubt that Wittgenstein was intent on showing that the goals of traditional philosophy were both overblown and predicated on deep mistakes about the proper function of words. Did he, however, hold in contempt the metaphysical systems he sought to undermine? Apparently, like Spengler, he did not. Drury reports what he took to be a paradoxical set of remarks that Wittgenstein made during one of their many conversations. First, he recollects

Wittgenstein saying, during a discussion of his later philosophy, "A philosopher should enjoy no more prestige than a plumber."[18] Then, Drury adds, "But then as against this I must record him saying: 'Don't think I despise metaphysics. I regard some of the great metaphysical writings of the past as among the noblest work of the human mind.'"[19] It is the second quote, in the present context, which is more interesting in that it expresses the same attitude toward the philosophical systems of the past that Spengler held. It indicates yet another Spenglerian feature of Wittgenstein's later thought: an abiding respect for the very philosophical systems his own philosophical inquiries were intent upon undermining. The first quote is harder to understand – especially when taken together with the second. As Drury reports Wittgenstein's remarks, he expresses an understandable sense of puzzlement. Why should an individual who produces writings that represent "the noblest work of the human mind" be given "no more prestige than a plumber"?

Before going on I would like to suggest, with less than full confidence, a way of unraveling this puzzle. My suggestion is this. Wittgenstein, in speaking of the "great metaphysical writings of the past" was writing of philosophers whose work, whatever its failures, embodied the spirit of a great culture. In contrast, when speaking of those philosophers who deserve no more prestige than a plumber does, he was thinking of the philosophers of his own time. Such philosophers repeat the mistakes of past philosophers while offering nothing of greatness to counterbalance them. Wittgenstein may even have thought that he, himself, deserved no more prestige than a plumber did. True, he at least hoped to correct philosophy's great mistakes – but he did so, by his own account, by offering truths of an ordinary and mundane sort. Difficult work, to be sure – but then so is that of a plumber.

In any event, further confirmation for the interesting possiblility that Wittgenstein held some of the systematic metaphysical systems of the past in high regard can be found in Waismann's interesting account of some of his own conversations with Schlick and Wittgenstein, as the latter returned to philosophy after his self-imposed post-*Tractatus* exile:

> Schlick and I … had no love for metaphysics or metaphysical theology. …Once when Wittgenstein talked about religion, the contrast between his and Schlick's position became strikingly apparent. Both agreed of course, in the view that the doctrines of religion, in their various forms had no theoretical content. But Wittgenstein rejected Schlick's view that religion belonged to a childhood phase of humanity and would slowly disappear in the course of cultural development. When Schlick, on another occasion, made a critical remark about a metaphysical statement by a classical philosopher (I think it was Schopenhauer), Wittgenstein surprisingly turned against Schlick and defended the philosopher and his work.[20]

---

18 M. O'C. Drury, "Notes on Conversations with Wittgenstein", in Rush Rhees (ed.), *Ludwig Wittgenstein – Personal Recollections* (Totowa, NJ, 1981), p 93.

19 Ibid.

20 Friedrich Waismann, "Intellectual Autobiography", in Paul Arthur Schilpp (ed.), *The Philosophy of Rudolf Carnap* (Library of Living Philosophers), (LaSalle, IL, 1963), p 25.

Two features of this exchange are especially pertinent. First, it may be seen again that Wittgenstein was inclined to see value in the work of the systematic metaphysicians even though he believed their work to be essentially flawed and even, on his view, devoid of meaning. Second, his attitude to the metaphysical systems of the past, as represented in this exchange and that described by Drury, is very much like Spengler's in that it both explicitly acknowledges their flaws and, yet, displays an obvious respect for them. It is worth noting too that Wittgenstein also held, on Waismann's account, a view of religion that is similar in important respects to his view of metaphysics. While acknowledging that neither had any theoretical content (indeed that their propositions lacked sense), he nonetheless regarded both with respect. More specifically, he explicitly rejected Schlick's tendency to see advances in science as threats to, and as improvements upon, religion and religious belief. I shall return to these matters in Chapters 5–7.

IV. Afterword: On What Has Not Yet Been Shown

I have tried to show, in these first three chapters, that Wittgenstein's view of his time was influenced by Spengler. Further, I have argued that Wittgenstein's philosophy has some pointedly Spenglerian features. This emerges, I have argued, in a number of ways. First, Wittgenstein remarks that what he called the spirit of his work is opposed to the civilized tendencies of his time. Wittgenstein never explains how his work opposes those tendencies and this matter must be taken up in the next chapter. Still, it is clear that there is a pointedly Spenglerian stamp in both his characterization of the civilization of his time and his opposition to it. Second, and, I believe more important, many of the most characteristic overall features of later Wittgensteinian thought fit Spengler's prescription for a philosophy of civilization. Establishing this latter claim has been the chief business of this short chapter.

Spengler's sketch of a philosophy of civilization, we have seen, addresses the goals and methods of philosophy rather than its actual content. As such, in discussing the remarkable fit between Spengler's sketch and Wittgenstein's later philosophical practices, I have focused primarily on the overall goals and some of the characteristic methodologies of the *Investigations*. This discussion has not touched on the *substance*, the *content* of that work.

Indeed, only briefly, in these first three chapters, have I addressed the substance, the direct content of the *Investigations*. In Chapter 1, section V, I did so, hypothesizing that Wittgenstein's later thoughts on meaning and context could be the result of a stronger, more direct Spenglerian influence. I shall return to this matter in Chapter 5. That, however, has, and will continue to be, a singular exception. If I am right, that represents the chief *explicitly Spenglerian idea* to be found directly in the *Investigations*. I also argued, in Chapter 1, section IV, that 1) Wittgenstein's well-known remarks on family resemblances and 2) his view of metaphysics as misconstrued grammar could well have had an origin in his reading of Spengler. This conclusion, however, was strongly qualified. Neither 1) nor 2), I claim, is, in any direct sense, a Spenglerian idea. Rather, these ideas appear to have occurred to Wittgenstein as a way of correcting confusions in Spengler. In these instances, Spengler appears to have served Wittgenstein not by expressing ideas that Wittgenstein accepted, but rather by making what Wittgenstein rejected as mistakes. His contemplation of these appears to have inspired some of the most powerful ideas to be found in his later philosophy. Wittgenstein, in discussing Spengler with Drury, emphasized some of Spengler's mistakes and spoke of the difficulty of expressing just what is right in Spengler. He even suggested that Drury attempt to do this. Drury did not. Could the *Investigations*, whatever else it sought to achieve, represent Wittgenstein's own attempt to show something right in Spengler?

It is also important to remember just what Wittgenstein indicates in the prefatory remarks about some of the Spenglerian ideas that he evidently accepted and which influenced him. These, he says, are "manifest" in the "spirit" of his work. If this is so, it should be possible to identify some characteristic "thought manoeuvres" in the *Investigations* that are offered, in part, as intimations or indirect evidences of what are recognizably Spenglerian ideas. Is there material in Wittgenstein's later work that can be seen as such?

This is the most difficult question I take up in this book. I seek to answer it by showing that there is a subtle Spenglerian influence in Wittgenstein's later work that concerns neither its overall character and intentions nor its direct content. Here the matter of the *spirit* of the work, of a "Spenglerian *valence*" must be taken up directly. I will address this in the next chapter. I begin by discussing Stanley Cavell's treatment of this question. His writings offer some strikingly imaginative and bold suggestions that point in the direction of an answer. Cavell's ideas, for all their daring, are, I think, plausible, and very likely correct. I don't believe they provide a *demonstrably correct* answer to the question at hand. I suspect that no such answer is possible. In what follows I will discuss and criticize Cavell's ideas carefully and seriously. I will offer further support for some of his claims. Finally, I will offer new suggestions of my own. Those suggestions can be seen as an attempt to advance in roughly Cavell's direction. In the end, I don't know whether the provisional answers Cavell and I offer to the question at hand are correct. They represent, at least, a serious attempt to do what has not been done in the first three chapters of this book.

Chapter 4

The *Investigations*
as a Philosophy of Culture

I. Introduction

In the first three chapters, I have taken seriously Wittgenstein's avowal that Spengler influenced his ideas. In Chapter 1, I identified some of Spengler's most prominent conceptions and began to discuss which of those may or may not have appealed to Wittgenstein. In Chapter 2, I focused on the prefatory remarks to *Philosophical Remarks*. I sought to show, point by point, how dramatically Spenglerian those remarks are. I focused also on a series of observations that Wittgenstein made over the following decades that, I argued, should be read as a continuation of the Spenglerian attitudes earlier expressed in those prefatory remarks. In Chapter 3, I identified five *desiderata* for a philosophy in a time of civilization recommended in Spengler's *Decline*. I showed, point by point, that Wittgenstein's later philosophy fulfills these *desiderata* uniquely well.

The discussions of the first three chapters show, if successful, that Wittgenstein's assessment of his own time was, in many important respects, influenced by Spengler. Beyond this, they show that this assessment of his time greatly influenced his attitude toward his own work, which often expressed itself in the form of grave misgivings about whether he would be understood. Finally, they show that Wittgenstein's later philosophy was, insofar as it fulfills Spengler's *desiderata* for a philosophy of civilization, Spenglerian in both what Wittgenstein calls its "spirit" and, to some extent, in its approach to philosophical problems.

We have seen that one of Spengler's *desiderata* for a philosophy in a time of civilization is that it "come to terms" with its time. It is clear enough that Wittgenstein intended to do this in his later writings because, on a number of occasions, he expresses just such an intention. What is not yet clear is how Wittgenstein sought to come to terms with his time in his later philosophical writings. It is the chief purpose of this chapter to take up this question.

To do so, I want to return to a problem that I raised in Chapter 1, III–*iii*. I asked there how the *Investigations* – which never explicitly mentions cultures, civilizations, or its own time in the main body of the work – can be, in any sense, a "philosophy of culture". This connects to the question of how the *Investigations* can constitute a philosophy for a time of civilization. I believe that Cavell has provided the best first steps toward answering this question. His suggestion is that Wittgenstein, in his characterizations of the misuses of language that lead to philosophical confusion and in his prescriptions for avoiding them, seeks also *in so doing* both to confront and combat conditions of cultural decline as they manifest themselves in those mistakes.

I seek, in this chapter, to clarify this aspect of Cavell's work, to elaborate upon his suggestions, and, finally, to offer fresh observations of my own.

II. The *Investigations* as a Spenglerian Portrayal of Cultural Decline: Cavell's Interpretation

i. Departures – Philosophical and Cultural

As we saw in Chapter 1, Cavell boldly interprets the *Investigations* as a "philosophy of culture", one which can be read as "a depiction of our times". He explicitly insists upon important connections between Wittgenstein and Spengler. He sees the *Investigations* as a work that addresses the wayward tendencies of traditional philosophy and intimates features of cultural decline that are reflected in those tendencies. Further, Cavell thinks, it seeks to combat those features of cultural decline. The main body of the *Investigations*, of course, never so much as mentions culture, civilization, cultural decline, or the time in which it was written. Cavell's chief task, then, is to show how Wittgenstein's primary philosophical preoccupation – that of gaining a perspicuous representation of the uses of words in order to identify and correct the misuses of language characteristic of philosophers – is also a preoccupation with a loss of culture embodied in those misuses. Cavell, in effect, seeks to give an account of how Wittgenstein's later philosophical writings fulfill Spengler's final *desideratum* for a philosophy of civilization. That is, it is an account of how specific philosophical observations found in the *Investigations* "absorb", "embody", or "realize" the prominent features of its civilized time. Beyond this, it is an account of how the *Investigations* opposes them. Cavell's main conclusions are, I believe, original, plausible, and ingenious.

In a somewhat confusing state of affairs, Cavell has published two papers on the subject at hand with the same title – "Declining Decline: Wittgenstein as a Philosopher of Culture". One appeared in the journal, *Inquiry*. It is a paper Cavell read at the international Wittgenstein seminar held in the town of Skibotn in Northern Norway.[1] The other appeared a year later in Cavell's book, *This New Yet Unapproachable America: Lectures After Emerson After Wittgenstein.*[2] More recently, it has been republished in a readily available, useful anthology, *The Cavell Reader.*[3] The latter is closely related to the former. Their primary claims and distinctions, the sequence of topics they take up, and their basic views on those topics are identical. The later paper, however, is more than twice as long as the earlier. Its main contentions are elaborated more fully and it contains more in the way of embellishments. Some of the extra length can be attributed also to a freer, more expansive form of writing. In consequence, it contains more in the way of those interesting asides characteristic

---

1   Stanley Cavell, "Declining Decline: Wittgenstein as a Philosopher of Culture", *Inquiry*, vol. 31, no. 3, September 1988, pp. 253–64 [hereafter referred to as "Declining Decline 1"].

2   Stanley Cavell, *This New Yet Unapproachable America: Lectures After Emerson After Wittgenstein* (Albuquerque, NM, 1989).

3   Stephen Mulhall (ed.), *The Cavell Reader* (Oxford, 1996) – includes Stanley Cavell, "Declining Decline", pp. 321–52 [hereafter referred to as "Declining Decline 2"].

of Cavell's writing: suggestions, questions asked but not answered, qualifications (sometimes themselves qualified), worthwhile tangents not fully explored, and frank admissions of the author's own ambivalences – even about his own views. In most respects, the earlier paper is a simpler, clearer work; the later one, richer but more daunting. Significantly, in what follows, I will draw upon points of agreement between the two papers, focusing upon shared claims and, most specifically, (with only one exception, that appears in the longer article, but not the shorter) exact quotations that appear in both.[4] This, it turns out, is not hard to manage. I am aware of no significant differences between the two works on any point of central significance.

Cavell explicitly holds that Wittgenstein's philosophy of culture is Spenglerian in nature – or, more exactly, that it has a "Spenglerian valence".[5] A key element in Cavell's interpretation is his focus upon Wittgenstein's characterizations of the misuses of language in which philosophers typically engage. As we have seen, Wittgenstein sees these as *departures from* correct usage, illicit attempts to use words outside the language games that provide the proper setting for their correct use. The *Investigations*, according to Cavell, links these philosophical departures to elements of cultural loss – and, in so doing, invokes a Spenglerian depiction of the latter. He explicitly claims, "both Wittgenstein and Spengler write of a loss of human orientation and spirit that is internal to human language and culture".[6] Cavell's Wittgenstein, then, writes of a loss of human orientation *both in language and in culture*. There is no doubt that the *Investigations* includes accounts of a loss of orientation in language. It is, however, essential to ask how Wittgenstein "writes of" a loss of orientation in human culture in the *Investigations*. Cavell explains this in two ways. He holds that there are two ways in which the *Investigations* links a disorientation in philosophers' uses of language with a disorientation in culture. The first link recognizes language itself to be a part of culture and, so, sees linguistic disorientation in philosophy to be, *ipso facto*, a form of cultural disorientation. The second link sees Wittgenstein's account of linguistic disorientation in philosophy to be what Cavell calls *a homologous form of* and also *an interpretation of* Spengler's depiction of cultural decline. I turn to these now.

The first of these links is fairly straightforward and offers relatively little in the way of difficulties. In a passage we shall examine more carefully in a subsequent section, Cavell claims, "[t]he *Investigations* is a work that begins with a scene of … the child's inheritance of language; it is an image of a culture as an inheritance".[7] This says, or seems to say, that Wittgenstein's representation of a child's inheritance of language is also a representation of a cultural inheritance. As such, a child's early experiences in learning the language of a community are also part of that child's early initiation into its culture. The language is part of a culture. This seems true to Wittgenstein's oft-repeated insistence that the uses of words are so inextricably bound

---

4   As such, I will footnote quotes from these articles, as they appear in "Declining Decline 2". All of them, with an exception that will be specified, can also be found, identically worded, in "Declining Decline 1".

5   Stanley Cavell, "Declining Decline 2", p. 337.

6   Ibid., p. 340.

7   Ibid., p. 341.

up with the forms of human interaction in which they play a role that their functions, their meanings, are inseparable from their relations to those forms. Human language, for Wittgenstein, is inextricably linked to a form of human life. In a crucial section of the *Investigations* that will be discussed in detail later in this chapter, Wittgenstein says, "to imagine a language is to imagine a form of life".[8] Cavell's central thought pervades both versions of "Declining Decline". It is that Wittgenstein sees word use – in its connections with rule-governed language games, social interactions, and a human form of life – as a *cultural* mode.

On such a perspective, one that identifies language as a component of culture, *linguistic deviations* would also count as *cultural deviations*. So for Cavell's Wittgenstein, philosophers' misuses of language, deviations from the rules governing the uses of words, are also deviations from established cultural norms. Every time Wittgenstein writes of disorientation in human language he is, *ipso facto*, writing of disorientation in human culture. On this view, his treatment of philosophy's linguistic transgressions, in part, invokes cultural decline by way of *synecdoche*.

The second link Cavell contends for is of a more subtle nature. Cavell's root idea is very original, penetrating, and, I think, plausible. In order to give a clear account of it, I will distinguish between *two conceptions of departure* upon which Cavell focuses. One is contained in Spengler's detailed account of cultural decline; the other, in Wittgenstein's many claims about philosophers' misuses of language. Briefly stated they are:

1) Spengler's account of a civilization's characteristic *departures* from the tendencies of the culture from which it declined.
2) Wittgenstein's account of the *departures* from the correct uses of words in traditional philosophical misuses of language.

For the sake of brevity and simplicity, I will frequently refer to 1) and 2) by number in what follows. The significance of the two for Cavell may be approached by focusing upon his most explicit statement on the relationship between 1) and 2):

> what Wittgenstein means by speaking outside language games … is a kind of interpretation of, or a homologous form of, what Spengler means in picturing the decline of culture.[9]

The terms "homologous form" and "interpretation of" in the context of this passage would seem to indicate something less direct than a *description* of cultural decline. The passage represents the *Investigations'* account of philosophical misuses of language as somehow similar or analogous to features of Spengler's depiction of cultural decline – enough so as to serve Wittgenstein as an "interpretation of" the Spenglerian picture of cultural decline. This means that Wittgenstein's conception of philosophical misuses of language bears an important relation to the generalized representation of cultural decline in Spengler. The nature of this relation will be explored. For now, it can be said that Cavell holds, at least, that Wittgenstein's

---

8   Ludwig Wittgenstein, *Philosophical Investigations* (New York, 1953), Pt I, paragraph 19.

9   Stanley Cavell, "Declining Decline 2", pp. 344–5.

descriptions of these linguistic misuses are designed to put us in mind of, or to evoke in us, something like a Spenglerian image of cultural decline. This, it seems, is part of what it means to say that they offer characterizations of philosophers' abuses of language which are "homologous to", or which can serve as "a kind of interpretation of ... what Spengler means in picturing the decline of culture". For Cavell, this evocation of cultural decline is internal to Wittgenstein's philosophical project. His account of it, in effect, provides his view of how the *Investigations* satisfies Spengler's requirement that philosophy in a time of civilization "absorb", "embody", or "realize" the tendencies of its epoch.

Cavell's suggestion is that a Spenglerian depiction of cultural disorientation is somehow evoked – by way of homology or interpretation – by Wittgenstein's account of philosophical disorientation in language. What specific links between 1) and 2) enable the latter to serve as a homologous form of, or an interpretation of the former? Cavell takes pains to identify and elaborate upon *a set of similarities* that can be noted between the departures cited in 1) and those cited in 2). These similarities take many forms – including structural, analogical, and metaphorical forms. Cavell's penetrating accounts of various similarities between 1) and 2), in effect, provide the substance of an answer to this question. They provide also a very important measure of support for his contention that Wittgenstein is "a philosopher – even a critic – of culture".[10] I will proceed, in the following subsections, to his accounts of those similarities. In so doing, I will focus upon details of Cavell's interpretation of the *Investigations* as a philosophy of culture with a "Spenglerian valence", as a work that, in part, functions as an interpretation of Spengler's depiction of cultural loss.

Before beginning, I want to present the greater part of a passage from both versions of "Declining Decline" which, I think, more than any other, summarizes Cavell's interpretation. In the following subsections I will often refer back to this passage, citing bits and pieces of it, and interpreting these, supporting those interpretations with other passages from Cavell. I present the passage now, and, from here on, will refer to it as "The Main Passage":

> Now take all this, the events of the *Investigations* – from the scene and consequences of inheritance and instruction and fascination, ... to the possibility of the loss of attachment as such to the inheritance; and these moments as tracked by the struggle of philosophy with itself, with the losing and turning of one's way... and conceive of it as a complete sophisticated culture, or say a way of life, ours ... Then I will suggest without argument that what Wittgenstein means by speaking outside language-games, which is to say, repudiating our shared criteria, is a kind of interpretation of, or a homologous form of, what Spengler means in picturing the decline of culture as a process of externalization.[11]

Two paragraphs later, in what I will consider a continuation of "The Main Passage", he adds:

> Wittgenstein in the *Investigations diurnalizes* Spengler's vision of the destiny toward exhausted forms, toward nomadism, toward the loss of culture, or say of home, or say

---

10 Ibid., p. 336.
11 Ibid., pp. 344–5.

community; he depicts our everyday encounters with philosophy ... wherein the ancient task of philosophy, to awaken us, or say bring us to our senses, takes the form of returning us to the everyday, the ordinary, every day, diurnally.[12]

ii. Departures from Home: A Loss of Home

For Cavell, an incisive way of characterizing both 1) and 2) employs the notion of *a loss of home*. He makes much of the fact that Wittgenstein and Spengler both explicitly use the term "home" in 2) and 1) respectively.

In this respect, the term "home", for Cavell, takes on a special, metaphorical, importance. To begin, he emphasizes that it is a key term in 2). As we have seen in the previous section, Wittgenstein, in the *Investigations*, asks his reader, regarding the philosopher's use of certain terms, "is the word ever actually used in this way in the language-game which is its original home?"[13] Cavell dwells upon that last word, and makes much of the fact that Wittgenstein describes the everyday uses of words as a "home".[14] In both versions of "Declining Decline", the first section of the article has the title "Everyday as Home", and, in both, Wittgenstein's use of the word "home" is stressed as an indication that he regarded the everyday uses of words metaphorically as a kind of home.

Given this characterization, what are we to make of Wittgenstein's diagnosis of the main failure of philosophers' uses of words – specifically, that they fail to jibe with the everyday uses of those words in the language games which are their original homes? Cavell sees in that diagnosis a vision of those misuses as departures from the everyday uses and, so, departures from home. This, he writes, "expresses a sense that in philosophy ... words are somehow 'away', as if in exile".[15] This, as it turns out, is important, for a number of reasons. For one thing, this image is central to Cavell's interpretation of the *Investigations*. For another, this vision of philosophy's linguistic disorientation is, he thinks, importantly similar to Spengler's vision of cultural loss and disorientation.

Before turning to Spengler and his use of the term "home" in 1), it is useful to note that Cavell explicitly claims in The Main Passage that the *Investigations diurnalizes* Spengler's vision of the "... loss of culture, or say of home". We shall later examine the passage's use of the strange term, "diurnalizes", more fully. For now, I would emphasize that Cavell sees in both 1) and 2) a vision of a *loss of home* and also sees an important connection between them. More specifically, he holds that Wittgenstein – in his own way, one that involves "diurnalization" – invokes a Spenglerian image of loss. Is it a stretch on Cavell's part, to characterize 2) in terms of *loss*? Perhaps not. In connection with this characterization, Cavell cites one of the *Investigations'* most striking passages – the one which claims, "a philosophical problem has the form: I don't know my way about".[16] Thus, in one of his most prominent and striking

---

12 Ibid., p. 345.

13 Ludwig Wittgenstein, *Philosophical Investigations*, Pt I, paragraph 47.

14 Stanley Cavell, "Declining Decline 2", pp. 322–7.

15 Ibid., p. 323.

16 Ibid., p. 325.

comments about the nature of philosophical perplexity, Wittgenstein represents the philosopher who loses track of correct word usage as someone who is *lost*. This provides straightforward and useful support for Cavell's characterization.

Turning now to Spengler, Cavell shows that the term "home" has an important function in 1). He focuses especially on Spengler's use of the term "home" in an important passage from *Decline*. Cavell quotes Spengler in this regard:

> Civilization is the inevitable destiny of the Culture ... Civilizations are the most external and artificial states of which a species of developed humanity is capable. They are a conclusion ... death following life, rigidity following expansion, petrifying world city following mother-earth. They are ... irrevocable, yet by inward necessity reached again and again ... a progressive exhaustion of forms ... This is a very great stride toward the inorganic... – what does it signify?
>
> The world-city means cosmopolitanism in place of "home". ... To the world city belongs [a new sort of nomad], not a folk but a mob.[17]

Significantly, with reference to this passage, Cavell immediately adds:

> In a footnote here Spengler declares "home" to be a profound word "which obtains its significance as soon as the barbarian becomes a culture-man and loses it again [with] the civilization-man ..."[18]

Thus, it is emphasized that there is a deep sense in which, for Spengler, a culture constitutes a *home* and a civilization does not. A people living during a time of civilization lack a home in this "profound" Spenglerian sense. Further, while they may live together in cities, they do not constitute "a folk" because their civilized condition prevents that. Why? The main passage makes it clear that a folk, for Spengler, must share a home. Spengler's explicit comment on the term "home", which Cavell takes pains to quote, shows that, in *Decline*, the term evokes one of the essential features that define a Spenglerian culture. These are, most notably, a community, a shared sense of life, and natural (as opposed to artificial) forms of interaction and expression. On this Spenglerian use of "home", a civilization's loss of a culture is represented as a *loss of home*. To sum up, Spengler in 1) sees cultural loss metaphorically as loss of home; Wittgenstein in 2) sees philosophical misuses of language, also metaphorically, as an abandonment of home, a kind of self-exile in which the philosopher becomes lost.

iii. Externalization

The penultimate passage cited in the preceding subsection represents civilizations as times of *externalization*, specifically stipulating that "[c]ivilizations are the most external ... states of which a species of developed humanity is capable". We have seen that The Main Passage addresses "what Spengler means in picturing the decline of culture as a process of externalization". What could that be?

---

17 Ibid., p. 345.

18 Ibid. (This passage is not included in "Declining Decline 1".)

Cavell emphasizes the role played by the notion of *externalization* in 1). In what sense did Spengler think a civilization, a culture in decline, represents externalization? The answer, in part, connects with another Spenglerian notion – that of *exhausted forms*. As we saw in Chapter 1, Spengler holds that every culture employs its own characteristic expressive forms in which its artistic accomplishments are carried out. These, he thinks, are understood and shared by those who participate in that culture. As cultures decline into civilizations these expressive forms become "exhausted" in two senses. First, their possibilities, the ways in which they can be used to create, become depleted with use. Second, and more important, these forms – having once been, in Spengler's terms, "living", "organic", unifying forces – become "dead" and "rigidified". They become increasingly powerless to maintain that commonality of perception and purpose necessary to hold a folk together a in a culture. In the autumn of a culture, these forms become less prominent, they lose their fascination. By the onset of winter, they are hardly accessible or even understandable.

This connects, or appears to, with another Spenglerian doctrine – that of the *prime symbol* of a culture. As we saw in Chapter 1, every culture, for Spengler, has a unique space-concept, a unique, shared perspective from which its people perceive and relate to the world. This Spengler calls the "prime symbol" of a culture. He asserts that it is not understandable from the perspective of another culture and also that it is no longer understood in the later, degenerated, civilized end-phase of its own culture.

In the terms of Spengler's vivid metaphors, certain forms of expression, unique to a culture, unify that culture. They hold it and its people together. They maintain it as a home within which a folk share their perception of, and characteristic responses to, the world. When cultures degenerate into civilizations, these forms become *exhausted*. They lose their influence, their power to unify, and, in the end, become virtually meaningless. When that happens, the greatest accomplishments of the culture, carried out within those forms of expression, are no longer possible. With the exhaustion of those forms comes a time of civilization in which the unified cultural perspective imposed by those forms is dissipated. The perspective of a high culture is fixed by such forms. It – in Spengler's sense – *exists within* those forms. With civilization comes a time when that cultural perspective is lost precisely because the perspective of individuals is no longer fixed by those forms. Their perspective becomes, in Spengler's terms, *externalized* with respect to those forms. Thus, the notions of exhausted forms and of externalization are key elements of 1).

Let us turn now to 2). Cavell thinks that Wittgenstein's special use of the term "home" and his interpretation of the everyday in Wittgenstein as a home connects interestingly with another feature of his thought. In the previous section we noted Wittgenstein's tendency both to characterize correct word usage with that which occurs *within*, or *inside of*, our natural language games, and also to equate certain philosophical misuses of words with those that take place *outside* any language game. Cavell sees a metaphorical connection here. The philosopher wrongly seeks to do outside what must be done inside, internal to, those language games. Externalization, in this sense, constitutes, for Wittgenstein, the most elemental transgression of wayward philosophy.

What of exhausted forms? Is there any sense in which that notion of Spengler has an analog in 2)? Cavell thinks so. For Wittgenstein, the philosopher mistakenly uses words outside the language games that fix their proper use. Further, this mistake proceeds on the false assumption that the limitations on proper usage imposed by those language games may be transcended by special philosophical uses of words. The temptation to think that there is something of philosophical importance that can only be said outside established language games, in a sense, regards those games as exhausted forms. The erroneous idea is that, from a philosophical standpoint, they are useless; they must be abandoned in order for philosophy to do its work. In the *Investigations*, this notion is dismissed as a vain philosophical conceit, a delusion. For Wittgenstein, our language games fix what can be said; outside of them there is nothing to say. This aspect of Cavell's interpretation may be something of a stretch. Specifically, the philosopher who imagines that the meanings of words must be expanded beyond their ordinary uses to make extraordinary philosophical statements does not so much regard those ordinary meanings to be *exhausted*, but, rather, to be *limited*. Perhaps Cavell's analogy limps a bit here. For me, it is hard to see how Wittgenstein's descriptions of philosophical misuses of language evoke, metaphorically or analogically, a sense of exhausted expressive forms. Certainly, the terms that are misused by philosophers, insofar as they are misused, would be better characterized as *empty* or *wayward* than *exhausted*.

With that caveat, it is now possible to summarize Cavell's view of externalization in 1) and 2). Spengler in 1) sees cultural decline as a process of externalization that connects to an abandonment of expressive forms. Wittgenstein in 2) metaphorically locates philosophy's linguistic transgressions as outside, external to, the language games which fix their proper use – in effect, seeing in them an illicit process of externalization which strays outside the proper locus of human expression.

iv. Repudiations of Community and Inheritance

Cavell also calls attention to a certain way in which, for Wittgenstein, everyday uses of words, inside their proper language games, connect importantly with what is *shared within a community*. This is not hard to understand. For Wittgenstein, the uses of words in language games are governed by criteria for their application that are common to, which are shared by, the community of language users who engage in those language games. For all his difficulties with essentialism, the later Wittgenstein famously claimed that language is essentially social. Cavell states explicitly that, for Wittgenstein, "speaking outside language games" amounts to "repudiating our shared criteria" for the correct use of words.[19] So, on Cavell's interpretation, Wittgenstein's wayward philosopher who abandons home by using words outside their proper language games, *ipso facto*, abandons their *shared* grammatical rules and also, in this sense, abandons *community*.

I want to focus upon a related term that Cavell uses in connection with 2). The term is "inheritance". We have already encountered this term in The Main Passage. Cavell's use of it, I think, establishes the strongest connection he offers between

---

19 Ibid., p. 325.

2) and straightforwardly cultural considerations. He notes that Wittgenstein begins the *Investigations* with a quotation from St Augustine's *Confessions*. The quoted passage offers Augustine's account of his earliest instruction in language, his recollected interactions with those of his elders who taught him. By most accounts, Wittgenstein uses this passage because he thinks Augustine's account incorporates deep philosophical mistakes that he seeks to combat. Cavell, however, claims a further significance for its use. He explains:

> The *Investigations* is a work that begins with a scene of inheritance, the child's inheritance of language; it is an image of a culture as an inheritance, one that takes place in ... the conflict of generations. ... Wittgenstein's heading his book with Augustine's paragraph ... sets the scene of inheritance.[20]

First, notice that Cavell explicitly says that the scene of a child's "inheritance of language" is "an image of a culture as an inheritance". Why does Cavell equate a scene of language-learning with one of an *inheritance*? This is not a term Wittgenstein himself uses.

The conception is, I think, defensible. As we have already noted, Wittgenstein believed that the proper uses of words occur inside the language games of everyday life. Words, when properly used, are done so in accordance with criteria. These are accepted and shared by the linguistic community that uses those language games. For Wittgenstein, language is a rule-governed, social activity and the use of language within a community is a natural part of its social fabric. It would certainly seem that the development of the rules that govern the uses of words in a linguistic community is part of the social history of that community. For persons born into the linguistic community, those rules constitute what can be thought of as social constructs that have been developed and handed down from generation to generation within the community – and metaphorically, at least, as an inheritance. In learning those rules, and complying with them, an initiate into the community accepts something provided by the community for the use of those born into it.

Granting this, how might Wittgenstein use this terminology to characterize the philosopher who persists in using words outside of language games, who, in effect, rejects the shared criteria for their proper use? Cavell's suggestion is that such a repudiation amounts to the repudiation of part of one's social inheritance. This application of the notion of a rejected inheritance is central to Cavell's interpretation of Wittgenstein.

So, Cavell seeks to convince his reader that 2) is an account of a loss, a repudiation, of community and of a social inheritance. His reasons for doing so are obvious. As we have seen, such an account is, in many respects, reminiscent of 1). It has already been noted that Spengler contends that it is an essential feature of a culture that it is populated by a "folk", a people, who not only live in the same place, but who share a community. This, in turn, means that they share forms of expression, interaction, perception, and goal-directedness. For Spengler, the decline of a culture into a civilization, by its nature, involves a loss of this. Those who once formed a "folk" come to lose what they once shared, their community dissolves, and social cohesion

---

20 Ibid., p. 341.

gives way to social fragmentation. Social decline has, as an essential feature, a disappearance of community and of the continuing social inheritance of cultural forms. Cavell, in both versions of "Declining Decline", interprets the *Investigations* as a work that invokes the same themes.

v. 1) and 2) as Homologous Forms

Let us sum up Cavell's case as I interpret it. First, it is one which represents 1) and 2) as homologous forms. Second, as we have seen, it asserts that Wittgenstein presents 2) *intentionally* as an interpretation of "what Spengler means in picturing the decline of culture as a process of externalization".

Cavell represents Wittgenstein as a writer who sought both to illuminate philosophical mistakes and also convey, albeit indirectly, his Spenglerian sense of a culture in decline. As such, Cavell's Wittgenstein intentionally constructed 2) in such a way as to make manifest its homological parallels with 1). He did so in order to present 2) as an interpretation of 1) and, thus, invoke his own Spenglerian sense of decline.

Spengler sees a form of externalization as a central feature of cultural decline; Wittgenstein sees a form of externalization as a central feature in philosophy's misuses of language. For Cavell, externalization is one of the parallel features of 1) and 2) in virtue of which 1) and 2) may be called, in an extended sense, homologous forms. Beyond this, consider other features of Cavell's interpretations of 1) and 2). In each, *a home is lost; an inheritance is repudiated; externalization leads to disorientation; shared modes of community expression are replaced by artificial ones*. To complete what I have started here, I offer a parallel display of Cavell's characterizations of 1) and 2) which elucidates the content of his claim that they are, in Cavell's sense, *homologous* forms:

1) Spengler's account of a civilization's characteristic *departures* from the tendencies of the culture from which it declined	2) Wittgenstein's account of the *departures* from the correct uses of words in traditional philosophical misuses of language
Philosophers use words *outside* the language games that are their *natural homes*.	Civilizations represent a *loss of home*. They are the most *external*, *artificial* states of which a species of developed humankind is capable.
Such uses are *artificial*, and stray *outside* the proper setting *within which* correct use must occur.	People who live in times of civilization *lose* what was once *shared within* the culture from which that civilization developed – a sense of community rooted, in part, in *shared* forms of expression.
They *repudiate* the rule-driven criteria for correct word usage. This, in turn, is a repudiation of something *shared* by the linguistic *community*. To that extent, it *repudiates the community itself*.	These shared forms, within the context of a culture, constitute part of a cultural *inheritance*.
The philosopher rejects a linguistic *inheritance* which is also a cultural inheritance failing to realize that it is impossible to use words at all in the face of such a rejection.	The shared forms, which help unite the community within a culture, become *lost* and, in effect, are *repudiated* in a subsequent time of civilization.
A philosophical problem has the form: I don't know my way around. The philosopher is like a nomad, a wanderer who has *lost* what was once a *home*, who becomes *disoriented*, and, so, cannot function.	The people of a civilized time, lacking a home, a shared inheritance, a community, become *lost*, *disoriented*, and can no longer find their way back to those shared forms of expression which once helped make a culture possible.

vi. Combating Cultural Decline

Cavell focuses on what he takes to be one of the most important of Wittgenstein's directly philosophical tasks in the *Investigations* – specifically, the attempt to identify and describe philosophical misuses of language. He thinks that Wittgenstein, in the performance of that task, indirectly confronts cultural decline. For Cavell, Wittgenstein's accounts of philosophers' misuses of language connect with cultural decline in two ways. First, he thinks, Wittgenstein represents those misuses in such a way as to show that they themselves constitute a form of cultural decline. Second, Cavell claims that Wittgenstein's account of those misuses functions in the *Investigations* as an "interpretation" or a "homologous form" of a Spenglerian picture of cultural decline.

It will be helpful here to review a number of points which I have tried to establish in previous chapters. To begin, there is no doubt that Spengler saw cultural decline as inevitable. He believed that it issued forth from a principle of historical necessity. In contrast, there is good reason to believe that Wittgenstein rejected this conception to be confused and held out some hope that cultural decline, or aspects of it, might be resisted. I have emphasized – citing Wittgenstein's own characterizations – that his own philosophical work was intended, in part, to oppose the spirit of cultural decline in his time. He was sometimes able to imagine that this feature of his work might come to have some influence. Especially pertinent here, in the *Investigations*, Wittgenstein seeks not only to identify the misuses of language characteristic of philosophy, but, quite straightforwardly, to *correct* them. As such, we can begin to appreciate Cavell's claim that the *Investigations* can be read as an attempt to *combat* cultural decline. If, as Cavell suggests, Wittgenstein saw these misuses as instances of cultural decline, then the directions he provides for correcting them can be interpreted also as a vehicle for the reversal of one form of cultural decline. Beyond this, if he also presented them as "interpretations of" or "homologous forms of" broader forms of cultural decline, his evident intention to reverse them could well represent some hope or determination that those larger forms of cultural decline might be reversed.

In any event, Cavell takes this into account in his interpretation of the *Investigations* as a philosophy of culture. He emphasizes that Wittgenstein, in the *Investigations*, intended both to *represent or intimate* cultural decline and also to *combat it*. The representation of cultural decline is somehow embodied in the descriptions of the ways in which philosophers misuse words. To the extent that the *Investigations* seeks to eradicate these misuses, it *ipso facto* embodies a rejection of and a response to cultural decline. Cavell cites Wittgenstein's claim that "[w]hat *we* do is bring [words] back from their metaphysical to their everyday use", adding:

> It would a little better express my sense of Wittgenstein's practice if we translate the idea of bringing words back as *leading* them back, shepherding them: which suggests not only that we have to find them, to go to where they have wandered, but that they will return only if we attract and command them, which will require listening to them.[21]

For Cavell, Wittgenstein not only seeks to identify just how philosophical word usage has gone wrong, but also to use what is thereby learned in an effort to gain sufficient "command" of language to re-establish proper usage. The latter task, on Cavell's view, functions as an attempt to reverse an instance of cultural decline. He regards this to be a very important, if latent, function of these discussions in the *Investigations*. As we shall see, he explicitly connects this with some of philosophy's oldest functions – those of awakening us and bringing us to our senses.

---

21 Stanley Cavell, "Declining Decline 2", p. 324.

Again, Cavell's account stresses two ways in which Wittgenstein combats cultural decline in the *Investigations*. First, to the extent that philosophy's misuses of language are themselves instances of cultural decline, he seeks, in correcting them, to combat them – both as linguistic misuses and as instances of decline. Second, there is the claim that Wittgenstein's characterizations of those misuses serve also as *interpretations of*, as *homologous forms of*, a full-blown Spenglerian image of cultural decline. This is important. Cavell, we have seen, believes that many of Wittgenstein's characterizations of philosophical waywardness in the *Investigations* serve to evoke a Spenglerian picture of cultural decline. These would include Wittgenstein's image of words being used outside of their original homes, his likening philosophical puzzlement to losing one's way, and his explicit complaint that philosophers, in rejecting shared and agreed upon criteria for the proper use of words, in effect, reject part of their natural, cultural inheritance. Cavell's suggestion is that these and other characterizations intimate Spengler's generalized picture of cultural decline and its most prominent features.

These characterizations are manifestly negative. Wittgenstein writes not only of words being used outside their original homes but also of a need to bring them back to those everyday uses which are their natural homes. What cultural significance, if any, does this have? On Cavell's view, Wittgenstein sought, in the *Investigations*, not only to evoke a full Spenglerian picture of cultural decline, but also to evoke, in opposition to it, a sense of redirection, an intimation of the sorts of measures that might reverse its tendencies. In his own words, he sees in the *Investigations* both "Spengler's vision of the destiny toward exhausted forms, toward nomadism, toward the loss of culture" and also a response in which "the ancient task of philosophy, to awaken us, or say bring us to our senses, takes the form of returning us to the everyday, the ordinary".[22]

Finally, there is the matter of Cavell's claim that "Wittgenstein in the *Investigations diurnalizes* Spengler's vision".[23] Wittgenstein was a most serious man and the seriousness that he attributed to his self-avowed task of confronting the spirit of his time must have been formidable. Spengler, imposing on himself a similar task, responded with a seriousness that, in *Decline*, often expressed itself as bombast and melodrama. Wittgenstein, in sharp contrast, detested bombast. He employed understated, indirect modes of expression toward this end. He believed a direct expression of his cultural purposes would not be understood. As a result, his cultural purposes are all but impossible to glean from his writing.

Cavell, recognizing this, focuses on Wittgenstein's restraint in pursuing his philosophy of culture. He notes that Wittgenstein's methods of combating cultural decline are never explicitly presented as such. They are manifest in his observations about the proper use of words, cautionary reminders about the ways in which philosophers stray from proper usage, and exhortations to resist temptations to so stray. Along these lines, Cavell sees in Wittgenstein's philosophical recommendations not only an emphasis on "returning us to the ordinary", to what is "natural", to what

---

22 Ibid., p. 345.
23 Ibid.

is "home", but also the determination to do so "every day, diurnally".[24] In this, there is not only an absence of any melodrama or bombast, but what can be thought of as form of humility. In the second version of "Declining Decline", Cavell characterizes this feature of Wittgenstein's procedures dramatically and incisively:

> Philosophers before Wittgenstein had found that our lives are distorted or waylaid by illusion. But what other philosopher has found the antidote to illusion in the particular and repeated humility of remembering and tracking the uses of humble words, looking philosophically as it were beneath our feet rather than over our heads?[25]

III. The *Investigations* as a Philosophy of Culture: More Evocations of Cultural Decline

I have shown in the previous section that Cavell seeks to identify a cultural component in Wittgenstein's writings by focusing on strong analogies between some of its strictly philosophical content and a Spenglerian picture of cultural decline. In this way, Cavell suggests, Wittgenstein offers philosophical remarks that serve also as intimations, evocations, or interpretations of cultural decline. This strategy, I think, is sound. It provides a sensible way of making sense of Wittgenstein's many suggestions that his work has a latent cultural component. Specifically, his suggestion is that Wittgenstein's descriptions of philosophical misuses of language represent both philosophical substance and also an intimation of cultural decline. We might say that Cavell presents Wittgenstein's discussion of philosophers' misuses of language as a locus of cultural concern. In what follows, I will offer two further suggestions that I believe fit Cavell's pattern of interpretation. I will argue that two well-known philosophical discussions within the *Investigations* may well function also to evoke a picture of cultural decline. The two discussions I have in mind are those that have come to be discussed under the headings "Wittgenstein's builders" and "the private language argument". Each, I think, can itself be seen – for reasons that I will explain – as a locus of cultural concern.

i. Wittgenstein's Builders: A Question and a Controversy – Rhees and Malcolm

In the second numbered section of Part I of the *Investigations*, Wittgenstein describes a language game (hereafter referred to as Language Game (2)):

> The language is meant to serve for communication between a builder A and an assistant B. A is building with building-stones: there are blocks, pillars, slabs and beams. B has to pass the stones, and that in the order in which A needs them. For this purpose they use a language consisting of the words "block", "pillar", "slab", "beam". A calls them out; – B brings the stone which he has learnt to bring at such and such a call.[26]

---

24 Ibid.
25 Ibid., p. 323.
26 Ludwig Wittgenstein, *Philosophical Investigations*, Pt I, paragraph 2.

This is straightforward and clear. It comes as a surprise, however, that Wittgenstein asks his reader to "[c]onceive this as a complete primitive language".[27] The request is a serious one. Wittgenstein believes that such a conception is possible. One page later, he is explicit on the point: "We could imagine that [Language Game (2)] was the *whole* language of A and B, even the whole language of a tribe".[28] There is textual evidence that Wittgenstein had believed this for years. In *The Brown Book* – for the most part, an early draft of Part I of the *Investigations* – he makes the same claim and even elaborates upon it. In the latter work, Wittgenstein describes Language Game (2) and writes: "Let us imagine a society in which this is the only system of language".[29] Several pages later in *The Brown Book* he writes sweepingly about the language games he has constructed – a remark which, therefore, plainly applies to Language Game (2):

> We are not … regarding the language games which we describe as incomplete parts of a language, but as languages complete in themselves, as complete systems of human communication. To keep this point of view in mind, it is very useful to imagine such a language to be the entire system of communication of a tribe in a primitive state of society.[30]

Could Language Game (2) be the entire language of a tribe? This question has divided commentators on Wittgenstein. Rush Rhees, Newton Garver, and others have argued that Wittgenstein's conception is misguided.[31] Norman Malcolm has offered an ingenious, though limited, defense of Wittgenstein's claim.[32] Cavell, who has focused extensively on other features of Language Game (2), frankly admits that his own responses are divided.[33] I will turn now to a brief account of the terms of disagreement between Rhees and Malcolm. My purpose is twofold. First, I seek to offer an overview of some of the issues that Wittgenstein's suggestion raises. Second, in explicating Malcolm's defense of Wittgenstein, I will focus upon what even he finds "most implausible about the people of Language Game (2)". This, in turn, will lead naturally to my own suggestion that Language Game (2) can be viewed as an analogy for cultural decline.

Rush Rhees, in his article, "Wittgenstein's Builders", concludes that Language Game (2), far from describing a complete language, fails to describe any language at all. Rhees raises three prominent interconnected objections to the notion that Language Game (2) describes a language.

---

27 Ibid., paragraph 16.

28 Ibid.

29 Ludwig Wittgenstein, *The Brown Book*, (Oxford, 1958), p. 77.

30 Ibid., p. 81.

31 See Rush Rhees, "Wittgenstein's Builders", in Rush Rhees (ed.), *Discussions of Wittgenstein* (London, 1970) and Newton Garver, *This Complicated Form of Life* (Chicago, 1994), Chapter 11, pp. 179–94.

32 Norman Malcolm, "Language Game (2)", in Georg Henrik Von Wright (ed.), *Wittgensteinian Themes – Essays 1978–1989* (Ithaca, NY, 1985).

33 Stanley Cavell, "Declining Decline 2", pp. 332–4.

First, Rhees focuses on the very limited use of the terms of Language Game (2). His objection is not that the vocabulary of the language game consists of only four terms but, rather, that A and B use those four terms "only to give these special orders on this job and otherwise never spoke at all".[34] It is this very strict limitation on the employment of the terms that bothers Rhees. Such a limited linguistic repertoire, he thinks, is not enough to constitute the speaking of a language. For example, Rhees thinks, if the four terms were really part of a language "it would be natural for the builders to use them in referring to the job when they had gone home".[35] Rhees does not want to make that particular extension of their use a requirement for language. His point is rather that the absence of any such extensions of the employment of the terms – beyond their very limited use at the building site – is a serious limitation.

It is worth noting in passing that this objection overlooks a detail that Wittgenstein explicitly includes in the *Investigations*. He specifically allows that the terms of Language Game (2) will be used in its teaching. He stipulates that in the teaching of the language game,

> the learner *names* the objects; that is, he utters the word when the teacher points to the stone – and there will be this still simpler exercise: the pupil repeats the words after the teacher.[36]

Wittgenstein, then, allows for the use of the four terms of Language Game (2) in language training, as well as at the building site to give and obey orders. Still, if these were the only settings in which they were used, Rhees' claim that their uses are unnaturally restricted would remain persuasive.

Rhees is bothered by a further limitation on the use of the four terms of Language Game (2). Specifically, he emphasizes the very limited use of the terms at the building site itself. He writes:

> If it is an actual building job, it will not always go according to plan; there will be snags. But when the builders come on a snag which holds up the work and baffles them, then although they have been speaking to one another in the course of their routine, they do not speak while they are trying to find out what the trouble is. What they have learned are *signals* which cannot be used in any other way … this will not do what Wittgenstein wanted.[37]

Second, Rhees thinks that there are no provisions in Language Game (2) to support a distinction between sense and nonsense. Specifically, he states:

> In our language as we speak it there are standards of what is correct and incorrect, and these come in when we say someone has misunderstood. But I do not see how there can be any such standard in the game Wittgenstein has described.[38]

---

34 Rush Rhees, "Wittgenstein's Builders", p. 76.
35 Ibid., p. 77.
36 Ludwig Wittgenstein, *Philosophical Investigations*, Pt I, paragraph 17.
37 Rush Rhees, "Wittgenstein's Builders", p. 77.
38 Ibid., p. 78.

and adds, "[i]n learning how to speak [one] learns what can be said; [one] learns, however fumblingly, what it makes sense to say."[39] Finally, he insists:

> If I know you can speak, then it makes sense for me to ask you what you mean, ... and to ask you questions about it: just as truly as it makes sense for me to answer you. The examples of the builders do not seem to allow of these.[40]

For Rhees, Language Game (2) lacks an important feature – namely provisions that enable the builders who employ it to communicate about what they mean and about whether, on a given occasion, one of them has succeeded in properly expressing his meaning.

Rhees does not appear to make it a formal requirement that the terms of a language be employed in a variety of contexts. He does not argue inductively that since all known natural languages have provisions for talking about meaning, sense, and nonsense, then every possible language must have such provisions. He never asserts anything like this. Still he is intent on emphasizing both that Language Game (2) limits the use of its terms to a single narrow setting and also that it has no provisions for speaking about meaning. These failures, taken together, Rhees thinks, somehow count strongly against Language Game (2) qualifying as a legitimate language.

This all connects with a third contention of Rhees – one that summarizes his thoughts on Language Game (2). Specifically, he insists that Wittgenstein's builders of Language Game (2) do not *converse*. Here, Rhees asserts a necessary condition for language, namely that it provide sufficient means to enable its speakers may hold *conversations*:

> Not all speech is conversation, of course, but I do not think that there would be speech or language without it. If there were someone who could not carry on a conversation, who had no idea of asking questions or making any comment, then I do not think we should say he could speak.[41]

Rhees thinks that the builders of Language Game (2) have so limited a linguistic repertoire, such limited interactions associated with their uses of words, that they do not display enough in the way of word-related interactions to qualify as speakers. They know what building pieces are called "slab", "block", "pillar" and "beams". They use these terms in an extremely limited manner that helps them accomplish an isolated, extremely limited, task. For Rhees, however, their described interactions do not even come close to qualifying as *conversation*s. Their word-related interactions are too mechanical for that. Rhees states that "[t]he description of them on the building site, if you add 'this may be all', makes them look like marionettes".[42]

Norman Malcolm, in his article, "Language Game (2)", admits "Rhees' criticism is acute" and adds, "I agree with it insofar as it is based solely on Wittgenstein's

---

39 Ibid., p. 79.
40 Ibid., p. 81.
41 Ibid.
42 Ibid., p. 83.

explicit description of Language Game (2) in the *Investigations*".[43] Still, Malcolm thinks, "there is something *in the background* of Language Game (2) which, when brought to the fore, makes it possible to view the builders and their helpers in a different light from that in which Rhees sees them".[44] This notion, that of something important in the background of Language game (2), is one that Wittgenstein himself explicitly takes up in *Zettel*. Malcolm responds to Rhees' criticism by identifying and effectively elaborating upon Wittgenstein's reflections on Language Game (2) and related subjects – not in the *Investigations*, but in *Zettel*.

Malcolm cites this passage from *Zettel*:

> (On language game no. 2) You are just tacitly assuming that these people *think*; that they are like people as we know them in *that* respect; that they do not carry on that language game merely mechanically. For if you imagined them doing that, you yourself would not call it the use of a rudimentary language.

> What am I to reply to this? Of course it is true that the life of those human beings must be like ours in many respects, and I said nothing about this similarity. But the important thing is that their language, and their thinking too, may be rudimentary, that there is such a thing as "primitive thinking" which is to be described via primitive *behavior*. The surroundings are not the "thinking accompaniment" of speech.[45]

Beyond this, Wittgenstein resists the suggestion in his own voiced objection that what is missing, what he must tacitly assume, in his description of Language Game (2) are "thinking accompaniments" of the builders' speech. Malcolm brings out this point nicely. He writes:

> he does *not* admit that he was making the unspoken "assumption" that those people *think*, in the sense of there being thinking concealed behind the outward behavior. But what he says has a bearing on the relevance of Rhees's criticism.[46]

If Wittgenstein was not tacitly assuming concealed thinking in his description of Language Game (2), then what was he assuming that avoids Rhees' charge that its builders behave too mechanically to count as speakers, as conversants? What else, if not concealed thought, might qualify their behavior as conversation? Malcolm rightly identifies Wittgenstein's answer to this question:

> He says: "the life of those human beings must be like ours in many respects, and I said nothing about this similarity". I will dwell on this remark.[47]

Malcolm focuses on the idea that the lives of the builders of Language Game (2) are "like ours in many respects" – something Wittgenstein presupposed, but did not spell out. Given this, he seeks to supply explicit background details to Wittgenstein's

---

43 Norman Malcolm, "Language Game (2)", p. 177.

44 Ibid.

45 Ibid.

46 Ibid.

47 Ibid.

account of Language Game (2) that would help meet Rhees' criticisms. One by one, he addresses Rhees' specific doubts.

First, let us return to Rhees' objection that the terms of Language Game (2) are used at the building site only to give or obey orders. This, he thinks, is too slim a repertoire to constitute conversation. He states that if the builders face a snag that holds up work, baffling them, they could not use words to seek out the nature of their problem. Language Game (2), Rhees thinks, allows only for mechanical interactions involving signals, but not words. Its speakers, as Wittgenstein describes them in the *Investigations*, do not interact in ways that even approach conversation. They do not engage in the sorts of flexible interactions that characterize speech. Against this, Malcolm cites another striking remark from *Zettel*:

> Were we to see beings whose *rhythm* of work, play of expression, etc., was like our own, except for their not speaking, perhaps we would say that they thought, considered, made decisions. For there would be a great *deal* there corresponding to the action of ordinary human beings.[48]

Malcolm takes this remark, along with the other from *Zettel*, to provide a way in which the setting for Language Game (2) might be embellished with enough details so that life at the building site would not seem so mechanical.

For example, Malcolm suggests the simple detail that when there are injuries at the building site, that other workers might show their concern, offer help, and sympathize. In many such ways that need not involve words, the builders could behave in recognizably human ways. What, however of Rhees' deeper objection, that the limitations of Language Game (2) would make it impossible for them to respond to work-specific difficulties, the "snags" which come up at the work site? Malcolm offers this:

> Suppose a builder is trying to fit a slab between two other slabs, but it will not go. He expresses frustration in sounds and gestures. After viewing the situation for a while, he proceeds to chip from one end of the slab until it finally fits   whereupon he laughs and claps his hands in satisfaction.[49]

Malcolm is trying to show that the building site snags that Rhees imagines need not cripple activities just because Language Game (2) is limited. In the passage above, Malcolm describes what Wittgenstein would think of as an example of primitive thought, which does not express itself in words. Malcolm might even have described not just one builder, but two, puzzling together, chipping away together (perhaps after one began to do so), gesturing to one another, and exulting wordlessly after their success. This might count as a primitive form of intelligent, cooperative interaction. Malcolm's point, in part, is that such wordless behavior need not be mechanical.

Then, there is Rhees' objection that the words of Language Game (2) (teaching aside) are used only at the work site. Malcolm makes the proper, if minor, objection that Wittgenstein does allow for the use of these words in language learning in the

---

48 Ibid., p. 179.
49 Ibid.

Investigations. His more important response to the objection is, again, within the spirit of Wittgenstein's *Zettel* remarks. Admitting that there is no provision for word use away from the building site (excluding teaching-related uses), Malcolm insists that the nonverbal behavior of the builders – and others of their tribe – away from the building site could still be like our own behavior in many respects. Their behavior could be recognizably human, albeit in primitive ways – enough so that we might not feel compelled to describe them as marionettes or mechanisms.

Let us turn now to Rhees' other objections – those which focus upon the nature of word use within Language Game (2). He claims that the language game is not rich enough to provide for the sort of give-and-take that would qualify as conversation. He is especially concerned that it cannot provide for communication about speaker meaning. Malcolm, mindful of Wittgenstein's remarks in *Zettel*, responds that we could imagine the following:

> If a builder says "Block" when a helper expected "Slab", the helper might say "Block?" with an expression of uncertainty. And the builder might repeat "Block!" with emphasis. Here would be something resembling question and reply. The helper would be asking the builder whether he *meant* "Block", and the builder would be saying that he did mean that. … [I]n Wittgenstein's bare description of Language Game (2) the only mentioned function of a builder's utterances is that they are *orders*; and no linguistic reply is assigned to a helper. But if the life of those people "must be like ours in many respects", then it would be natural enough that a helper should sometimes question the meaning of an order, and that a builder should answer the question. This enriching of their utterances would not require an expansion of their vocabulary.[50]

Malcolm here is suggesting one way in which Language Game (2) might provide for both something like the give-and-take of questions and answers and also meaningful, if crude, interchanges about speakers' meanings on Wittgenstein's tacit assumption that its builders behave as we do "in many respects".

This connects with Rhees' related objection that Language Game (2) offers no standards for distinguishing sense from nonsense, that it is not rich enough to support exchanges about whether a particular use of words constitutes nonsense. Malcolm admits that this is so insofar as the language game is described in the *Investigations*. He thinks, however, that the *Zettel* remarks suggest that the account of the surroundings of the language game can be enriched in ways that would represent its speakers differently – as people capable of primitive behavior that is straightforwardly analogous to conversation about conversation. To support this, he suggests and comments upon this case:

> Let us suppose that a worker is building a wall. Only slabs are used in walls: beams are used only in roofs. We may even suppose that beams physically *cannot* be used in walls. …Now this builder, at work on a wall, calls out to his helper "Beam". The helper looks at him in astonishment – then bursts into laughter. The startled builder looks at the helper, then at the wall, then back at the helper with a grin of embarrassment. He slaps himself on the head, and then calls out "Slab". The chuckling helper brings him a slab. …Cannot we say that the builder's original call, "Beam", was, in that situation, *nonsense*. The utterance

---

50 Ibid., p. 180.

"Beam" was "incompatible" with the situation. ...It is true that those people do not have conversation. But this exchange was similar to conversation. ...Rudimentary thinking occurred on both sides, thinking that was exhibited in the rudimentary behavior.[51]

Malcolm's point is that his imagined embellishment offers not only an example of crude verbal give-and-take, but also of communication that – however crudely – addresses whether one of the speakers' utterances made sense. While the builder's miscue in this scenario may seem more analogous to a procedural mistake than to an expression of nonsense, Malcolm's conclusion that the ensuing exchange presents something analogous to a conversation about the builder's original call seems right. I will not address the question of whether Malcolm's imagined give-and-take is a primitive counterpart to a conversation about whether the builder's first call was *nonsense*. I note only that Malcolm thinks that it is.

In summary, Malcolm thinks that one could successfully add enough in the way of details to the *Investigations'* extremely sparse account of the lives and interactions of the builders of Language Game (2) that their behavior would no longer seem mechanical. Their uses of the four terms at the work site, in conjunction with appropriate behavior, could strongly suggest intelligent behavior, cooperative action, and primitive forms of conversation – even conversation about their own utterances. Their nonverbal behavior away from the work site could also suggest at least primitive forms of thought, cooperative interaction, and human emotions. In a passage that may stand as the best expression of Malcolm's considered view of the matter, he re-emphasizes the remarks from *Zettel* that he deems so important in respect to this problem:

> From the cue that the life of the builders "must be like ours in many respects", and that there will be "a great deal there corresponding to the actions of ordinary human beings", I think we can fairly conclude that there is no justification for supposing that the workers of Game (2) will always work "mechanically" or that on the building sites they will "look like marionettes".[52]

Before leaving this subject, I want to emphasize two interesting remarks Malcolm makes after spelling out his response to Rhees. They concern the obvious and dramatic limitations upon the lives of the people of Language Game (2) imposed by the austere simplicity of their linguistic repertoire. First, Malcolm concedes that there is something that "we may find most implausible about the people of Language Game (2)".[53] He characterizes this implausibility as follows:

> they have words *only* for building stones – but none for food or danger, day or night, sleeping or waking, illness or death, or changes of weather. The people do not have names, nor are there words for parents or children. They do not even have a word for the activity of building, nor for the purpose of it.[54]

---

51 Ibid., p. 179.
52 Ibid.
53 Ibid., p. 180.
54 Ibid.

Malcolm is struck by the extremely unnatural circumstance that Wittgenstein's imaginary tribe have no words for those things that we take to be most basic in human life. Equally odd, alongside this strikingly impoverished vocabulary, they do have words for their building materials.

Malcolm notices a second "implausibility". It is, given my purposes, the more important of the two. Specifically, he notes that the tribe – while they have words for their building materials – have no words for either the *activity* of building or for its *purpose*. Malcolm finds this especially striking. He muses about what the purpose of that activity, given its surroundings, could be. His only attempt at a suggestion is this:

> Why is the activity of building so important for them that their only words are the names of building stones? And what is the purpose of the buildings? Well, let us think of the adults of the tribe as like our small children, who delight in creating structures out of sand or from little blocks of wood – but for no purpose other than the activity itself. The people of the tribe do not use the buildings, but sometimes they like to look at them.[55]

This is worth reflecting upon. Malcolm is best able to make sense of the behavior of the builders by likening it to the behavior of children. They have no purpose in building what they build. They simply build. This is a natural enough interpretation of the builders' strange behavior. Why, after all, would they have words for building materials but no words for the activity of building or its purpose? It is natural to imagine that they are focused more on the details of building than they are on the purpose, if they have any, of building. This is deeply puzzling. Indeed, in all these respects, the builders' behavior seems – to our way of thinking – alien, unnatural, and oddly misfocused.

ii. Wittgenstein's Builders: A Cultural Analogy?

Wittgenstein wrote in opposition to the spirit of his time. We have seen that there are persistent indications throughout the thirties and the forties that he understood his own work in this way. More specifically, he saw his own time as one that represented characteristics of cultural decline. In Chapters 1–3, I have presented a great deal of evidence that he conceived of his mature philosophy, especially as expressed in the *Investigations*, in part as a coming to terms with cultural decline. This coming to terms, he thought, was not a subject that his writings take up directly, but rather, something to be gleaned from what he described as the "spirit" of his writings – something not stated, but evoked indirectly. In this respect, I have argued, he regarded the *Investigations*, in part, as a Spenglerian philosophy of culture.

It has been the task of this chapter to give a plausible account of *how* his later philosophical writings address his cultural concerns – how their direct philosophical content might have served also to intimate Wittgenstein's self-avowed preoccupation with cultural decline. In the previous section, I examined Cavell's interesting account of how one feature of the *Investigations* – its account of philosophical misuses of language – may constitute one *locus* of cultural concern. In this subsection, and

_____
55 Ibid., p. 181.

the next, I seek to identify two more. They are Wittgenstein's discussions of a) the builders of Language Game (2) and b) the philosophical presumption that there can be a metaphysically private language.

I begin with the builders of Language Game (2). I want to suggest that Language Game (2) (and the slightly more detailed variants of it discussed in subsequent sections of the *Investigations*) functions not only to begin the development of a perspicuous representation of human language, but also to evoke another Spenglerian image of cultural impoverishment.

What do Wittgenstein's discussions of the builders of Language Game (2) – and especially his repeated suggestions that it could be the entire language of a tribe or a society – have to do with cultural decline or an image of cultural decline? To answer this question, we must return to the dramatically Spenglerian prefatory remarks to *Philosophical Remarks*. More specifically, I will revisit one of Wittgenstein's most negative characterizations of his own civilization, first cited above in Chapter 2, II–*iii*:

> Our civilization is characterized by the word "progress". Progress is its form rather than making progress being one of its features. Typically it constructs. It is occupied with building an ever more complicated structure. And even clarity is sought only as a means to this end, not as an end in itself. For me on the contrary clarity, perspicuity are valuable in themselves.

These words provide a dramatic description of a defining feature of his civilization that Wittgenstein found both mystifying and uncongenial. It describes what, for him, is something basic to cultural decline in his time – a preoccupation with building, with construction. This, he thinks, represents a corruption of genuine progress. Building, he thinks, has become the dominant activity of civilization – but it is an activity which is performed unreflectively, in a manner which values building as an end-in-itself and clarity, if at all, as a means to that end. Against this, Wittgenstein expresses his contrary stance. Genuine progress, he holds, requires both that building be done reflectively and construction should not be regarded as an end-in-itself. His sense is that a time of real progress would regard building as a means toward independent ends that are settled upon by the kind of thinking which values clarification itself. His sense is that his civilization is misfocused. Its primary focus on building itself – with no clarification of its point – constitutes something akin to a collective form of heedless behavior. It is blindly unreflective – perhaps even reckless or compulsive.

I emphasize, as Wittgenstein himself does in the passage cited, that this sort of misfocused, unreflective building is not merely a feature of his civilization, but constitutes *its form*. If Wittgenstein's mature philosophy were written, as he says it was, in part, to come to terms with his civilization, then one would expect that his writings would somehow address what he takes to be its form. It is fair then to ask how the *Investigations* achieves this. What features of the *Investigations* might evoke an image of Wittgenstein's conception of the form of his civilization?

I want to suggest that Wittgenstein's discussions of the people of Language Game (2) were presented, in part, to evoke an image of the form of civilization. Of course, those discussions more clearly connect with Wittgenstein's more direct and straightforwardly philosophical intentions. These can easily be enumerated: They help introduce Wittgenstein's central notion of a language game. They help convey the instrumentalist conception of language in the *Investigations*; it is in those discussions that he first likens words to tools. They help focus on the social, interactive function of language that Wittgenstein stresses in his later writings. My suggestion here, however, is that, in addition to all this, Wittgenstein employed his descriptions of the people of Language Game (2) also to present an image of a much simpler, more primitive variant of the misfocused, unreflective, purposeless features of the civilization of his time. By doing so, I am suggesting, he sought, indirectly, to address those features of the time.

Remember, Cavell claims that Wittgenstein's descriptions of philosophers' misuses of language serve to evoke a Spenglerian image of cultural decline as a process of externalization. In a like manner, I am suggesting that Wittgenstein's descriptions of the people of Language Game (2) serve to evoke a negative image of what Wittgenstein thought of as the form of the civilization of his time. How do those descriptions evoke such an image? Presumably, by way of striking similarities and analogies. Beyond this, Wittgenstein describes the lives of the people of Language Game (2) in such a way as to elicit a sense of puzzlement, even vexation, in his reader that is strikingly similar to his own sense of puzzled vexation with his time. Let me elaborate.

In pondering Wittgenstein's builders we are confronted with details similar to those which Wittgenstein confronted in regarding the form of his civilization: a society engaged in a process of building which is pursued unreflectively, with no apparent purpose, but with an intensity of focus which far exceeds any focus on things which are manifestly more important than building. The society of Wittgenstein's builders strikes us, quite naturally, as alien, misfocused, and lacking in any overall purpose that we can understand, much less admire. These are, of course, the very terms of Wittgenstein's characterization of what he identified as the form of the civilization of his time.

My suggestion, then, is that the discussions of Language Game (2) constitute another locus of cultural concern in the *Investigations*. They serve not only to directly engage Wittgenstein's straightforwardly philosophical concerns, but, also, to confront – less directly, by way of image and evocation – the form of his own civilization. I note also that the passage in Wittgenstein that I have cited in this respect comes from the prefatory remarks to *Philosophical Remarks*. We have seen in Chapter 2 that those remarks are the most Spenglerian of Wittgenstein's writings and that the passage in question has striking correlates in Spengler's *Decline*. If I am right that Language Game (2) connects with Wittgenstein's cultural concerns, then it also connects with Spengler's influence upon Wittgenstein. Of course, I realize all too well that my suggestion is highly conjectural and may well be wide of the mark. Still, I suggest it seriously as an interesting possibility.

Have I placed too much weight on the passage from the prefatory remarks in which Wittgenstein identifies unreflective building as the form of his civilization? That remark was written in 1930, while the *Investigations* were published more than twenty years later. Is it too much of a stretch to suggest that Wittgenstein still held to its Spenglerian conception of the form of his civilization while he was writing the

Investigations? I think not. There are two reasons for taking my suggestion seriously. First, Wittgenstein described Language Game (2) in lectures delivered in 1934. It is described very early in *The Brown Book* – a work based upon notes dictated in 1934 and 1935. It is quite possible that Wittgenstein first conceived of Language Game (2) even earlier than that. As such, it is not at all hard to imagine that Wittgenstein began to have the thoughts upon which his more formal presentations of Language Game (2) are based at a time when the Spenglerian conceptions of the prefatory remarks were demonstrably still very much with him. Indeed, this seems far more likely than not. The gap is not one of twenty years, but, rather, one of fewer than four years. Second, I have taken some pains in Chapter 2 to show that Wittgenstein continued to hold many of the central contentions of the prefatory remarks for many years thereafter – even well into the 1940s. In doing so, I have shown that some of Wittgenstein's explicit thoughts about the *Investigations* and its relationship to its time – most of which he expressed in the late 1940s – are similar to those expressed in the prefatory remarks.

Finally, in the *Investigations'* discussion of the builders, Wittgenstein asks, and leaves unanswered, an interesting question. As we have seen, in *The Brown Book*, he claims that language game (2) can be seen as "a complete system of communication". This was certainly his view in the *Investigations* as well. Before even suggesting it, however, he anticipates an obvious objection:

> Do not be troubled by the fact that languages (1) and (2) consist only of orders … It easy to imagine a language consisting only of orders and reports in battle. – Or a language consisting only of questions and expressions for answering yes or no. And innumerable others.[56]

Relative to this, Wittgenstein asks a leading question:

> If you want to say this shows them to be incomplete, ask yourself whether our language is complete; – whether it was so before the symbolism of chemistry and the notation of infinitesimal calculus were incorporated into it; for these are, so to speak, suburbs of our language.[57]

In part, Wittgenstein is urging his reader to understand that such questions about the "completeness" of the builders' language – or of our own language – are non-starters. Without some clear criterion for the completeness of a language, no clear answer can be given. His evident suggestion is that no such criterion has been provided. Still, there is something more. It can be gleaned from the passage that one can *stipulate* a respectable sense in which our language, as well as the made-up languages, (1) and (2), *are* incomplete. For the passage shows that, at any point in the development of a language, there are possibilities for extending that language, for extending the activities in which its words play a role, and extending the uses of its words (perhaps adding others) to accommodate them. Some of these possibilities, in time, might become actualized, others not. In this sense, it might be supposed that no language

---

56 Ludwig Wittgenstein, *Philosophical Investigations*, Pt I, paragraphs 14 and 15.
57 Ibid., paragraph 19.

is "complete" – that is, there is always more that we can do with any language, including (1), (2), and our own. This much seems clear enough.

Is there however, in Wittgenstein's musings, a further Spenglerian intimation? Could he be suggesting to his reader that there is *a more specific sense* in which our own language, like that of the builders, is incomplete? I want to suggest this and suggest further, that this provides a measure of support for my interpretation.

In the *Investigations*, immediately following the quotation above, Wittgenstein says, "And to imagine a language is to imagine a form of life"[58] Thus, one might say that a language is incomplete if the form of life in which it is rooted is, in some respectable sense, incomplete. This is exactly what one wants to say about the builders. Malcolm pinpoints incisively what it is about the builders' "form of life" that strikes us as incomplete. They build, but without any ultimate purpose – as it were, blindly. This, of course, is strikingly similar to Wittgenstein's complaint about his own civilization in the 1930 prefatory remarks. If such thoughts still occupied Wittgenstein when he conceived of his builders a few years later, then one can imagine an intended "Spenglerian valence" here: an intimation of the decline of a culture into a civilization. I take seriously the possibility that Wittgenstein intended to intimate a clear sense in which the form of life of the builders might be said to be incomplete that can be extended equally to the form of our own civilization as well. On this conjecture, Wittgenstein used the discussion of his builders not only to make some important observations about language that are characteristic of his later view, but, also, to present a simplified image of an incomplete form of life that captures a pervasive feature of our own far more complicated civilization. I am making a suggestion about how to read a portion of the *Investigations*: if the form of life of the builders is incomplete in the sense that Malcolm so well articulates, then so, on a Spenglerian conception, is the form of the civilized world in what Wittgenstein explicitly referred to as "the darkness of this time". In asking his reader whether our own language is complete, what is Wittgenstein hoping his reader will think? Certainly he is guiding his reader towards the perspicuous view of language that the *Investigations* seeks to illuminate. If I am right, he is also trying to lead his reader, less explicitly, by means of intimation and analogy, to a certain vision. It is a vision of pointless construction – building that is accompanied and abetted by a pervasive blindness and an unreflective absence of purpose – that characterizes our time.

Wittgenstein, after all, explicitly *invites* his reader to compare the truncated language of the builders with our own language by raising the issue of whether either should be thought of as complete. In an adjacent remark, he explicitly states that to imagine a language is to imagine a form of life. So, quite conceivably, he is directing us to compare the builders' truncated, unreflective form of life with our own. Is it unreasonable to think that Wittgenstein was offering an oblique hint that our own form of life is truncated in ways that are analogous to that of the builders? I think not. And this suggestion becomes far more plausible when one considers that Wittgenstein, not very long before constructing the *gedanke* experiment involving his builders, had emphatically articulated a clear sense in which he felt that the civilization of his time was so truncated.

---

58 Ibid.

One final point: In Chapter 3, I showed that Spengler enumerated a number of *desiderata* for a philosophy of civilization, almost all of which seem to have shaped Wittgenstein's later philosophy. One of those *desiderata* is that philosophy should come to terms with its time, its epoch. Spengler characterizes this "coming to terms" in a way that suggests not that it take the form of a description of its time or epic; rather, he suggests some sort of indirect manifestation of that time or epoch. More specifically, he writes about an *absorption*, a *realization*, or an *embodiment* of it. If I am right in suggesting a cultural intimation in Wittgenstein's characterization of the builders in the *Investigations*, that would jibe perfectly with this Spenglerian requirement. For, on my view, this intimation would involve just such a coming to terms with the times. In the *Investigations*, Wittgenstein never mentions the blind, unreflective building that he had previously identified as the form of his civilization. Against this, the builders' activities invoke it by way of analogy. They intimate, absorb, realize, or embody what we know Wittgenstein had seen to be the most characteristic negative aspect of the civilized time in which he wrote.

iii. Private Language: A Philosophical Concern

Commentators on the *Investigations* are in general agreement that its discussion of a logically private language and its rejection of that conception is one of the most important, if not the most important, philosophical features of the work. The focus of this discussion is the nature of the words we use to speak of our sensations. Wittgenstein's discussion and rejection of private language for sensations has come to be known as "the private language argument". Most commentators, though not all, locate the private language within sections #243 to #301 of Part I of the *Philosophical Investigations*. Beyond this, there is far less agreement about just what the argument is and how it works. Almost fifty years after the publication of the *Investigations*, there are still nearly as many interpretations of Wittgenstein's discussion as there are interpreters. Some have doubted whether the private language argument is actually an argument. Those who harbor no such doubts, almost inevitably disagree on just what its conclusion is and what premises are offered in its support.

Certainly if we take Wittgenstein's own accounts of his philosophical procedures seriously, we would expect to find, within sections #243–#301, not arguments, but, rather, a series of grammatical reminders – careful descriptions of the actual workings of the common language we use to refer to sensations. To a great extent this is so. Wittgenstein, in these sections, is often focused upon both the ways in which this portion of human language is tied to, and depends upon, the natural expressions of our various sensations and, to a lesser extent, to the natural responses to those expressions by others which are an integral part of human behavior. He sees our actual linguistic ability to speak about our own sensations and those of others to be grounded in a common form of human life which includes shared primitive, pre-linguistic forms of expressive behavior and in rule-guided linguistic practices – language games, which enhance the expressive possibilities embodied in that form of life. Much of Wittgenstein's focus, in the these sections, concerns the public, interactive nature of sensation language, the communal nature of the rules and criteria which fix the meanings of sensation terms, and shared forms of behavior upon which this area of our language depends.

Wittgenstein makes these observations about actual sensation language not only because he thinks they are true, but because he hopes they will loosen the hold of what he takes to be a compelling, but false, picture of sensation language. It is this false conception that finds its expression in Wittgenstein's hypothesized private language. This picture or conception has its expression in section #243:

> we could imagine human beings who spoke only in monologue; who accompanied their activities by talking to themselves. – An explorer who watched them and listened to their talk might succeed in translating their language into ours ...
>
>   But could we also imagine a language in which a person could write down or give vocal expression to his inner experiences – his feelings, moods, and the rest for his private use? – Well can't we do so in our ordinary language? – But that is not what I mean. The individual words of this language are to refer to what can only be known to the person speaking, to his immediate private sensations. So another person cannot understand the language.[59]

This conception of a language in which an individual refers to her/his own private sensations, to what is inaccessible to anyone else, is far from a mere flight of fancy. Wittgenstein certainly did not regard it as such. It has served, within modern philosophy, as a model for the actual language of sensations. It is deeply embedded in the thought of the most influential Western philosophers of the seventeenth and eighteenth centuries: Descartes, Berkeley, Hume, and (at least when he adheres to his basic principles) Locke. In the twentieth century, it motivated many forms of phenomenalism and of sense-data theory. It has great appeal. I will suggest without argument that, for Wittgenstein, the conception of a private language depends, in part, on a tendency to misconstrue grammar as metaphysics – a subject already discussed in Chapter 1 in connection with the metaphysical notion of the privacy of experience. The picture of a private language is, perhaps, one of those misleading "illustrated turns of speech" – false metaphysical pictures imposed upon us when simple grammatical truths misrepresent themselves to us as supposedly deep metaphysical pictures. Be that as it may, Wittgenstein, not content to offer his own observations about sensation language, seeks also to undermine this conception of a *metaphysically* private language. He takes pains to show that it is incoherent.

These efforts come to a head in section #257 and, more dramatically, in section #258. It is there, if at all, that Wittgenstein offers what might reasonably be identified as an argument. I will offer only an outline of his discussion. I believe it to be, at least, correct as far as it goes. I recognize in advance that I do not address in detail some of the most important features of these passages. Having offered this modest outline, I will try to connect the philosophical discussion of private language, as I see it, with its cultural component. In effect, I want to show that the sections of the *Investigations* that discuss private language constitute yet another *locus* of cultural concern.

---

59 Ibid., paragraph 243.

In section #258, Wittgenstein takes the idea of a metaphysically private language, with a private grammar, seriously. He imagines himself to be a diarist who undertakes to write a certain sign, "E", in his diary each day that he has a certain sensation. This diarist's method is to inwardly connect his private sensation with the sign "E" in a private, ostensive definition, and, then, to use the sign consistently with that definition. The section begins as follows:

> Let us imagine the following case. I want to keep a diary about the recurrence of a certain sensation. To this end I associate it with a sign "E" and write it down in a calendar for every day on which I have the sensation. – I will remark first of all that a definition of the sign cannot be formulated. – But still I can give myself a kind of ostensive definition. – How? Can I point to the sensation? Not in the ordinary sense. But I speak, or write the sign down, and at the same time I concentrate my attention on the sensation – and so, as it were, point to it inwardly.[60]

However plausible this may seem, Wittgenstein holds that the diarist's attempt at an ostensive definition fails. Part of his reason for this is hinted at in the previous section, #257, in which a similar conception is entertained – that of a "genius child" who shows no outward signs of toothache, but nonetheless "invents a name for" that sensation. This conception too, Wittgenstein thinks, is incoherent. In #257, he objects to it: "When one says 'He gave a name to his sensation' one forgets that a great deal of stage-setting in the language is presupposed if the mere act of naming is to make sense."[61] His point is that an ostensive definition presupposes existing linguistic practices, that ostensive definitions cannot succeed in the absence of pre-existing linguistic "stage-setting". This plainly refers back to sections #27–36. In those sections Wittgenstein explicitly sets out to show that ostensive definitions cannot be, as it were, the first move in a language game. He says, in section #29, "the ostensive definition depends on … the circumstances under which it is given" and, in section #30, "the ostensive definition explains the use – the meaning – of the word when the overall role of the word in language is clear". In section #33 he characterizes the view he is putting forward as follows: "you must already be master of a language in order to understand an ostensive definition".

The diarist of #258 (and, it seems, the genius child of #257) seeks to establish the meaning of the term of his private language by connecting it, via an ostensive definition, with the private object it purports to name. This, Wittgenstein thinks, conflicts with his "stage-setting" requirement concerning ostensive definitions. So, part of his objection to the hypothesized ostensive definition of #258 appears to be that it lacks the necessary stage-setting preconditions for successful ostensive definition.

Section #258 itself contains another objection to its hypothesized private language. It is, I think, Wittgenstein's major objection. It seeks to undermine, more directly, the proposed ostensive definition which gives the diarist's sensation term "E" its meaning. It may have some interesting connections with his observations about the surroundings – the "stage-setting" necessary for ostensive definitions to

---

60 Ibid., paragraph 258.
61 Ibid., paragraph 257.

come off. I shall not pursue this. I will address it as an independent and much more direct objection which is based upon a deeper observation about ostensive definitions themselves.

Having hypothesized the diarist's procedures in #258, Wittgenstein goes on to express a fundamental objection. It specifically concerns the diarist's private ostensive definition of "E":

> But what is this ceremony for? For that is all it seems to be! A definition surely serves to establish the meaning of a sign. – Well, that is done precisely by the concentrating of my attention; for in this way I impress on myself the connexion between the sign and the sensation. – But "I impress it on myself" can only mean: this process brings it about that I remember the connexion *right* in the future. But in the present case I have no criterion of correctness. One would like to say: whatever is going to seem right to me is right. And that only means that here we can't talk about "right".[62]

For the diarist's ostensive definition of "E" to work – for it to "establish the meaning of" "E" – it must be remembered correctly. More specifically, the *connection between* "E" and the private sensation it would name must be remembered correctly. Wittgenstein, however, thinks that, in the truncated context of his example, the very question of whether the connection is remembered correctly is entirely empty. Why? Wittgenstein remarks that there is *no criterion* for remembering the connection correctly in the future. Why is this relevant? A criterion, for Wittgenstein, fixes the applicability of the terms or expressions for which it is the criterion.[63] A criterion (or the criteria) for the use of an expression constitutes our means of distinguishing situations to which the expression applies from those to which it does not. Without a criterion, there is no way of making such a distinction. Expressions, generally speaking, need criteria in order to have an application and, so, it seems, in order to have a meaning. With respect to the diarist, Wittgenstein's point is that there is no criterion for "he remembered the connection correctly". That expression, then, lacks applicability and meaning. It cannot be said that the diarist remembered (or failed to remember) the connection correctly and, so, the ostensive definition fails.

Why, however, does Wittgenstein think that "he remembered the connection correctly" *requires* a criterion in the context of #258? Wittgenstein did not think, after all, that *all* expressions have criteria for correct usage.[64] Why is this expression not one of the exceptions he allows for? What is it about this case and this expression that makes a criterion necessary? A completely satisfactory account of the so-called private language argument would provide an accurate and complete answer to this question. It is fair to say that there is nothing approaching a consensus on this point.

---

62 Ibid., paragraph 258.

63 For incisive discussions of this, see Newton Garver, *This Complicated Form of Life*, Chapter 11, and John V. Canfield, *Wittgenstein, Language and World* (Amherst, MA, 1981), Part 1, Chapters 3–6.

64 For a very complete discussion of this point, see Newton Garver, *This Complicated Form of Life*, pp. 179–94.

It is also unclear just why Wittgenstein believes that there is no criterion for "he remembered the connection correctly" or how exactly that claim should be understood. One suggestion about this specific issue that has been especially influential, and will prove useful for my purposes, is worthy of special mention. First articulated publicly by Saul Kripke in his seminal book, *Wittgenstein on Rules and Private Language*, the suggestion has been taken up by many commentators. It should be noted that Kripke's overall view of Wittgenstein's private language argument has not proved as influential as his specific suggestion about the issue at hand. I shall discuss only the latter – namely, Kripke's take on the claim in #258 that there is no criterion for the diarist remembering the connection between "E" and, so, for the correct use of 'E'.

Kripke sees the attempt of Wittgenstein's diarist in #258 to give himself an ostensive definition for "E" in terms of *rules*. It is natural to interpret the diarist's ostensive definition as an attempt to establish a criterion, or a *criterial rule* for the use of "E" – namely, "use 'E' on all and only those days on which I have *this* sensation". The diarist has endeavored to give himself a criterial rule for the use of "E". His subsequent use of that term is legitimate only if it is in accordance with that rule. As Kripke reads #258, the question "does the diarist remember the connection established by his ostensive definition correctly in using 'E'?" may be recast as something like "does the diarist follow the criterial rule established by his ostensive definition in using 'E'?". But, on Kripke's view – of this point, at least – Wittgenstein does not think that *any* rule can be followed privately. Kripke writes:

> following #243, a "private language" is usually defined as a language that is logically impossible for anyone else to understand. The private language argument is taken to argue against the possibility of a private language in this sense. This conception is not in error, but it seems to me that the emphasis is somewhat misplaced. What is really denied is what might be called the "private model" of rule following, that the notion of a person following a given rule is to be analyzed simply in terms of facts about the rule follower and the rule follower alone, without membership in a wider community …[65]

For Kripke's Wittgenstein, an individual, considered in isolation from a wider community, cannot follow a rule. Rather, rule following requires that there be a certain sort of agreement between the behavior of the individual and that of the wider community.

Wittgenstein, on Kripke's view, regards the private model of rule following as a philosophical false start – an illusion, which obscures a *necessarily social* component of rule following. Thus, the private model deceives us into thinking that an isolated individual can be said to follow a rule. Kripke is explicit that Wittgenstein means to deny that an isolated individual can be said to follow a rule: "The falsity of the private model … [means] that an individual, *considered in isolation* (whether or not he is physically isolated), cannot be said to do so."[66] Thus, Wittgenstein's diarist cannot be said to use "E" in accordance with his own internal ostensive definition. Given the nature of the case, as it is hypothesized by Wittgenstein, he could be said

---

65 Saul Kripke, *Wittgenstein on Rules and Private Language*, reprint edition (Cambridge, MA, 2004), p. 109.

66 Ibid., p. 110.

to do so only on the private model of rule following. For Kripke's Wittgenstein, no fact about the diarist and the diarist alone, in isolation from a wider community, could count either for or against his following his own private rule. This, in the context of Kripke's overall interpretation, is tantamount to there being no criterion for the diarist "remembering correctly" the connection purportedly established by his ostensive definition.

Many interpreters who reject Kripke's overall interpretation have agreed with his claim that Wittgenstein's central point in his denial of a private language is that private rule following is impossible.[67] One such commentator is A. C. Grayling, author of *Wittgenstein*, a respected introductory study of Wittgenstein's philosophical thought and development. Grayling characterizes Wittgenstein's view of rules and rule following as follows:

> What Wittgenstein emphasizes is the crucial fact that what *constitutes* a rule is our *collective use* of it; rule-following is general established by agreement, custom, and training. Therefore, although rules indeed guide us and afford us with our measures of correctness, they are not independent of us ...[68]

Grayling goes on to apply this to a reading of Wittgenstein's rejection of a logically private language, and, as context makes clear, of his remarks in #258:

> The reason for this has already been given: to understand a language is to be able to follow the rules for its use, and nothing can count as private rule-following for otherwise there would be no distinction between following a rule and merely *thinking* – perhaps mistakenly – that one is following a rule.[69]

On this interpretation of Wittgenstein, using a language involves following rules. Following rules is essentially a social activity, an activity that cannot be done by an individual in isolation from a wider linguistic community. Thus, private rule following and private language are rejected. There is much I have left out of my account of Kripke's provocative interpretation of Wittgenstein – indeed, Kripke's account amounts to much more than the point I have attributed to him. I have not touched upon some important features of his reading of Wittgenstein's view of rules and its account of how these relate to the so-called private language argument. These raise important questions that remain very much open. Still, the details of his interpretation that I have addressed here are plausible. They offer a way of reading #258 that has influenced many commentators who have rejected other features of Kripke's view. At least equally important, they further illuminate Wittgenstein's many suggestions that language is essentially social, that our common sensation language depends upon shared modes of behavior and shared interactive practices, and that the notion of a private language incorporates a deep misunderstanding of

---

67 This interpretation, for example, can be found in Norman Malcolm, *Nothing is Hidden* (Oxford, 1986), Chapter 9; A. C. Grayling, *Wittgenstein* (Oxford, 1988), pp. 77–86; Marie McGinn, *Routledge Philosophy Guidebook to Wittgenstein and the* Philosophical Investigations (London, 1997), pp. 89–106.

68 A. C. Grayling, *Wittgenstein*, p. 80.

69 Ibid., p. 86.

the real workings of language. I will take this influential feature of Kripke's view seriously, assuming it, without further argument, to be roughly correct, in what follows.

I have now discussed, albeit briefly and incompletely, the so-called private language argument. I have offered sketchy remarks concerning Wittgenstein's philosophical procedures in combating the notion of a private language. I want now to consider these questions: 1) In what ways, if any, do the discussions in #243–#301 embody or evoke Wittgenstein's cultural concerns? 2) In what ways, if any, do Wittgenstein's efforts to combat the notion of a logically private language serve also as an attempt to come to terms with and/or express his opposition to the civilized tendencies of his own time?

iv. Private Language: A Locus of Cultural Concern?

I begin by focusing upon the contrast these sections emphasize between a) our actual, common sensation language and b) Wittgenstein's hypothesized logically private language of #258. I would suggest that the former, a), serves to evoke, by way of analogy, the functioning of a culture; the latter, b), by way of exaggeration, the conditions of civilization and cultural decline. Indeed, the conception of a logically private language, I will suggest, may well serve to present, also by way of analogy, a kind of dystopian image of those conditions of civilization that Wittgenstein plainly deplored. I will proceed now to explain this suggestion.

For Wittgenstein, the actual functioning of that portion of our common language in which one can communicate about one's own sensations and those of others depends upon a shared form of life, accepted community practices, and behavior that accords with rules which themselves constitute accepted social constructs. I think Cavell's notion of the acceptance of a *social inheritance* may be invoked here without distortion. The cultural significance of these philosophical observations is that they direct the reader's attention to what is natural, what is shared, to social agreement and cohesion, and to community. All these, of course, are important features of the Spenglerian conception of a culture which impacted upon Wittgenstein. Transporting more of Cavell's terminology from its original context, one might say that Wittgenstein's account of our common language of sensations serves as a "homologous form of" or "an interpretation of" a Spenglerian image of a culture.

In direct contrast, Wittgenstein's conception of a private language points in an opposite direction. There, nothing depends upon what is shared by members of a community, upon practices which have developed over generations, which are agreed upon and accepted, or upon that form of community agreement which underlies rules and rule following. One might say that all this, in effect, points to a rejection of a social inheritance. To this extent, the logically private language of #258 points to a movement away from these features of a culture and, so, represents a rejection or loss of culture. Again, in Cavell's terms, we might say that part of the cultural component of Wittgenstein's conception of a private language is that it serves as a homologous form of, or an interpretation of, a Spenglerian image of a loss of culture.

If the foregoing is correct, then there is a clear way in which Wittgenstein, in passages #243–301, is *both* attempting to remedy philosophical confusion *and also*, indirectly, invoking and combating the conditions of cultural loss. In directing his reader to focus on the essentially public underpinnings of language, even of sensation language, he is exhorting his reader to focus upon what is shared, what is common, and to reject an illusory picture that rejects these as irrelevant. The mistake he seeks to avoid evokes (perhaps by way of Cavellian "homology") some of the tendencies of our time that typify cultural loss. Wittgenstein discourages his reader from alienating his efforts from shared, inherited, agreed upon social practices. He emphasizes, in a philosophical context, the importance of agreement and cohesion between the language user and the larger community. In Spenglerian terms, such a shift of emphasis is one that points away from civilization in the direction of culture.

Beyond this, the conception of a private language may have added significance. Wittgenstein's conception of a private linguist is, he thinks, a representation of a full-blown philosophical illusion. I would suggest that it might serve also as a depiction of cultural disfunction.

We might approach my suggestion by picturing a human being intent on setting up a private language. To the onlooker, he yammers to himself nonsensically, in stark isolation from his fellow human beings and the community practices that make communication possible. "E", he says to himself in a tone of seriousness, mystifying the onlooker who is witness to what Wittgenstein would characterize as an idle ceremony. Could this not have been for Wittgenstein a nightmare vision – a Spenglerian caricature – which represents the conditions of culture *giving way entirely* to the very worst conditions of civilization? It depicts a situation in which an individual's alienation from his community is so complete that meaningful communication is no longer even possible. In it, the minimal agreement between individuals necessary to talk sense has been abandoned. The conditions of a civilized time, in which, say, artistic communication is no longer possible, have worsened to the point where even ordinary communication is no longer possible. Seen in this way, the image is both Spenglerian and dystopian. It is an image of an individual in a kind of hyper-civilization – one in which social fragmentation is so complete as to undermine any possibility of meaningful expression. I am contending, then, that Wittgenstein's remarks on private language were intended to combat not only a mistaken picture of the functioning of sensation language but also, more indirectly, the tendencies of his time – what he refers to in the Preface of the *Investigations* as "the darkness of this time".

Before concluding this section, and this chapter, I want to indicate one more feature of Wittgenstein's discussion in #258 that I find fascinating. It concerns his characterization of the hypothesized inner ostensive definition of that section as a *ceremony*. As we have seen, his exact words are: "what is this ceremony for? For that is all it seems to be!" In the light of his rejection of this attempt at a definition, it is clear that he is likening it to a ceremony that has no point, which fails to come off, to an *idle ceremony*. I shall only note this here. Later, in Chapter 6, I shall argue that there is good reason to think that the conception of an idle ceremony may have served, for Wittgenstein, as a representation of the irreligiousness of his time – a feature that both he and Spengler believed to be characteristic of civilization and cultural decline.

Chapter 5

Religious Inexpressibility: Continuity and Change from Wittgenstein's Early to Late Views

I. Introduction

Throughout his life, Wittgenstein was concerned both with language and with religious approaches to life and its problems. Naturally enough, he pondered the matter of religious expression: how, if at all, can that which is religious be expressed in language? His persisting tendency was to doubt the possibility of meaningful religious expression in language. In this chapter, I seek to give an account of his doubts as he expressed them during his lifetime. In so doing, I distinguish between the doubts that are characteristic of his early work and those that he expressed in his later work and toward the end of his life. I offer a standard account of his early misgivings. My account of his later thought on the subject is original. First, I will offer an overview of my full account. Having done so, I shall elaborate upon it and defend it.

The notion that religion somehow defies expression in language appears to have appealed to Wittgenstein throughout his life. In his early work, he articulated and defended a boldly radical version of this notion. He held that any attempt to express in words anything of or about religion unavoidably results in nonsense. This remarkable view was a consequence of the view of language that he presented in the *Tractatus*. There, convinced that there are limitations upon what language could do in virtue of its very nature, he offered a denial of sorts (in the form of Tractarian "elucidations") of the possibility of religious expression. In "A Lecture on Ethics", delivered later in the 1920s, he articulated and defended this notion in a manner intended to be more accessible. Any attempt to write or talk about religion, he said there, is an attempt "to run against the boundaries of language", boldly adding, "This running against the walls of our cage is perfectly, absolutely, hopeless."[1]

Wittgenstein's later view of religious expression remained pessimistic and doubtful about the possibility of religious expression. While he continued to hold that there is something deeply problematic about religious expression, his diagnosis of the difficulty changed dramatically. Religious expression, on the later view, is

---

1   Ludwig Wittgenstein, "A Lecture on Ethics", in James Klagge and Alfred Nordman (eds), *Ludwig Wittgenstein – Philosophical Occasions 1912–1951*, (Indianapolis and Cambridge, 1993), p. 44.

problematic due to obstacles posed by modern civilization – the "darkness of this time".

Specifically, Wittgenstein believed that the conditions of cultural decline in which he lived and worked represented a setting against which it had become all but impossible for religious expression to succeed. Implicit in this view are two components. First, there is the view, familiar to readers of the *Investigations*, that meaning is – in a variety of important ways – dependent on context. The same symbol, action, or utterance may have a certain meaning in one setting, while having a significantly different meaning, or no meaning at all, in a different contextual setting. Second, he held that the obstacles to religious expression were not intrinsic to the nature of language itself, but, rather, consequences of his civilized time. He believed that surroundings very different from his own, and, more notably, past epochs of the culture from which his civilization proceeded, provided settings against which religious expression is not only possible, but entirely natural. This conception is, of course, Spenglerian and may well have been influenced by Spengler. This later view on religious expression reflected both an important change in his view of language and an intensifying of his deeply pessimistic attitudes toward his own time as one of cultural decline.

II. Religious Inexpressibility in Wittgenstein's Early Thought

i. Religious Inexpressibility in the Tractatus

Wittgenstein's early view of religious inexpressibility, at least in outline, presents little in the way of difficulties. The *Tractatus* and "A Lecture on Ethics" point in the same direction. I will offer a brief account of the view that emerges from the two works. What I offer should be familiar enough to most readers who are acquainted with Wittgenstein's early views.

Wittgenstein explains in a short preface that the *Tractatus* seeks to show that there is a limit upon "what can be said" – by which he means, of course, on what can be said *meaningfully*. Employing the metaphor of a limit, he writes, "on the other side of the limit will be simply nonsense".[2] In outline, at least, his overall strategy emerges fairly clearly: in showing the limits upon what can be meaningfully expressed in language, it will become clear that metaphysics, ethics, aesthetics, and religion lie on "the other side" – and, so, are "simply nonsense". Wittgenstein intended nothing less than to show that those philosophers who tried to write metaphysical, ethical, aesthetic, or theological works could never succeed. On Wittgenstein's view, they quite straightforwardly *had nothing to say* because *there was nothing to say*.

Wittgenstein's specific rejection of religious expression in the *Tractatus* was connected to the work's novel view of language. He believed that all meaningful propositions are truth-functions of elementary or atomic propositions. To this, he added a strikingly new idea: atomic propositions are *pictures* of atomic facts.

---

2   Ludwig Wittgenstein, *Tractatus Logico-Philosophicus* (Routledge Classics edition, London, 2002), p. 4. All further references to the *Tractatus* are indicated in the text using that work's numbering system.

The details of this claim are intricate and difficult, but he was explicitly clear on one consequence of it: the truth or falsity of an atomic proposition can never be established *a priori*. Each is a picture, and, so, its truth or falsity is a matter of whether it accurately depicts some fact that is in the world. Wittgenstein, in the second sentence of the *Tractatus*, identifies the world with "the totality of facts". Ascertaining the truth or falsity of an atomic proposition requires *comparing* the proposition with the world. The truth or falsity of each is an empirical matter. An atomic proposition is true if and only if it depicts some fact in the world.

Believing that all propositions are either atomic or else truth-functions of atomic propositions, Wittgenstein called the latter "molecular" propositions. He took great care to explicate the notion of a *tautology* – that is, a molecular proposition that is true no matter what the truth or falsity of its components. For example, suppose **P** is an atomic proposition and consider the proposition '**P** or not-**P**'. This very simple molecular proposition will be true whether its single atomic component, **P**, is true or false. It is a *logical* truth. Its truth is a matter of its logical structure and is compatible with any factual situation in the world. It is certainly true, but it is an empty or trivial truth that really gives us no direct factual information about the world. Similarly, Wittgenstein recognized that there are logical falsehoods ('both **P** and not-**P**' is an example) that are false in virtue of their logical form alone, which – like tautologies – convey no factual content.

Wittgenstein made the powerful claim that tautologies constitute the only species of *necessary, a priori* truth. All other truths depend upon the factual nature of the world. First, atomic propositions either correctly picture the world or they don't. Their truth depends, at bottom, upon what the world is like. Those molecular propositions which are not tautologies (and not logical falsehoods) will turn out to be true just on certain specific patterns of truth or falsity among their atomic components. The truth or falsity of each depends on which of its atomic components are true and which false. This, in turn, is inevitably a matter of fact – a matter of what the world is like.

In overview, then, Wittgenstein held that there are just two sorts of truths. Tautologies are *a priori*, necessary truths – but they are devoid of factual content, being consistent with any set of facts. All other truths require, in effect, that the world be a certain way – which is a contingent, empirical, *a posteriori* matter. He was clear and explicit that this left no room for metaphysical truths, aesthetic truths, theological truths, or religious truths. These, he thought, purport to be both necessary and also to convey meaningful truths that transcend mere facts. For him, all necessary truths are empty and all truths of substance are merely factual. There can be no significant truths beyond empirical facts. Traditional metaphysics and theology claimed to establish substantial, trans-empirical truths – an impossibility on the *Tractatus* view. Ethical and aesthetic truths were traditionally thought to hold no matter what the world is like and theological truths were certainly thought to transcend empirical facts. Wittgenstein's scheme, then, leaves no room for traditional metaphysics, theology, or for an expressible body of religious doctrine.

Why exactly did Wittgenstein himself believe that religious and theological discourse, by its nature, purported to go beyond empirical propositions? After all, there is a longstanding tradition in which philosophers and theologians – those who accept "natural theology" as a legitimate endeavor – employ factual propositions to support (or undermine) religious claims. For example, attempts to argue for the existence of God *a posteriori* have been, and continue to be, taken seriously. Why did Wittgenstein, in effect, reject all this?

The *Tractatus* does not offer much in the way of clear answers. The last few pages of the book offer some scattered intimations regarding ethics, aesthetics, God, and religion. What is offered is written in the stark, oracular style that is characteristic of the work. It certainly doesn't help that Wittgenstein believed that these intimations were themselves nonsensical by the book's own tenets. I think that "Lecture" provides a clearer expression of this same tendency of thought, providing some helpful material that the *Tractatus* leaves out.

It is well documented that Wittgenstein took religious matters seriously throughout his life. I discuss this matter further in the next chapter. In the *Tractatus*, and later in "Lecture", he concluded that any attempt to give expression to that which is religious would need to capture within propositions that which is of the highest importance. Such an attempt, he believed, should connect with absolute values, with what is of ultimate importance, with the deepest problems of human life, with the meaning of life, and with the meaning of the world itself. However, he did not believe that such matters *could* be put into words. This emerges very clearly in "Lecture", but indications of this tendency can be seen in the *Tractatus* – expressed in that work's characteristically truncated form. The *Tractatus* provides intimations concerning "what is higher", "the problems of life", "the sense of the world", and even God. It does so in a way that suggests that these are all interconnected and, equally important, that they transcend that which is merely factual. On the Tractarian view of language, these things cannot be meaningfully expressed. Here are some quotes:

> The sense of the world must lie outside the world ... If there is a value which is of value, it ... cannot lie *in* the world. [6.41]

> Propositions cannot express anything higher. [6.42]

> *How* the world is, is completely indifferent for what is higher. God does not reveal himself *in* the world. [6.432]

> We feel that even if *all possible* scientific questions be answered, the problems of life have not been touched at all. [6.52]

Wittgenstein's intimations, then, might be given expression as follows: the things which religious discourse would need to express lie outside the Tractarian boundary of what *can be* meaningfully expressed.

ii. Religious Inexpressibility in "A Lecture on Ethics": The Impossibility of Expressing Ultimate Values

In contrast to the removed, oracular tone of the *Tractatus*, "Lecture" is down to earth. Wittgenstein's approach there is personal and autobiographical. He enacts his own attempts to give expression to some of his own religious impulses. He makes it clear that these are powerful tendencies with important consequences for him. Having done so, however, he emphatically condemns all such expressions as nonsensical. In fact, it is exactly such attempts at expression which, we shall see, he believed to be "perfectly, absolutely, hopeless" in "Lecture". It is worth noting that what is being condemned as nonsense here is not only high-minded theology, but also the attempts of earnest individuals, like himself, to express deeply felt religious tendencies.

"Lecture" was first presented as a talk in 1929 and later published. It is an informal presentation and lacks the rigor of the writings Wittgenstein intended for publication. On a reasonably charitable reading it provides an outline of Wittgenstein's thoughts about ethics, religion, and their inexpressibility. In that respect, it may be seen as a less daunting attempt to illuminate what is intimated in the *Tractatus*.

"Lecture", I think, is best interpreted as a Tractarian demonstration of the impossibility of ethical statements and, as the discussion continues, of religious statements too. It begins with a *prima facie* characterization of what ethics would be, if it were possible. It seeks to show that ethics, as he would like to characterize it, could not sensibly be expressed in language. Finally, and most important for my purposes, Wittgenstein links the inexpressibility of ethics and ethical values to the inexpressibility of religion and religious values. Considerations that weigh against the possibility of ethical expression, he holds, weigh equally against the possibility of religious expression.

Beginning with a *prima facie* characterization of ethics, "Lecture" claims that ethics, if it is anything at all, must be concerned with values of a certain sort. Wittgenstein says:

> to make you see as clearly as possible what I take to be the subject matter of Ethics I will put before you a number of more or less synonomous [sic] expressions, and by enumerating them I want to produce the same sort of effect which Galton produced when he took a number of photos of different faces on the same photographic plate in order to get the picture of the typical features they all had in common. ...Now instead of saying "Ethics is the enquiry into what is good" I could have said Ethics is the enquiry into what is valuable, or, into what is really important, or I could have said Ethics is the enquiry into the meaning of life, or into what makes life worth living, or into the right way of living. I believe that if you look at all these phrases you will get a rough idea as to what it is that Ethics is concerned with.[3]

Wittgenstein wants also to say that ethics, as he thinks of it, is concerned with values such as goodness or rightness as *absolute* values. Ethics, he thinks, purports to express absolute values – but this, he seeks to show, cannot be done. Admitting that he himself is initially inclined to think that he can sensibly express absolute values, he ultimately comes to the conviction that any such expression is impossible. In "Lecture", he tries to take the purported notion of an absolute value seriously. In the end, however, he wants to show that it is "a chimera". He begins by attempting to distinguish between *relative* and *absolute* values and between a relative and absolute sense of evaluative terms like "good" and "right":

---

3   Ludwig Wittgenstein, "A Lecture on Ethics", p. 38.

I will [speak of] the trivial or relative sense on the one hand and the ethical or absolute sense on the other. If for instance I say this is a *good* chair this means that the chair serves a certain predetermined purpose and the word here has meaning so far as this purpose has been previously fixed upon. In fact the word "good" in the relative sense simply means coming up to a certain predetermined standard.[4]

He goes on to explain that "good runner" or "good pianist" uses "good" in the relative sense and that "right way to Granchester" uses "right" in a similar relative sense. These terms of mere relative value do not, Wittgenstein explains, express an ethical value. He explains,

[T]his is not how ethics uses them. Supposing that I could play tennis and one of you saw me playing and said "Well, you play pretty badly" and suppose I answered "I know but I don't want to play any better," all the other man could say would be "Ah, then that's all right." But suppose I had told a preposterous lie and he came up to me and said "You're behaving like a beast" and then I said "I know I behave badly, but then I don't want to behave any better," could he then say "Ah, then that's all right"? Certainly not; he would say "Well, you *ought* to want to behave better." Here we have a judgment of absolute value, whereas the first instance was one of a relative judgment.[5]

Ignoring that some of what Wittgenstein says in this informal presentation of the distinction is imprecise and in need of amendment, his intended meaning may nonetheless be grasped. Playing tennis well is not an absolute value. Since ethics deals with absolute values, it may be ethically acceptable for someone to play tennis badly. Playing tennis badly (normally) does not constitute behaving badly; bad tennis may be "all right" from an ethical viewpoint. In contrast, *behaving well*, in Wittgenstein's account, *is* an absolute value, an ethical value. On that account, it is not ethically acceptable to behave badly; bad behavior is never "all right" from an ethical viewpoint.

Having proffered a distinction between relative values and absolute ethical values, Wittgenstein then proceeds to what stands, in "Lecture", as a pivotal claim. He maintains that statements of relative value can be expressed as factual statements but that statements of absolute value cannot.

Instead of saying "This is the right way to Granchester," I could equally well have said, "This is the right way to go if you want to get to Granchester in the shortest time"; "This man is a good runner" simply means that he runs a certain number of miles in a certain number of minutes, etc. Now what I wish to contend is that, although judgments of relative value can be shown to be mere statements of facts, no statement of fact can ever be, or imply, a judgment of absolute value.[6]

There is a bit of sloppiness in this too. In the Granchester case the word "right" is not eliminated in the supposedly purely factual restatement of the original statement of relative value. In addition, the purported factual reformulation of "This man is a

---

4   Ibid.
5   Ibid., pp. 38–9.
6   Ibid., p. 39.

good runner" is not convincing as it stands. I shall not pursue these points. His claim that statements of relative value can be reformulated in a factual form is a familiar one. It could surely have been more carefully spelled out and, no doubt, would have been in a more formal setting. As such, I will take the claim seriously here without further comment.

Returning to the further contention that statements of absolute value cannot be reformulated as factual statements, Wittgenstein supports it by posing a striking thought experiment:

> Let me explain this: Suppose one of you were an omniscient person and therefore knew all the movements of all the bodies in the world dead or alive and that he also knew all the states of mind of all human beings that ever lived, and suppose this man wrote all he knew in a big book, then this book would contain the whole description of the world; and what I want to say is, that this book would contain nothing that we would call an *ethical* judgment or anything that would logically imply such a judgment. It would of course contain all relative judgments of value and all true scientific propositions and in fact all true propositions that can be made. But all the facts described would, as it were, stand on the same level and in the same way all propositions stand on the same level. There are no propositions which, in any absolute sense, are sublime, important, or trivial.[7]

Wittgenstein holds that this world-book would "contain all relative judgments" because it contains all factual statements and relative judgments can be expressed as factual statements along the lines of his examples. In contrast, he explicitly denies that the world-book would contain any ethical judgments or judgments of absolute value. Those familiar with Hume's ethical writings would, I think, see striking similarities to Hume's various presentations of his problem about the gap between facts and values, the "is" / "ought" distinction. Wittgenstein's elaboration upon his denial is also reminiscent of a very similar observation of Hume:

> If for instance in our world-book we read the description of a murder with all its details physical and psychological, the mere description of these facts will contain nothing which we could call an *ethical* proposition. The murder will be on exactly the same level as any other event, for instance the falling of a stone.[8]

Why is Wittgenstein so confident of this? First, the passage suggests, as does the *Tractatus*, that he believed that it is the purpose of language to express factual or empirical propositions. A subsequent passage in "Lecture", we shall see, confirms this explicitly. Second, he contends that ethical statements, if there were any, would serve to express what he would like to think of as a necessity:

> The right road is the road which leads to an arbitrarily predetermined end and it is quite clear to us all that there is no sense in talking about the right road apart from such a predetermined goal. Now let us see what we could possibly mean by the expression, "*the absolutely right road*". I think it would be the road which *everybody* on seeing it would, *with logical necessity*, have to go, or be ashamed for not going. And similarly, the *absolute*

---

7   Ibid.
8   Ibid., pp. 39–40.

good, if it is a describable state of affairs, would be one which everybody, independent of his tastes and inclinations, would *necessarily* bring about or feel guilty for not bringing about.[9]

Finally, Wittgenstein insists, no factual statement – and, so, no statement at all – can express what he would like to think of as an ethical necessity. Language can only express facts or states of affairs, and these, he thinks, are all contingent. A mere description of contingent fact cannot express what Wittgenstein wants to express in the above passage – his presumed notion of ethical necessity. The following passages provide confirmation:

> And I want to say that such a state of affairs is a chimera. No state of affairs has, in itself, what I would like to call the coercive power of an absolute judge.[10]

> And now I must say that if I contemplate what Ethics really would have to be if there were such a science ... [i]t seems to me obvious that nothing we could ever think or say should be *the* thing.[11]

> Our words ... are vessels capable only of containing and conveying meaning and sense, *natural* meaning and sense. Ethics, if it is anything, is supernatural and our words will only express facts; as a teacup will only hold a teacup full of water and I were to pour a gallon of water over it.[12]

Wittgenstein's position in "Lecture" is dominated by 1), his early philosophical view that the business of language is to express facts and by 2), his denial that statements of absolute value, if there were any, could be in any way expressed by factual descriptions. Finally, there is his belief that theological propositions, if there were any, would themselves need to be statements of absolute value. Hence, in overview, an argument like this is suggested:

1) All meaningful statements are factual statements.
2) No purported statements of absolute value are factual statements.
3) All purported theological statements are purported statements of absolute value.

Therefore, no purported theological statements are meaningful statements.

This may serve, as an illuminating outline of Wittgenstein's thought on religious expression at the time he produced "Lecture". The argument presented has a valid form. Strictly speaking, Wittgenstein, consistent with his *Tractatus* view, would neither accept the premises nor the conclusion as meaningful propositions. Presumably, he would accept them and the purported argument as useful "elucidations".

One final point: It is worth noting that Wittgenstein, faced with something like Hume's conundrum about facts and values, *wholly rejects* anything along the

---

9   Ibid., p. 40.
10 Ibid., p. 40.
11 Ibid.
12 Ibid.

lines of a Humean "skeptical solution" to the problem – and, more specifically, the well-known Humean claim that ethical values have their source in certain kinds of subjective feelings of approval and disapproval. Without mentioning Hume (perhaps even unaware of the close and striking similarities in the way they pose this problem), he explicitly considers this line of thought.

> Now perhaps some of you will … be reminded of Hamlet's words: "Nothing is either good or bad but thinking makes it so." But this again could lead to a misunderstanding. What Hamlet says seems to imply that good and bad, though not qualities of the world outside us, are attributes to our states of mind.[13]

Wittgenstein holds that such a response fails to recognize the source and scope of his problem. It is at this point that he introduces his example of a factual description of a murder, claiming that such a description has no ethical content. For emphasis, he adds:

> Certainly the reading of this description might cause us pain or rage or any other emotion, or we might read about the pain or rage caused by this murder in other people when they heard of it, but there will simply be facts, facts, and facts but no Ethics.[14]

Wittgenstein's problem is that absolute values, unlike relative values, cannot be reduced to facts. The view of Hume, attributed also to Hamlet, cannot be considered a solution to that problem because emotions and other subjective states, whatever their content, occur wholly within the realm of facts. They cannot be the ground of absolute values.

iii. Case Studies in Inexpressibility of Absolute Value in "A Lecture on Ethics"

The previous subsection gives a rough account of what might be thought of as Wittgenstein's demonstration in "Lecture" of the impossibility of ethics or – what amounts to the same thing – his demonstration of the impossibility of expressing absolute values. No doubt, he recognized that his main claim was a radical one and that it was contrary to the tendencies of most philosophers. More important, I think, he recognized that it was contrary to one of his own deepest personal tendencies. He saw an evident tension between it and his determination both to ponder and to articulate thoughts about the right way to live, what gives life meaning, what is ultimately most important, and whether anything one may experience in life might have "the coercive power of an absolute judge".[15] This tendency, for Wittgenstein, manifested itself as a persisting, sometimes urgent, lifetime preoccupation. His demonstration in "Lecture", the confident finality with which he presents it, must have been unsettling to him. It undermined one of his fondest hopes. Surely, Wittgenstein *wanted to* reach and articulate conclusions about what is most valuable, most important, in life. The

---

13 Ibid., p. 39.
14 Ibid., p. 40.
15 Ibid.

philosophical stance of the *Tractatus* and "Lecture" convinced him that he could not.

Wittgenstein might have stopped at this point. He did not. In the last few pages of "Lecture", Wittgenstein, convinced that there can be no meaningful talk of absolute values, provides accounts of his own attempts to do so, describing some of them in detail. Why did he do this? For one thing, I think he recognized that a mere philosophical demonstration might not be sufficient to quiet such tendencies. For another, he seemed to think that clarity might be further served by attending, *in specific detail*, to his own attempts to express absolute values and to show, *case by case*, that they come to nonsense. These discussions are interesting in their own right. In addition, they lead to further discussions that specifically address religious expression and why Wittgenstein thinks that it, like the ethical, lacks sense.

As soon as he completes his demonstration, he says:

> Then what have all of us who, like myself, are still tempted to use such expressions as "absolute good", "absolute value," etc., what have we in mind and what do we try to express? Now whenever I try to make this clear to myself it is natural that I should recall cases in which I would certainly use these expressions …[16]

He cites two cases that come to his mind when he is so tempted. Of the first, he says:

> in my case … one particular experience presents itself to me which … is, in a sense, my experience *par exellence* and … I will use this experience as my first and foremost example. …I believe the best way of describing it is to say that when I have it I *wonder at the existence of the world*. And I am then inclined to use such phrases as "how extraordinary that anything should exist" or "how extraordinary that the world should exist."[17]

He characterizes the second as follows:

> I will mention another experience straight away which I also know and which others of you might be acquainted with: it is, what one might call, the experience of feeling *absolutely* safe. I mean the state of mind in which one is inclined to say "I am safe, nothing can injure me whatever happens."[18]

With respect to both, he says:

> Now let me consider these experiences, for, I believe, they exhibit the very characteristics we try to get clear about. And the first thing I have to say is, that the verbal expression which we give to these experiences is nonsense![19]

Wittgenstein offers extremely brief accounts of why the expressions of each of these two experiences are indeed nonsense. As for the first, he says:

---

16 Ibid.
17 Ibid., p. 41.
18 Ibid.
19 Ibid.

If I say "I wonder at the existence of the world" I am misusing language. …To say "I wonder at such and such being the case" has only sense if I can imagine it not to be the case. …But it is nonsense to say that I wonder at the existence of the world, because I cannot imagine it not existing. I could of course wonder at the world round me being as it is. If for instance I had this experience while looking into the blue sky, I could wonder at the sky being blue as opposed to the case when it's clouded. But that's not what I mean. I am wondering at the sky being *whatever it is*. One might be tempted to say that what I am wondering at is a tautology, namely that the sky is blue or not blue. But then it's just nonsense to say that one is wondering at a tautology.[20]

I do not want to take up the merits of this passage. It certainly seems to presuppose some unexpressed principles. In addition, it does not explain why one cannot imagine the world not existing or just why it is nonsense to speak of "wondering at a tautology". For this discussion, it is enough to show that Wittgenstein was persuaded that the expressions used in connection with the first experience come to nonsense.

He thinks much the same thing about attempts to give expression to the second experience and, more specifically, about the words "absolutely safe".

We all know what it means in ordinary life to be safe. I am safe in my room, when I cannot be run over by an omnibus. I am safe if I have had whooping cough and cannot therefore get it again. To be safe essentially means that it is physically impossible that *certain* things should happen to me and therefore it's nonsense to say that I am safe *whatever* happens.[21]

This account is incomplete and raises questions that I shall not take up. The important thing, for my purposes, is that Wittgenstein thought it is nonsense to speak of being "absolutely safe". The intended point here appears to be that any purported statement to the effect that someone is absolutely safe would be consistent with *any* state of affairs and, so, empirically meaningless, not factual.

More generally, Wittgenstein explicitly states, "I want to impress upon you that a certain characteristic misuse of our language runs through *all* ethical expressions."[22] He goes on to elucidate the "characteristic misuse" of language shared by all would-be ethical expressions. He offers no arguments here – only what might be thought of as a sketch of his considered viewpoint. He writes:

All these expressions *seem*, prima facie, to be just *similes*. Thus it seems that when we are using the word *right* in an ethical sense, although, what we mean, is not right in its trivial [relative] sense, it's something familiar, and when we say "This is a good fellow," although the word here doesn't mean what it means in the sentence "This is a good football player" there seems to be some similarity. And when we say "This man's life was valuable" we don't mean it in the same sense in which we speak of some valuable jewelry but there seems to be some sort of analogy.[23]

---

20 Ibid., pp. 41–2.
21 Ibid., p. 42.
22 Ibid.
23 Ibid.

The key word here is "seems". Wittgenstein is suggesting an account of ethical (and also, as it turns out, religious) language here. It is an account which he is *tempted* to give. It *seems* right, at first glance. He offers it, I think, as a *prima facie* plausible account of ethical (and religious) statements: ethical talk of absolute values is meaningful in virtue of some *similarity* to talk of relative values. This account is offered, only to be rejected.

Wittgenstein's rejection of his own suggestion follows almost immediately:

> in ethical and religious language we seem constantly to be using similes. But a simile must be a simile for *something*. And if I can describe a fact by means of a simile I must also be able to drop the simile and to describe the facts without it. Now in our case as soon as we try to drop the simile and simply state the facts which stand behind it, we find that there are no such facts.[24]

The thought here is this: If statements of absolute value were to bear the needed similarity to statements of relative value to support his suggestion, then there would need to be some similarity between what the two forms of expression describe. Statements of relative value, at bottom, describe facts. So, for purported statements of absolute value to be in some way similar or analogous to them, they too would have to describe facts that are similar or analogous. But, of course, earlier in "Lecture", Wittgenstein explicitly denies that purported ethical statements of absolute values are factual descriptions. In the above passage this is reflected in his concluding remark that "there are no such facts".

We could put Wittgenstein's point in another way: factual statements of relative value and ethical statements of absolute value, as he is inclined to think of them, *can't be analogous* because the former deal with natural facts, while the latter, if they were possible, would describe nothing of the kind. We have seen that he explicitly insists that "[e]thics, if it is anything, is supernatural". Now Wittgenstein remained vexed by this result – he found it neither welcome nor congenial. It is equally plain, however, that he saw no way to avoid it:

> And so, what at first appeared to be a simile now seems to be mere nonsense. Now the … experiences I have mentioned to you … seem to those who have experienced them, for instance to me, to have in some sense an intrinsic, absolute value. But when I say they are experiences, surely, they are facts; they have taken place then and there, lasted a certain definite time and consequently are describable. And so from what I have said some minutes ago I must admit it is nonsense to say that they have absolute value.[25]

iv. The Transition from Ethical Inexpressibility to Religious Inexpressibility in "Lecture"

Having offered both a demonstration of the inexpressibility of absolute value and a vivid rejection of his own attempts to express absolute values as nonsense, Wittgenstein ends "Lecture" with a consideration of religious expression. Wittgenstein explicitly

---

24 Ibid., pp. 42–3.
25 Ibid., p. 43.

asserts that what he claims about the impossibility of ethical statements applies in the same way to religious statements. He poses, and then rejects, a suggestion about the meaning of religious statements that closely corresponds to his suggestion about the meaning of ethical statements that we have just examined. In so doing he ties the two forms together, concluding that both come to nonsense:

> all religious terms seem in this sense to be used as similes or allegorically. For when we speak of God and that he sees everything and when we kneel to pray to Him all our terms and actions seem to be parts of a great and elaborate allegory which represents Him as a human being of great power whose grace we try to win etc., etc. But this allegory also describes the experience which I have just referred to. For the first of them [wondering at the existence of the world] is, I believe, exactly what people were referring to when they said that God had created the world; and the experience of absolute safety has been described by saying that we feel safe in the hands of God.[26]

This passage immediately precedes the last two passages cited in the previous subsection. For Wittgenstein, religious terms, like ethical terms, *seem* to function as similes – but this appearance is deceptive. So conceived, attempts at religious expression fail for the same reason that attempts at ethical expression fail: no similarities can underlie the apparent similes. Hence, with religious terms too, "what appeared to be a simile" in the end can be seen "to be mere nonsense". Wittgenstein never spells out what he means by "a great and elaborate allegory" in connection with religious terms in the above passage, nor does he explain why he is inclined to think that all religious expressions function as similes. Thus, it is not clear just why he thinks that all religious language is nonsensical in just this way. There is no doubt, however, that he did think it. His dramatic closing remarks in "Lecture" certainly leave no doubt:

> For all I wanted to do with [ethical and religious terms] was just *to go beyond* the world and that is to say beyond significant language. My whole tendency and I believe the tendency of all men who ever tried to write or talk Ethics or Religion was to run against the boundaries of language. This running against the walls of our cage is perfectly, absolutely hopeless. Ethics so far as it springs from the desire to say something about the ultimate meaning of life, the absolute good, the absolute valuable [sic], can be no science. What it says does not add to our knowledge in any sense.[27]

This is an astonishing conclusion, one that seems consistent with the scattered intimations of the *Tractatus* while providing a somewhat more helpful, if less rigorous, sense of his overall thoughts and even a rough indication of how he came by them. "Lecture", like the *Tractatus*, ends with an indirectly expressed intimation that the most important things in life may be too deep for words. Wittgenstein ends "Lecture" with a claim about the human tendency to express absolute and religious values that immediately follows the passage cited immediately above:

---

26 Ibid., p. 42.
27 Ibid., p. 44.

But it is a document of a tendency in the human mind which I personally cannot help respecting deeply and I would not for my life ridicule it.[28]

III. The Problem of Religious Expression in the Later Work

i. A Weakening of the Earlier View of Religious Expression: A Lesser Form of Pessimism?

The conclusion of "Lecture" can be seen as Wittgenstein's clearest expression of his early view of the impossibility of religious expression. Attempts at religious expression are "perfectly, absolutely hopeless", because they seek to overstep "the boundaries of language", to use language to perform a task which, by its very nature, it cannot perform.

Wittgenstein's later views on religious expression continued to be pessimistic about its possibility. His later pessimism, however, was very different in character from that of the *Tractatus* or of "Lecture". The most important factor in this change was the dramatic change in Wittgenstein's treatment of language as his early philosophy gave way to his later one. In the thirties and forties, Wittgenstein had given up the treatment of language that supported his early view that religious expression must come to nonsense. That treatment, and its attendant conviction that the function of language is to state facts, gave way to a very different view that emphasized that language has many functions. The mature Wittgenstein no longer accepted the view of the *Tractatus* and of "Lecture" that religious expression is absolutely impossible given the very nature of language. He came to think that those works endorsed a misguided and oversimplified treatment of language against which much of the later writings were directed.

It is noteworthy that Wittgenstein never addressed questions of God and religion in the *Investigations*. The only evidence of a direct and public philosophical treatment of religious subjects by the late Wittgenstein comes in the form of fewer than twenty pages of notes taken by his students during some lectures and discussions of religious belief given in 1938. These were published as part of a very short book, *Lectures and Conversations on Aesthetics, Psychology and Religious Belief*. His views, insofar as they emerge in this work, retain an important feature of his early view: he continued to hold that expressions of religious belief are not expressions of factual belief. On the early view, this, of course, insured that such expressions are nonsensical, since, on that view, the only meaningful statements were factual. In *Lectures and Conversations*, no such claim is made and the discussion takes a different turn. The tendencies of *Lectures and Conversations* are consistent with and partially confirmed by passages from *Culture and Value* written during the same and subsequent times.

Wittgenstein's later view notoriously emphasized the many different functions of language. Far from holding that the single business of language is to state facts, the new view emphasized that language consists of a plurality of different language games, each regulated by its own set of rules, its own "grammar". Where the

---

28 Ibid.

early view offered a singular, unified view of language, the later view emphasized multiplicity and differences. In *Lectures and Conversations*, Wittgenstein explicitly emphasized the differences between typical expressions of factual belief and those of religious belief. Beyond this, he focused upon the very different ways in which factual and religious beliefs are justified or grounded. In these discussions, Wittgenstein never comes close to claiming that expressions of religious belief are nonsense. His discussion, rather, presents expressions of religious belief as natural expressions that are easily misunderstood. He emphasizes that they are different from expressions of factual beliefs and, to a great extent, a misunderstood sector of language. He seeks to gain some understanding of its nature and to guard against the temptation to think of religious belief and its grounds on an analogy with factual, especially scientific, beliefs and their grounds. Nowhere does he suggest that there is anything illegitimate or nonsensical in expressions of religious belief.

With respect to the differences between religious and factual belief, Wittgenstein begins his lectures with a striking example:

> Suppose someone were a believer and said: "I believe in a Last Judgment," and I said: "Well, I'm not so sure. Possibly." You would say that there is an enormous gulf between us. If he said "There is a German aeroplane overhead," and I said "Possibly, I'm not so sure," you'd say we were fairly near.[29]

Wittgenstein focuses on the source of these differences between religious and factual assertions. He emphasizes how the tendency to think of religious belief as a type of factual belief leads to mistakes and misunderstandings. This tendency, he thinks, is, in part, a function of surface similarities between factual and religious discourse. Within both, we can speak of "reasons" or "grounds" for belief. These similarities, he thinks, obscure deep differences. Later in the lecture, Wittgenstein says:

> In a religious discourse we use such expressions as: "I believe that so and so will happen," and use them differently to the way in which we use them in science.
>
> Although there is a great temptation to think we do. Because we do talk of evidence, and do talk of evidence by experience.[30]

There is no doubt that Wittgenstein believed that the subject of religious belief and its grounds is extremely difficult. There, one is often misled: surface features of religious discourse and their similarities to those of other, very different, sorts of discourse are deceptive. I will address this matter in more detail, albeit in a different context, in this book's final chapter. At any rate, it is most noteworthy that nowhere in *Lectures and Conversations* does Wittgenstein suggest that religious discourse is meaningless or that it runs hopelessly against some presumed boundary of language. The entire discussion presumes that religious language has its own grammar, its own function – one that is deceptively and interestingly different from other forms. Did

---

29 Ludwig Wittgenstein, *Lectures and Conversations on Aesthetics, Psychology and Religious Belief* (Berkeley, CA, 1967), p. 54.

30 Ibid., p. 57.

he believe that religious language then is meaningful and legitimate? It would appear so, though, I will offer an important qualification to this in what follows.

There is also direct evidence that Wittgenstein came to reject his early views on the inexpressibility of religion. In personal conversations with Drury, Wittgenstein explicitly rejected his early view that theology is impossible. Indeed, Drury reports that Wittgenstein, near the end of his life, characterized his earlier expression of that view as "stupid".[31] Also important, Wittgenstein agreed to have discussions about religion with Drury. The details of this, as Drury reports them, are interesting,

> I had begun to attend Professor Moore's lectures. …At the commencement of his first lecture Moore had read out from the University Calendar the subjects that his professorship required him to lecture on, the last of these was "the philosophy of religion." Moore went on to say that he would be talking about all of the previous subjects except this last concerning which he had nothing to say. I told Wittgenstein that I thought a Professor of Philosophy had no right to keep silent concerning such an important subject. Wittgenstein immediately asked me if I had a copy of St. Augustine's *Confessions*. I handed him my Loeb edition. He must have known his way about the book thoroughly for he found the passage in a few seconds.

> WITTGENSTEIN: "You are saying something like St. Augustine says here. 'Et vae tacentibus de te quoniam loquaces muti sunt.' …It should be translated, 'And woe to those who say nothing concerning thee just because the chatterboxes talk a lot of nonsense.' …I won't refuse to talk to you about God or about religion."[32]

Here Wittgenstein appears to be saying that the prevailing nonsensical talk of "chatterboxes" notwithstanding, it is possible to talk sense about God and religion – at least with people of substance, such as Drury. Subsequently, true to his word, he discussed religion with Drury on many occasions. Throughout the thirties and forties, Wittgenstein continued to pursue religious subjects. *Culture and Value* contains many observations about religion, religious conviction, and even religious doctrine. He also discussed religion with O. K. Bouwsma. One of these discussions, I shall try to show, is especially helpful in clarifying his later view of religious expression. It is noteworthy that Wittgenstein was *generally reluctant* to discuss religion. He might occasionally hold discussions one on one, or with small numbers of trusted friends or students. He made a number of interesting journal notations. Still, never again, after he delivered "A Lecture on Ethics", did Wittgenstein return to the subject of religious expression in works intended for publication.

Wittgenstein's attitude toward religious expression remained one of pessimism, if not of *absolute* pessimism. While he no longer regarded religious expression to be nonsensical and he retained a desire to express religious thoughts, he rarely did so. His reluctance, however, was no longer a matter of believing that only nonsense could come of it. What, then, was its source? Part of the answer is that he came to think that his own attempts at religious expression would go almost entirely *misunderstood*. More important are his reasons for thinking so.

---

31 M. O'C. Drury, "Conversations with Wittgenstein", in Rush Rhees (ed.), *Ludwig Wittgenstein – Personal Recollections* (Totowa, NJ, 1981), p. 113.
32 Ibid., p. 104.

One of the most dramatic indications – though, by no means the only one – of Wittgenstein's conviction that his own expressions of religious attitudes would go misunderstood are found in the prefatory remarks to *Philosophical Remarks*. There he confesses a desire to dedicate that book "to the Glory of God", but adds immediately that "nowadays, this would be the trick of a cheat". He does not further explain the latter observation except to add, "it would not be correctly understood". This remark deserves and will receive a thorough discussion. For now, it is interesting because it may well stand as Wittgenstein's first statement of a new attitude toward religious expression. I say this in part because the remark, while pessimistic about his desire to begin *Remarks* with a religious dedication, does not claim that the dedication would be a misuse of language. That appears not to be the source of his pessimism. Instead, he writes of his sense that the dedication would not be *correctly understood*. This suggests a different sort of pessimism: his religious dedication may well have had a meaning, but not one that could be grasped by many readers – at least not "nowadays". In what follows I will discuss this remark in depth.

I want to suggest a way of thinking about Wittgenstein's continued pessimism about religious expression. I maintain that it is analogous to the pessimism he expressed with respect to the arts in the Spenglerian prefatory remarks to *Remarks*, and later, in scattered observations over the next two decades. Let us recall some of what I showed in Chapter 2. Wittgenstein, like Spengler, believed that artistic expression – which had flourished at the highpoint of modern culture – had all but died out entirely as that culture began to rigidify into twentieth-century civilization. We saw that Spengler was explicit about this, writing that "[o]f great painting or great music there can no longer be" in the West and that its "architectural possibilities have been exhausted these hundred years". Similarly, Wittgenstein's prefatory remarks echoed this striking pessimism, explicitly referring to "the disappearance of the arts".

This shared pessimism, it must be noted, involved no claim about the *absolute impossibility* of artistic expression. On the contrary, Spengler and Wittgenstein saw the obstacles to artistic expression in his time as a particular condition of civilization. They were both explicit that artistic expression is a characteristic of a time of high culture. Their conceptions were similar: the forms of artistic expression which had once stood at the center of a high culture had lost their power, had almost entirely withered away, as that culture died and gave way to a civilization. In overview, they believed that a time of civilization did not provide the sort of background against which attempts at artistic expression could succeed. Art, which once helped express the shared life stance of a cultured people, expressed little, if anything, to the alienated people of a civilization. Convinced that this was so, both Spengler and Wittgenstein urged the individuals of their own time to abandon the arts.

In Chapter 2, we also noted that, for Spengler, religion undergoes the same fate as the arts as cultures decline into civilizations. He believed that times of high culture and their artistic achievements are rooted in religion and religious expression. We have seen Spengler's characterization of a culture as a setting in which "[a]ll living forms in which it expresses itself – all arts, doctrines, customs … every column and verse and idea – are ultimately religious, and *must* be so." He believed that cultures are *essentially* religious. In contrast, he believed that religion slowly withers away in a time of civilization. Civilizations are characteristically irreligious. Religious practices lose their life, their vitality, and, eventually, their meaning in civilized times – they cannot survive in the final stages of civilized decline. Cultures are essentially religious for Spengler, but we must remember his qualification: "from the setting in of Civilization, they *cannot* be so any longer." Spengler believed that the West was advancing toward its decline into civilization in which religion would no longer be possible. Interestingly, there are indications that Spengler did not think that such a point of complete irreligiousness had yet occurred during his lifetime, but he believed that such a time would inevitably come. While he saw signs that most of what passed for religion in his time was a counterfeit of the real thing, he did admit that scattered pockets of legitimate religious practice could still be found in the West. These, he thought, would die out soon enough in subsequent times as the early phases of a civilized time evolved into a time of complete decline into full civilization. I shall take this up in detail in Chapter 7.

Could this radical view, or a near variant of it, have been shared in some form by Wittgenstein? There is some reason to think so and I want to pursue it. Assuming that Wittgenstein, in his later period, did come to share something like Spengler's view, then his diagnosis of religious inexpressibility would have changed dramatically. Having once held that religious expression is absolutely impossible, he came to hold the more Spenglerian view that religious expression, like artistic expression, cannot long endure in a time of civilization and that the West was approaching such a time.

ii. Two Divergent Tendencies in Wittgenstein's Later Remarks on Religion

I have discussed two distinct sorts of observations in Wittgenstein's later remarks on religion that have not heretofore been clearly distinguished. Once identified, the two may seem to be in conflict. Careful analysis, I think, will show that they are not. Appropriate to the project of this book, I have focused almost exclusively on one such set of remarks. I take seriously, emphasize, and try to illuminate Wittgenstein's many indications of his continuing doubts concerning the expressibility of the religious. We have seen that this is the clear tendency of the early work. I have focused – and will continue to focus in what follows – on a similar tendency in the later remarks. I have shown that religious inexpressibility in the early work is seen as an absolute, built-in limitation given the very nature of language. I shall argue that, in the later work, religious inexpressibility, while remaining a problem for Wittgenstein, is not absolute. Instead, it is a consequence of the nature of the time – of the surroundings of early civilization within which religious expression, which might succeed during a time of high culture, is increasingly more likely to misfire. It is this facet of the later work that most interests me. It connects directly to Wittgenstein's cultural concerns.

Against this, there is another tendency in Wittgenstein's later observations about religious language and religion – one I have touched upon and will take up again in a different context. Wittgenstein expresses, in both *Lectures and Conversations* and *Culture and Value*, a more or less consistent set of observations about religious language. They indicate that expressions of religious belief have a different grammar from expressions of factual belief and that, to the extent that one can speak of evidence in connection with the former, it is evidence of a very different sort than those that typically operate in the factual realm. They suggest that expressions of religious belief have a hidden motivational and exhortational function that is obscured by similarities in surface grammar between religious and factual claims. I will return to this specific claim, and to some of the remarks that support it, in this book's final chapter. For now, I will suggest that those remarks about religious language are predicated on a presupposition that the more pessimistic remarks about religious inexpressibility do not. Let me explain.

There seems to be a tension between the two tendencies of Wittgenstein's later observations about religious expression that I have begun to discuss. If Wittgenstein had doubts about religious expression – and he clearly expressed such doubts – why then did he seek to clarify religious usage and its correct grammar? Wittgenstein, in *Lectures and Conversations* and in *Culture and Value*, addresses the real grammar of religious language and its proper function, correctly understood; yet, elsewhere, he expresses serious worries about whether religious discourse is even possible. It is worth asking how he was able to do both without feeling a tension between the two.

I would propose a solution. It seems to me the best way to make sense of these two seemingly incompatible tendencies. When Wittgenstein addresses the logic of religious discourse in *Lectures and Conversations* and in *Culture and Value*, he certainly treats such discourse as if it is meaningful. On my view, Wittgenstein did believe that such discourse *is meaningful and unproblematic in the right cultural setting*. The analysis of religious language he offers is best viewed, I think, as *presupposing that such a cultural setting is in place*. When he wrote or spoke of the real nature of religious discourse, his attitude, I am suggesting, can be expressed roughly as, "in those times and settings when religious discourse is capable of successfully doing its job, the grammar of such discourse works something like this…". In effect, Wittgenstein's analyses of the real function of religious discourse presupposed a background against which such discourse can work.

Viewed in this way, there is no mystery about how Wittgenstein could have gone on to express reservations about religious expression in his time. The mystery disappears when one considers that those very reservations were based on his worry that the surroundings, *the externals necessary for successful religious discourse*, were in the process of vanishing. Even when religious discourse correctly follows its *internal* grammar, it will misfire if these *externals*, the needed cultural surroundings, the forms of life, the background against which religious expression has its meaning, are absent. A significant component of Wittgenstein's focus on cultural decline included his conviction that such surroundings were indeed disappearing – that is, that the *externals* necessary to support the function of religious discourse even when one does one's best to observe its *internal* rules of grammar, are withering away and, with them, the possibility of meaningful religious discourse. I will discuss this further in Chapter 7. It will prove helpful first to proceed to support the contextual component of my reading of Wittgenstein's view. This I do in the following subsections.

First an observation of some importance: Some interpreters of Wittgenstein, focusing on Wittgenstein's remarks on the grammar of religious language – and especially on some of the differences he cites between religious claims, factual claims, and their justifications – have taken his position to be one of fideism and even see him as an apologist for religion. This position has considerable merit and I will revisit it in Chapter 7. I believe that such an interpretation is viable and quite possibly correct as a reading of Wittgenstein's later remarks about religion and religious language. I cannot, however, accept such a view without a significant caveat – one that recognizes and explains away the tension between such an interpretation of Wittgenstein's thought and his powerfully stated doubts about religious expression in his own time. I shall make this case in Chapter 7.

iii. A Connection with Wittgenstein's Later Contextualism

Wittgenstein's later view of religious language and religion are connected with an important tendency of Wittgenstein's later philosophy – one that I noted in Chapter 1, section IV. It is one of the most dramatic departures from the doctrines of the *Tractatus* to be found in the *Investigations*. I will revisit and further develop my view of this matter.

In the *Tractatus*, the meaning or sense of a proposition depended almost entirely on its logical form and on a small number of naming and projection conventions. A proposition, in his words, *showed its sense*. On that view, anyone able to ascertain the logical form of a proposition and the immediate conventions regarding its use will be able to master its sense. Nothing else mattered. While Wittgenstein believed that logical form itself was inexpressible, this posed no practical problem because he also believed that logical sense can be *shown*. In the early work, propositions, which included thoughts, functioned quite naturally as pictures or representations of possible facts. The sense of a proposition was simply the picture it naturally conveyed. In the *Investigations* all this changes. The meaning of an expression in language (the highly technical Tractarian notions of *propositions* and of *sense* were, of course, dispensed with) was largely determined by factors external to it. These include the language game in which it plays a role, the rules governing the use of the expression in that language game, and the way in which the language game is embedded in the wider practices, including the form of life, of those who employ those expressions. For the later Wittgenstein, linguistic and other meanings are bound up in the most complicated ways with these social practices and human forms of life. Wittgenstein thought it important to see this in order to gain philosophical clarity. He never so much as suggested, nor did he appear to believe, that a complete theory of language – a total description of all the practices and rules governing the expressions in a language – was possible. He insisted repeatedly in the *Investigations* that he had no theory of language, but only grammatical remarks helpful to those in philosophical perplexity. Far from believing, as he did in the *Tractatus*, that a proposition showed itself, he came to believe that any meaningful expression bears its meaning largely in virtue of complicated background and surrounding conditions.

These two conceptions – the early and the late – are radically different. What is remarkable is that Wittgenstein, having dramatically altered his conception of meaning, was still left with a conception that left him doubtful about the meaningfulness of religious expression. A major line of continuity endures through the striking discontinuities that Wittgenstein's conception of language underwent.

Religious expressibility is highly problematic in both the *Tractatus* and the later work – but the nature of the problem shifted. In the *Tractatus*, religious expression is impossible because the very nature of language cannot accommodate it. Language, by its nature, seeks to picture facts in the world and there are no religious facts in the world for language to picture! In his later thought, as we have seen, there are clear indications that religious expression is problematic. He came to reject the view that language, by its nature, cannot accommodate religious expression. Rather, he came to believe that the cultural surroundings necessary for meaningful religious expression have all but disappeared. I have suggested earlier that Spengler may have directly influenced the shift in Wittgenstein's conception of meaning. I will argue too, that Wittgenstein's worries about religious inexpressibility – as they express themselves in the later work – also bear a distinctly Spenglerian mark. To help show this, let us return to the major Spenglerian theme of cultural insulation and its affinities with Wittgenstein's views.

We have seen that Spengler endorsed a radical conception of cultural insularity. He regarded it to be all but impossible for individuals immersed in one culture or civilization to understand another culture – its religion, its art, its values, or its conception of the world and of humanity. Beyond this, he claims that it is virtually impossible for people who inhabit a civilization to understand the culture that has declined into that civilization.

I believe that the idea of cultural insularity – especially as expressed in Spengler – is one that probably always held some appeal for Wittgenstein. It appears, however, to have especially appealed to him at the time when he was in transit between the early philosophical conceptions of the *Tractatus* and the late *Investigations* views. It is worth noting, for example, that Wittgenstein, beginning about the time that he was first influenced by Spengler, explicitly expressed such thoughts about culture on a number of occasions.

Wittgenstein expressed extreme disapproval of writers and even friends who, to his mind, failed to appreciate the huge differences separating them from people living in fundamentally different cultural surroundings. The best-known example, perhaps, comes from his "Remarks on Frazer" in which he takes Frazer to task for doing just this in presuming to understand the significance of certain primitive religious practices in the terms of his own time and culture. Wittgenstein wrote, "how impossible for him to understand a different way of life from the English one of his time!"[33] It is not clear that Wittgenstein saw this "impossibility" as intrinsic to the task – he explicitly chides Frazer for a "narrowness of life" and adds, "Frazer cannot imagine a priest who is not basically an English parson of our times."[34] These remarks are open to two possible readings. First, Wittgenstein may have believed that Frazer might have understood these practices with more care and less "narrowness"; then again, he may have thought that neither Frazer nor any of his contemporaries could understand them owing to the huge cultural gulf separating them from their own.

---

33 Ludwig Wittgenstein, *Remarks on Frazer's "Golden Bough"*, Rush Rhees (ed.), (Retford, 1979), p. 5.

34 Ibid.

Wittgenstein admonished Drury under similar circumstances. Drury describes a fiery outburst in which his teacher chided him for "just the sort of stupid remark an English parson would make!"[35] Drury's offense was belittling the religious practices of a tenth-century sect. He said to Drury, "What do you know about the problems of those people or what they had to do about them?"[36] Here, it seems, Wittgenstein was acknowledging a built-in difficulty in trying to understand or assess the lives and practices of those in alien cultures. Again, it is not clear whether he thought the difficulty insuperable. There is, I think, at least a suggestion here that he felt Drury (whom he did not regard as hopelessly narrow) should not have formed conclusions about the practices and customs of people who lived lives so very different from his own. At the least, he seems to think that Drury should not have done so without having fully, empathetically, and carefully attended to the particulars of the lives of those monks.

It is significant that so much of this discussion of cultural insularity focuses on religious expression. Frazer and Drury are criticized for what Wittgenstein took to be shallow remarks about the religious practices of people who lived in very different times and places. A similar thought emerges in a description by Bouwsma of a conversation he had with Wittgenstein. In it, he explicitly attributes to Wittgenstein that the practices of religious groups during a period of high culture become unintelligible at a later time, after the social surroundings which characterize that culture have disappeared. I shall address this in detail, in subsection *iv.* below. For now, it can be said that Bouwsma took Wittgenstein to be saying that the meaning of certain religious expressions and practices are so bound up in a culture, in social surroundings, that they cannot be understood outside that setting.

But, there is more to it than that. Spengler's doctrine of cultural insularity has very strong affinities with more central ideas in the later Wittgenstein. Spengler emphasized the radical differences between the character of human life and its practices in different cultures. Dray and I have emphasized that one of his most important claims is that an individual not immersed in a given culture couldn't understand the prime symbol of that culture. This is connected to his belief that the meaning of a prime symbol is internally linked to cultural context. Those immersed within a culture can understand its prime symbol; those who stand outside it cannot. I showed in Chapter 1 that, for Spengler, this is also emphatically true of its expressions of art and, most notably in the context of this discussion, religion. This Spenglerian belief about the cultural embeddedness of the meanings of prime symbols – as well as those of artistic and religious expression – is startlingly similar to many of Wittgenstein's later pronouncements about meaning in general and to religious expressibility in particular. It has strong affinities with a basic theme of the *Investigations* and, of course, contrasts starkly with those of the *Tractatus*.

---

35 M. O'C. Drury, "Conversations with Wittgenstein", p. 128.
36 Ibid.

iv. A New Sort of Pessimism: A Spenglerian View of Religious Expression?

I have already suggested that one of the first indications that Wittgenstein had abandoned his early views on religious inexpressibility may be found in the prefatory remarks for *Philosophical Remarks*. This is not surprising, given that the *Remarks* showed signs of breaks with some of the central views of the *Tractatus*. It is worth noting also that the prefatory remarks were written less than two years after "A Lecture on Ethics" was delivered. Among Wittgenstein's writings, they show the most direct and obvious Spenglerian influence.

We have seen that Wittgenstein's prefatory remarks are in agreement with Spengler's views about the withering away of the arts in their time of civilization. What about Spengler's very similar views about the withering away of religion? In the prefatory remarks, Wittgenstein invokes the subject of religion only indirectly. Both the preface and the proto-preface contain an interesting sentence. Here is the Rush Rhees translation:

> I would like to say, "this book is written to the glory of God", but nowadays this would be the trick of a cheat, i.e. it would not be correctly understood.[37]

I want to show that this puzzling passage can be interpreted as a Spenglerian statement. First, Wittgenstein describes his desire to express a religious thought and then indicates that such an attempt would not be understood. In this, at least, the passage reminds us of the closing passages of "Lecture". Unlike "Lecture" however, this passage does not account for the futility of the religious expression in question with anything like the claim that it is absolutely inexpressible in language. On the contrary, the passage suggests that the difficulty is not with any intrinsic limitation on language, but rather, with *the times*. He explicitly states that his attempt to express his religious sentiment cannot "nowadays" be rightly understood. This is interesting for a number of reasons.

The term "nowadays" suggests that, while such a remark might be rightly understood in another time, the same remark made in his own time was likely to be largely misunderstood. This is suggestive of Spengler's beliefs that 1) a religious sensibility is typical of a time of high culture, but cannot endure in a time of civilization, and 2) that the West was nearing such an irreligious, civilized time. I am suggesting that religious discourse, for Wittgenstein, was becoming increasingly problematic as the cultural background against which it gained its meaning slowly disappeared in consequence of Western culture devolving into Western civilization.

The passage in question is certainly consistent with such a view and, in context, seems to suggest it. Elsewhere in the prefatory remarks Wittgenstein explains that even the most talented people in whom remnants of artistic sensibility still exist must leave the arts behind in a civilized time. In such a time – one in which the conditions for real artistic appreciation have all but vanished – their artistic efforts will not likely be appreciated or rightly understood. In consequence, an outright charlatan could expect to fare as well. Wittgenstein had such concerns about his

---

37 Ibid., p. 93.

own artistic tendencies. The passage in question could well be taken to express a very similar attitude toward religious expression in general and Wittgenstein's own desire to invoke "the glory of God" in particular. Such expressions in a civilized time, even when made by those very rare individuals who can still discern in their surroundings something reminiscent of those of an earlier cultured time, will not be rightly understood – or, at best, only equally rare individuals will understand them. To most, they would be indistinguishable from similar words uttered by a complete charlatan, a cheat who uses such words without understanding.

v. Further Support for a Spenglerian Interpretation

Drury, alert to Wittgenstein's less overt intentions, was convinced that the sentence focused upon in the previous subsection is an important one. His comment:

> I would dwell on this quotation for a moment. It implies that words which in one age could be correctly used can at a later time be "the words of a cheat"; because if these words are constantly used in a superficial way they become so muddied that the road can no longer be trod.[38]

Here Drury comes close to attributing to Wittgenstein the view that his proposed dedication of *Remarks* to "the glory of God" would employ a religious expression that has all but lost its meaning. I think this reading is correct as far as it goes. But Drury may mislead in suggesting the source of that loss of meaning is careless or "superficial" usage. Drury's interpretation suggests that careless people rob religious expressions of their original meanings by making a wrong choice between the open alternatives of using them incorrectly to say something superficial and using them correctly to say something important. On a Spenglerian interpretation the diagnosis would be more radical: as culture gives ways to civilization, the conditions under which genuine religious expression is possible begin to change into conditions in which it is not. Against the background of a culture Wittgenstein's words can be understood; against the background of a civilization, they will (to borrow an appropriate term of Austin) misfire. I am suggesting that Wittgenstein came to believe something very much like this.

This, however, must be qualified. Wittgenstein certainly thought that the surroundings of his time made meaningful religious discourse highly problematic, but he never appears to have come to the utterly defeatist conclusion that religious discourse in his time was impossible. As mentioned, he was pessimistic that any public expression of a religious nature that he might make would be understood. Still, he did discuss religion, religious belief, and the requirements of a religious life privately with a small, select group of individuals. So just what was the nature of his pessimism?

One possibility is this: we can imagine a smooth continuum from a cultured time against whose surroundings religious expression gains rich meaning to a time of total decline against whose surroundings religious expression is devoid of any meaning at all. Most likely, Wittgenstein believed that the West had traveled *nearly*

---

38 Ibid., pp. 93–94.

all the way from the former end to the latter. He appears to have believed that the cultural situation of his time made attempts at religious expression difficult, but not impossible. Evidently he felt strongly that the great majority of the people of his time had no understanding of real religion or of religious expression. Still, in his actions, he proceeded as if there were individuals – such as Drury, Rhees, Malcolm, Bouwsma – whom he deemed sufficiently serious, intelligent and discerning that they might still discern meaning in religious expression. Such people, at least, may have understood his desire to dedicate the *Remarks* to "the Glory of God". They, perhaps, could discern enough in the way of remnants of their past culture in their surroundings, against which they could find meaning in religious expression. Such people, however, were the exception. Wittgenstein feared that the great majority of his contemporaries could not find in their surroundings a background against which religious expression could derive any meaning at all and so, for them, religious expression had become meaningless. The surroundings of his civilization increasingly militated against meaningful religious discourse.

The best evidence for this suggestion may be found in a remarkable passage from Bouwsma's *Wittgenstein – Conversations 1949–1951*. Bouwsma describes a conversation with Wittgenstein in which the latter discussed religious matters, focusing on what he took to be the lifeless, moribund character of Judaism and Anglicanism in their day. Bouwsma represents Wittgenstein's view as follows:

> a religion is bound up with a culture, with certain externals in a way of life, and when these change, well, what remains? … [O]nce the sacrifices, whatever there was in Greek religion, and the ceremonies and rituals in Anglicanism, were entered into with earnestness and serious intent, with spirit. At a later time, they were done listlessly, mechanically, and as unessential. Once this happens, it is finished.[39]

Note the flow of ideas here. Bouwsma represents Wittgenstein as holding that "at a later time" religious practices lack the life, spirit, and earnestness that they once had. Drury might read these remarks as suggesting only that these practices are done carelessly and without serious intent. I will suggest something more: that for Wittgenstein, these practices – in losing their "seriousness and earnest intent" and in becoming listless and mechanical – approach meaninglessness. Bouwsma represents him as saying that the "culture" which provides the "background" and the "externals" with which such religious practices are inextricably bound up has vanished – and, consequently, virtually *any* attempt to duplicate the practices of the earlier times will typically result in (to appropriate a wonderfully appropriate expression of Wittgenstein taken from a different context) *an idle ceremony*.

The passage from Bouwsma does not explicitly mention *linguistic* forms of religious expression. This is not, I think, a serious difficulty. It may even strengthen the force of Wittgenstein's observations. The passage implicitly mentions religious expressions as they take place in religious rituals and ceremonies. Typically these include, but are not limited to, linguistic forms. Think, for example, of the ceremonies in an Anglican church or that of other Christian sects. The participants might typically recite prayers together – perhaps "The Apostles' Creed" or some

39 O. K. Bouwsma, *Wittgenstein – Conversations 1949–1951* (Indianapolis, 1986), p. 34.

other expression of belief. Alternatively, we could focus on the gestures used in the proceedings – kneeling, bowing, genuflecting, and so on. Or, again, we might think of the formalized activities according to which the ceremony proceeds – collective activities performed in accordance with agreed upon practices. If I am right, all of these are forms of religious expression that are carried out in an earnest spirit in a time of culture which affords the background conditions, the externals, against which these derive their meaning. When, however, the latter conditions disappear at a later time – as they do in a time of civilization – these expressive forms lose their life, their spirit, and, presumably, in the later stages of a civilization, even their meaning. Having lost their meaning, the ceremonies in which they play a role are, in effect "finished" as expressions of a viable human tendency.

This, I think, may help clarify somewhat Wittgenstein's later thoughts on religion. It provides a clear view of both continuities and discontinuities with his earlier thoughts. The idea that there is something about religion that defies significant expression always appealed to Wittgenstein. In his early work – in the *Tractatus* and the "Lecture on Ethics" – he had a most radical view of the matter. In those works, he held that any attempt to express anything of or about religion in words must result in nonsense. This, he believed, derived from a built-in limitation on what language could do in virtue of being language. What I am suggesting is that the later view – as expressed in the important passages I have examined – was quite different. He continued to hold that there is something deeply problematic about religious expression, but the diagnosis of the difficulty changes dramatically. Religious expression is problematic not because of necessary limits on expressibility, but only in times of cultural decline. Again, religious expression is not perfectly, absolutely impossible; but in a civilized age, the cultural surroundings needed for religious expression – the "externals" against which religious expression has its meaning when it does have meaning – have all but disappeared.

There is irony in this. Wittgenstein discussed religion with Bouwsma. During one such discussion – the one cited above – he indicated his concern that religious expression, in times like theirs, was highly problematic. Why then bother to discuss religion with Bouwsma? Again, my conjecture is that Bouwsma was, in Wittgenstein's estimation, a rare individual – an exception to the trends of their time. He was among the few of those in his civilized time who were still capable, at least to some degree, of apprehending the expressive modes of the culture from which their civilization evolved. Perhaps he thought that enough in the way of scattered remnants of his civilization's prior culture had survived to enable such serious, discerning, and exceptional individuals to practice religion and communicate their religious beliefs meaningfully to one another. Be that as it may, it is clear enough that, for Wittgenstein, genuine religion and religious expression, while not extinct, were certainly high on the list of endangered forms of life.

Chapter 6

A Religious Viewpoint in Wittgenstein's Later Writings?

Norman Malcolm's Four Analogies

I. Introduction

Do Wittgenstein's late philosophical writings represent a religious point of view? There is a good deal of evidence – including a number of Wittgenstein's own avowals – for an affirmative answer. Against this, there is the stark fact that Wittgenstein's late philosophical writings never directly discuss questions of God and religion. So, if they do represent a religious viewpoint, a correct account of it would presumably need to address elusive subtleties and hidden tendencies. While a number of philosophical authors have sought to identify such a viewpoint, nothing resembling a consensus has so far emerged.

In this chapter, I will critically address what I take to be one of the best and clearest discussions of this problem – that offered by Norman Malcolm in his short book *Ludwig Wittgenstein – A Religious Point of View?*[1] I do so in part because I do not think the book and the views it presents have received the attention they deserve. Far more important, I believe that some of what Malcolm has to say on the subject – while not fully developed – is both insightful and correct. I seek to explain Malcolm's approach to the problem at hand, focusing especially on those of his views that I believe to be correct. With respect to the latter task, I shall carefully articulate those of his ideas that I take to be correct, defend them from criticisms to which they have been subjected, and, finally, expand upon and strengthen them while remaining within their spirit.

Ludwig Wittgenstein – A Religious Point of View? is a significant contribution to the literature on a daunting subject. Its posthumous publication represented the results of the last philosophical project taken on by its author prior to his death in 1990. While not satisfied that he had completed his thoughts on the book's subject, Malcolm felt that he had brought those thoughts far enough so that he was willing have them published. He was convinced that the question he takes up is an important one. He worked on the project, striving to improve it until shortly before his death. His writings were edited into publishable form by his friend Peter Winch, who also appended a careful, extended critique of the views they express. Malcolm's total contribution is only ninety-two pages; the entire book, including Winch's critique

---

1 Norman Malcolm, *Wittgenstein – A Religious Point of View?* (Ithaca, NY, 1992), edited with a response from Peter Winch.

and an appendix, one-hundred-forty pages. Its brevity and the uncompleted state of Malcolm's thoughts notwithstanding, it represents, I think, a clear-headed examination of its subject matter. In what follows, I seek, in effect, to help complete some of Malcolm's best thoughts. I do so in a spirit of humility. It is unlikely that my attempt to improve what he started could measure up to what he might have achieved, had he had the opportunity to do so.

II. Malcolm – A Problem and his Approach

In Chapter 2 I discussed a sequence of remarks made by Wittgenstein in a conversation with Drury. Discussing his later work, he told Drury, "My type of thinking is not wanted in this present age. I have to swim so strongly against the tide."[2] Later in the same conversation he added, "I am not a religious man, but I cannot help seeing every problem from a religious point of view."[3] Malcolm was fascinated by this latter remark. Made in connection with a discussion of his later philosophy, Malcolm, following Drury, took it to mean that Wittgenstein viewed *philosophical problems* from a religious point of view in his later writings. This, however, presents a serious problem. On one hand, Malcolm knew that Wittgenstein was interested in and attracted to religion, that he had what could be described as religious tendencies and concerns, and that he was often absorbed by religious ways of thinking and religious ways of engaging the problems of everyday life. Given this, and given the religious focus of the later paragraphs of the *Tractatus*, it would seem natural to suspect that Wittgenstein's later philosophy might also have had a religious dimension. Against this suspicion, however, there is the powerful consideration that there is virtually nothing in *Philosophical Investigations* or in any of his other late philosophical writings that in any direct way addresses problems of God or religion. This can hardly be ignored. It would seem then, that if the later work does contain a religious dimension, it would have to be of a subtle and unstated nature. Malcolm undertakes to show that Wittgenstein's later thought does indeed represent an unstated religious viewpoint and strives to articulate clearly in just what sense that viewpoint is religious.

Malcolm's strategy is threefold. First, he seeks to detail some of the prominent and persistent themes to be encountered in Wittgenstein's religious thoughts and concerns. Here, he makes frequent use of materials from *Culture and Value*, *Personal Recollections* (especially the contributions of Drury and Fania Pascal), and the first volume of Brian McGuinness' *Wittgenstein – A Life*.[4] (It is worth noting that Ray Monk's biography, *Ludwig Wittgenstein – The Duty of Genius*, published only briefly before Malcolm's death, is not cited.) This he accomplishes in the book's first chapter, called "A Religious Man?" Second, he carefully explores a number of the central themes of Wittgenstein's later philosophy. This occupies the book's second through sixth chapters. Finally, Malcolm seeks to show that there are similarities

---

2   Rush Rhees (ed.), *Ludwig Wittgenstein – Personal Recollections* (Totowa, NJ, 1981), p. 94.

3   Ibid.

4   Brian McGuinness, *Wittgenstein: A Life* (Berkeley, CA, 1987).

or analogies to be noticed which link Wittgenstein's philosophical and religious thinking. Specifically, he says:

> there are four analogies between Wittgenstein's conception of the grammar of language, and his view of what is paramount in a religious life.[5]

and then muses, with nearly self-effacing modesty:

> Do these analogies present the meaning of Wittgenstein's remark that he saw philosophical problems from a religious point of view? I do not know. I cannot answer with any confidence. The analogies are there, and are worthy of reflection. But as an interpretation of Wittgenstein's surprising statement, they may be wide of the mark.[6]

One final preliminary point: There appears to be some ambiguity in Malcolm's statements of his overall view of the book's central problem. At one point he states that in Wittgenstein's late philosophy there is "*not* strictly a religious point of view, but something *analogous to* a religious point of view."[7] Elsewhere he writes as if there is a religious point of view in Wittgenstein's later philosophical thought *in virtue of* its many analogies to his explicitly religious thoughts. In Winch's response to Malcolm, he subjects the former, weaker, statement to criticisms that would not apply to the latter, stronger, conclusion. For this reason, and for reasons I will explain later in section VI, I prefer the latter conclusion – both as the better expression of Malcolm's thoughts and as a closer approximation of the truth.

I shall, in the next two sections, give a straightforward, descriptive account of Malcolm's views on the book's central question. As such, I shall postpone my criticisms of those views until my discussion of Winch's response to Malcolm, in subsequent sections.

III. Malcolm on Wittgenstein's Religious Life

In the book's first chapter, Malcolm effectively demonstrates that religious concerns played an extremely important role in Wittgenstein's life. Indeed, he succeeds in raising doubts about Wittgenstein's assessment that he was not himself a religious man. Malcolm states his own strong belief that Wittgenstein "was more deeply religious than many people who correctly regard themselves as religious believers."[8] He adds emphatically that "Wittgenstein was as qualified as any philosopher has ever been, to understand what it might mean to see the problems of philosophy from a religious point of view."[9] I think he succeeds in supporting these claims. He summarizes his reasons for his conclusions near the end of the chapter:

---

5   Norman Malcolm, *Wittgenstein – A Religious Point of View?*, p. 94.

6   Ibid.

7   Ibid., p. 10.

8   Ibid., p. 21.

9   Ibid., p. 23.

The feeling of being "absolutely safe", which first came to him at about age 21, exerted some hold on him throughout most of his life. The desire to become "a decent human being" was vividly expressed in his prayers during the First World War, and in his volunteering for a dangerous post. The act of renouncing his inherited wealth probably had, in part, a religious motive. At the end of the war his first preference for a vocation was to be a priest. His discussions with Drury contained many reflections on religious matters. His "confessions" belonged to a hope for "a new life". He expected and feared a Last Judgment. He read and reread the Gospels and knew them thoroughly. His desire for his philosophical work was that it should be "God's will". He thought it would be of value only if it received "a light from above". His conception of the meaning of Christianity stressed human "wretchedness" and "anguish" – and the necessity of "turning around" and "opening one's heart". This surely expressed an awareness of his own state and his own need.[10]

While Malcolm supports his view more than adequately in the main body of the chapter, the summary above passes over some of the strongest points he makes. I will mention a few here.

In 1931, Wittgenstein went to Norway in order to work on the *Investigations*, free of distractions. Upon his return, he informed Drury, as the latter tells it, that "he had done no writing there but had spent his time in prayer."[11] Indeed, it was during this time in Norway that Wittgenstein conceived the need to begin "a new life" with a confession. In another remarkable conversation with Drury, Wittgenstein expressed his hopes for a "religion of the future ... without any priests or ministers," a religion that is "extremely ascetic; and by that I don't mean just going without food and drink."[12] Equally intriguing, later in the same conversation, he said to Drury, "There is a sense in which you and I are both Christians."[13] This last statement is especially important; since it provides direct support for Malcolm's sense that Wittgenstein was – his own disavowals notwithstanding – in certain respects, a religious man.

I would note also that Malcolm's summary does not mention the *Tractatus*. His chapter mentions only in passing some of the striking sentences near that book's conclusion that strongly suggest that there is a religious point of view – in Wittgenstein's early work. This is puzzling. Malcolm, in what may be his most penetrating book on Wittgenstein's thought, *Nothing Is Hidden*, argues that a full understanding of Wittgenstein's later philosophy is only possible against the background of his early work. That book admirably demonstrates the truth of his contention. It is surprising then, that Malcolm, in a book-length study of Wittgenstein's religious point of view, shows little interest in the religious focus of Wittgenstein's early writings as a background against which the religious viewpoint of the late writings might be explored.

Malcolm not only seeks to show that Wittgenstein had deep and persistent religious concerns. He also takes pains to highlight some of the central and persistent themes

---

10 Ibid., p. 21.

11 M. O'C. Drury, "Conversations with Wittgenstein", in Rush Rhees (ed.), *Ludwig Wittgenstein – Personal Recollections*, p. 135.

12 Ibid., p. 129.

13 Ibid., p. 130.

that occur in Wittgenstein's more general discussions of religious life and in his writings about Christianity. For this, he leans heavily on passages from *Culture and Value*. He focuses especially on four that he finds strongly analogous to philosophical themes in Wittgenstein's later philosophy. Explaining these and emphasizing their analogies to those philosophical themes constitutes Malcolm's central task. The completion of this task occurs in the book's seventh chapter, "Four Analogies". In what follows, I offer a brief account of each of Malcolm's four analogies.

IV. Malcolm's Four Analogies

i. The First Analogy

Malcolm spends a good deal of time focusing on Wittgenstein's thoughts on explanation. In the end, he wants to note a strong parallel between Wittgenstein's later views of explanation in philosophy and a familiar religious attitude toward explanation. In religion it is common to refer to "the will of God". Malcolm accepts a view that he rightly attributes to Wittgenstein that "at the deepest religious level there is no asking for God's reason or justification."[14] Malcolm also claims that to say that something is the will of God is not to invoke a final explanation – or, for that matter, any explanation at all. On the contrary, he states:

> The words, "It is God's will", have many religious connotations: but they also have a logical force similar to "That's how it is!" Both expressions tell us to stop asking "Why?" and instead to *accept a fact*![15]

Malcolm clearly believes that in many difficult situations, such an attitude – one of acceptance, one that does not demand explanations – is an appropriate one. He seems to think that one benefit of religion can be to invoke such an attitude when it is needed.

Malcolm sees this religious theme to be strongly analogous to a philosophical theme from *Philosophical Investigations*. He approaches this theme in a discussion that spans the book's second, fifth, and sixth chapters – titled, respectively, "The Search For Explanation", "Failed Explanations", and "The Limit of Explanation". The discussion reaches its terminus in the latter chapter. Malcolm makes much of Wittgenstein's oft-repeated warnings in his later work that philosophy must replace misguided searches for explanation with *descriptions*. These descriptions are of the language games that are the natural homes for the words in which philosophical problems are couched and of the rules – Wittgenstein calls them "grammatical" rules – governing those language games. These descriptions serve as useful reminders about the actual uses of these words and their connections to specific forms of human interaction. Wittgenstein believed that these descriptions of the uses of words have two useful functions. First, they show that philosophers characteristically misuse words – that is, use words outside the language games in which they have their

---

14 Norman Malcolm, *Wittgenstein – A Religious Point of View?*, p. 85.

15 Ibid., p. 86.

natural home – when doing philosophy. Second, he believed that they serve to promote a better understanding of the nature of the language games and the forms of life to which they are connected. For Malcolm, a proper understanding of the language games in which explanation plays a role illuminates an important truth about a certain demand for explanation in philosophy. In Malcolm's words:

> Wittgenstein regarded the language-games, and their associated forms of life, as beyond explanation. The inescapable logic of this conception is that the terms "explanation", "reason", "justification", have a use *exclusively within* the various language-games. The word "explanation" appears in many different language-games, and is used differently in different games ... An explanation is *internal* to a particular language game. There is no explanation that *rises above* our language games, and explains *them*. This would be a *super-concept* of explanation – which means that it is an ill-conceived fantasy.[16]

This is, on Malcolm's reading, part of Wittgenstein's view of explanation.

It is worth noting that Malcolm is not merely content to claim that Wittgenstein regarded *philosophical* explanations of language games to be impossible. He explicitly adds the stronger claim, that, for Wittgenstein, no explanations at all are possible for language games – that neither the hard nor soft sciences can explain them. The culmination of this discussion is Malcolm's claim that there is an important connection between Wittgenstein's philosophical pronouncements on the explanation of language games and the attitude of religious acceptance. Interspersing short quotations from the *Investigations*, he tries to emphasize the analogy between that religious attitude and Wittgenstein's recommendations about the proper understanding of language games:

> stop trying to satisfy this craving for explanation. "The question is not one of explaining a language game by means of our experiences, but of noting a language game" (PI I, 655). "Look on the language game as what is *primary*!" (PI I, 656) You make a study of a particular language-game. Then you can say to someone: "Look at it! That's how it is! Don't ask why, but take it as a fact, without explanation!" We need "to *accept* the everyday language game." (PI, p. 200)[17]

In both, Malcolm thinks, there is an emphasis on bringing the demand for explanation to an end and upon the need to simply accept some things.

ii. The Second Analogy

Malcolm's second analogy is connected to the first. He emphasizes a certain religious tendency of Wittgenstein to which the latter gave expression both in conversations with intimates and, more formally, in his "A Lecture on Ethics". Wittgenstein often expressed a sense of wonder at the existence of the world. In "Lecture" he both identifies this as a religious feeling and likens it to seeing the world as a miracle. Malcolm adds:

---

16 Ibid., pp. 77–8.
17 Ibid., p. 86.

> In scientific, cosmological speculation there are theories about "the origin" of the universe. ...But, in so far as I can understand them, these are theories about "the first state" of the universe. ...They are not theories as to *why anything exists at all*; and it does not seem that it could be the business of science to offer a theory about that.[18]

So, for Malcolm, there is no explaining the existence of the world. Lacking any explanation for it, one may or may not regard it with an attitude of wonder. While neither attitude is incumbent, Wittgenstein was clearly struck in this respect by a certain attitude of wonder – an attitude that he saw as religious in character.

Malcolm tries to show an analogy between this attitude and one that Wittgenstein expresses relative to language games:

> In the *Investigations* and other late writings, Wittgenstein sometimes expressed a kind of wonder at the existence of the various language-games and their contained forms of human action and reaction. "Let yourself be *struck* by the existence of such a thing as our language game of: confessing the motive of my action" (PI, p. 224). ...A language-game simply *is there*. You can observe it, describe it – but not explain *why* it is there.[19]

Malcolm sees in Wittgenstein an attitude of existential wonder relative to language games and the forms of life they embody which is analogous to his often-stated feelings of wonder at the existence of the world. He concludes that, for Wittgenstein, "The religious sense of seeing the world as a miracle has its analogue in a kind of astonishment at the inexplicable existence of the human language games."[20]

iii. The Third Analogy

Malcolm's third analogy cites an attitude that Wittgenstein describes both in connection with religious life and in connection with his own later philosophical procedures. First, Malcolm correctly attributes to Wittgenstein, frequently citing *Culture and Value*, the thought that:

> religious emotion, thinking, practice, are an expression of the conviction that something is *basically wrong* with human beings. ...There is a kind of moral and spiritual illness that possesses us, even when we think we are healthy. ...This is how a genuinely religious person thinks and feels about *himself*. As Wittgenstein puts it: "People are religious in the degree that they believe themselves to be not so much *imperfect*, as *ill*" [*Culture and Value*, p. 45].[21]

In comparison with this, Malcolm emphasizes a recurrent theme in Wittgenstein's later philosophy. It identifies the techniques of the *Investigations* and other later works of Wittgenstein as a kind of *therapy* that is needed to cure pathologies *of thought* that are characteristic of philosophy. Malcolm states, "it is interesting that Wittgenstein employs the terms 'illness' and 'disease' (*Krankheit*), when he is trying

---

18 Ibid., pp 86–7.
19 Ibid., p. 87.
20 Ibid.
21 Ibid.

to characterize the manoeuvres and expedients to which we resort in philosophical theorizing."[22] For Wittgenstein, both religious progress and philosophical progress require not only dealing with internal defects, but *turning around one's whole viewpoint or orientation*. In his late philosophy, these are just the terms in which he thought of his overthrow of the *Tractatus'* view of language, the terms in which he thought of philosophical progress.

It should be noted that Malcolm is careful here to emphasize a point of disanalogy:

> Wittgenstein was a serious man, and he took philosophy seriously. Although he sometimes compared the repetitious movements of philosophical thinking to an "illness" of the understanding, he did not of course consider this as having anything like the deadly gravity of the moral and spiritual illness to which religion speaks. He could joke about philosophical problems, but not about religious ones. He created new methods for treating philosophical questions. ...But he did not think that he had any capacity for dealing with religious problems.[23]

iv. The Fourth Analogy

Malcolm's last analogy cites the role of *action* in both Wittgenstein's religious and philosophical thought. On the religious side, he notes two points. First, there is Wittgenstein's sense that most theological formulations, especially the theological demand for proofs of God's existence, have very little value in religion. Second, and more important, is his emphasis on the importance of changing one's life, on the importance of *deeds* in religious life. He writes:

> For Wittgenstein the essential thing in a religious life was not the acceptance of doctrines or creeds, but *works*. To Drury he said that his belief was that "only if you try to be helpful to other people will you find your way to God."[24]

He continues, in a similar vein, "Wittgenstein would agree with St James that 'Faith without works is dead.'"[25] In these and other ways, Wittgenstein consistently emphasized the importance of certain kinds of acts and de-emphasized – as we shall see, sometimes to the point of ridicule – the importance of dogma, thought, reasoning, theology, and proof in religious life.

This, Malcolm thinks, has a striking analogy to a philosophical tendency of the later Wittgenstein. Citing *On Certainty*, he writes this:

> In Wittgenstein's post-*Tractatus* philosophical work a main current of his thinking is the insistence that our everyday concepts require a base of *acting*, *doing*, rather than reasoning or interpreting. This is one reason why his comparing our employment of language to playing games – for in games the players act and react. He says that instead of

---

22 Ibid., p. 88.
23 Ibid., p. 89.
24 Ibid., p. 20.
25 Ibid., p. 90.

the weighing of grounds or of making inferences from evidence, "it is our *acting*, which lies at the bottom of the language game" (OC, 204).[26]

Malcolm sees the similarity or analogy here to be a striking one: on important problems in both his religious and philosophical thought, Wittgenstein – against the tendency of many other thinkers – insisted upon the importance of action and discouraged a focus upon thought, reflection, or reasoning. This observation and the analogy it emphasizes, completes Malcolm's substantive case for his overall view of the religious perspective in Wittgenstein's later work. I turn now to Winch's response to Malcolm's views. I shall offer some of my own assessments of Malcolm's views along with my discussion of Winch's criticisms.

V. Winch's Response: A Fundamental Criticism of Malcolm's View

Peter Winch's response to Malcolm offers well-considered rebuttals to Malcolm's views. While his writing lacks Malcolm's clarity and focus, and is occasionally even daunting, his essay offers more in the way of subtlety, more of a spectrum of the issues underlying the difficulties inherent in the book's subject. Winch, I think, does succeed in showing that part of Malcolm's view of the nature of a religious viewpoint in Wittgenstein's later philosophy is, indeed, wide of the mark. He offers both a bold general criticism of Malcolm's overall approach to the book's problem and also many detailed critical comments on its execution. For me, the former is unsuccessful; some of the latter, more compelling. Winch's best critical strategy, I think, is to identify, for each of Malcolm's proposed analogies, powerful points of disanalogy. In this, Winch is forceful, perceptive, and clear. In the end, I think, the second and third of Malcolm's four analogies can be reasonably defended from Winch's criticisms.

At the end of his essay, Winch also offers a brief and sketchy set of comments on his own sense of the nature of the religious viewpoint in Wittgenstein's late philosophy. In the remainder of this section, I want to take up Winch's first prolonged criticism of Malcolm's view and show a fundamental difficulty with it. I will devote the next two sections to a discussion of Winch's many specific objections to Malcolm's four analogies, and, in the final section, to some aspects of Winch's own view of the book's main problem.

The part of Winch's response takes up the question of Malcolm's interpretation of Wittgenstein's remark: "I am not a religious man: but I cannot help seeing every problem from a religious point of view" (hereafter referred to – inelegantly, but in the service of much-needed stylistic simplicity – as "the LW remark"). He writes:

> Malcolm's essay rests on the assumption that Wittgenstein meant that he saw an *analogy* between philosophical and religious problems and his discussion is carried out on that supposition. But the supposition is only plausible as long as we take Wittgenstein to be speaking of philosophical problems in an exclusive way. We may perhaps allow that he was singling out his attitude to philosophical problems for special attention, but there is no

---

26 Ibid.

reason to think that he was not also expressing an attitude to many other sorts of problems as well. Once this is acknowledged, it becomes almost senseless ... to suppose he was talking of an analogy between philosophical and religious problems. Are we to say that he saw an analogy between religious problems and problems of decency in one's manner of life? If we do so, we are in danger of losing our grip on any manageable question.[27]

Here, Winch tries to reduce Malcolm's position to a kind of absurdity. It is the absurdity that would supposedly result from extending Malcolm's account of the religious point of view in Wittgenstein's philosophy to a parallel account of Wittgenstein's religious viewpoint toward the central problems of human life. The absurdity would be that of ascribing to Wittgenstein a view that regards religious problems as *analogous to* the problems of decency in one's manner of life. For Winch, these problems cannot even be separated – they are not analogous, but identical. Presumably, this shows a conceptual confusion in Malcolm's view.

This argument is well structured and has some initial plausibility, but I want to look at his reasoning carefully. I believe it rests on a number of weak premises, trades on an ambiguity, and represents a surprisingly unsympathetic and unhelpful reading of Malcolm. As such, I will pursue in some detail what Winch presents in this passage.

First, Winch writes as if the plausibility of Malcolm's views on the religious point of view in Wittgenstein's philosophy rests entirely upon the truth of his interpretation of the LW remark. This is too strong. The LW remark both called Malcolm's attention to the possibility of a religious point of view in Wittgenstein's late philosophy and also set him to wonder specifically about what Wittgenstein meant by this remark. With respect to the former, Malcolm devotes the greater part of seven chapters to his attempt to identify and articulate a religious point of view in Wittgenstein's later writings. It would be best if his account of that point of view jibed perfectly with what Wittgenstein intended by the remark, but surely the account could be true independently of whatever support it receives from the LW remark. Indeed, it could be true if Wittgenstein meant something quite different by the LW remark – or even if he had never made the remark at all.

Second, I think it is more likely than not that Malcolm's assumption that Wittgenstein was referring *exclusively* to philosophical problems in the LW remark is *correct*. It is true that Malcolm does not argue for it and Winch is right to point this out. It is also fair for Winch to question Malcolm's assumption that the problems referred to by the LW remark are exclusively the problems of philosophy. Wittgenstein did, after all, explicitly use the words "every problem" in the LW remark. This, in the absence of contextual considerations, suggests that Wittgenstein did not mean to limit his reference to philosophical problems. On the other hand, what is known about the nature of the conversation in which Wittgenstein made this remark, *does* suggest such a limitation. Wittgenstein was talking with Drury *about his philosophical work.* He was in the process of finishing the *Investigations*. As already noted, he stated his conviction that his kind of thinking is "not wanted in this present age," and indicated that he had to "swim so strongly against the tide." Evidently, he was acknowledging

---

27 Ibid., pp. 96–7.

a concern – one that he expressed on many other occasions in connection with his late philosophy – that his work was contrary to the spirit of his time. Then, later in the conversation, he made the LW remark. Given the setting, it is reasonable to take the remark to be a continuation of his earlier observations, one that cites an important aspect of his philosophical work – the religious point of view from which he engaged its problems – which, he believed, was indeed alien to the spirit of his time. As we have seen, Drury certainly understood the remark in this way. On this reading, the remark is concerned with the problems taken up by Wittgenstein in his late writings – philosophical problems. Indeed, I regard this as the most natural – though, by no means the only possible – reading of Wittgenstein's remark. The vagaries of context preclude a definitive reading of the remark's intended scope.

Finally, I disagree with Winch's claim that Malcolm's overall view requires his assumption that the LW remark refers *only to* philosophical problems. Even if that restrictive assumption were wrong, Malcolm could, making only minor modifications, interpret the remark consistent with his overall views. I shall now explain this.

Winch, in a different context, correctly criticizes Malcolm for not distinguishing carefully enough in his discussion of Wittgenstein between 1) thoughts on religion itself and 2) identifiably religious thoughts on other subjects. The latter might naturally include religious thoughts about the important problems of everyday life. Without ever distinguishing, Malcolm discusses examples of both types of thoughts in connection with Wittgenstein. He refers to both 1) and 2) using the expression "religious thoughts". Notably, when Malcolm cites analogies between Wittgenstein's "religious thoughts" and his philosophical thoughts, he includes both sorts of religious thoughts. First, he saw analogies between some of Wittgenstein's thoughts on religion and his philosophical thoughts; second, he saw analogies between some of Wittgenstein's characteristically religious thoughts about the problems encountered in everyday human life and his strictly philosophical thoughts. Winch is right that it would have been better had Malcolm made this distinction and incorporated it into his book.

Nonetheless, with these points out of the way, it may be seen that Malcolm could have made sense out of the LW remark even had he concluded, as Winch does, that the remark referred to *all* the problems Wittgenstein encountered in life. Winch thinks not and asserts strongly, in the passage quoted at the beginning of this section, that absurdities would result for Malcolm on this alternative reading. To show this, he anticipates – I believe wrongly – how Malcolm would interpret the LW remark on this reading. Apparently Winch assumes that Malcolm's account of the religious point of view in Wittgenstein's late philosophy in terms of certain analogies must serve as his model for giving an account of the religious point of view he employed in engaging life's other problems. He seems to think that since Malcolm interprets the religious point of view *in* Wittgenstein's philosophy in terms of certain analogies that he is somehow committed to interpreting Wittgenstein's religious point of view *outside* philosophy in terms of parallel analogies. I think that this assumption is unjustified and that it does not do justice to the substance and detail of Malcolm's views.

Compared to Malcolm's more restrictive assumption about the scope of the LW remark, Winch's contrary assumption – that the LW remark refers more widely to *both* the vital problems of human life *and* the problems of philosophy – changes the logic of the remark. It reads the remark as one about problems in general – including, but not restricted to, philosophical problems. As such, it would require Malcolm to structure his interpretation of the remark differently in order to accommodate its significantly extended subject. Let me suggest how Malcolm could, quite naturally and fully within the spirit of his overall view, interpret the LW remark to meet this wider reading of it. Such an interpretation of the remark represents Wittgenstein as making two claims: 1) There is a tendency on his part to see the central problems of human life from a point of view that is, in important and specifiable ways, religious. 2) There are analogies between his religious thoughts – *both* his religious thoughts about the problems of life *and* his thoughts about religion – and many of the thoughts characteristic of his late philosophy. This interpretation of the LW remark would be plausible and in no way incoherent. It is certainly true to the particulars of Malcolm's overall account. His book can be seen as an extended exercise in citing important details of Wittgenstein's life and writings that confirm the truth of 1) and 2). Roughly, in the first chapter he defends 1); in Chapters 2–7 he defends 2). Indeed, I believe that much of what Malcolm says in Chapter 1 of his book would have met with Wittgenstein's approval as an account of the ways in which he brought a religious point of view to his own life. While I have ultimate doubts about Malcolm's interpretation of the LW remark and his account of the religious point of view in Wittgenstein's later philosophy, it is not on the basis of the argument just discussed from the first section of Winch's response. Winch's best and most penetrating arguments against Malcolm concern his specific criticisms of Malcolm's analogies. I turn to these now.

VI. Winch's Response: Rebutting Malcolm's Analogies

i. A Basic Strategy

Winch's discussion of Malcolm's four analogies, for the most part, showed breadth and depth in Wittgenstein. Its tone, especially considering Malcolm's recent death and the personal friendship Winch shared with him, was surprisingly and needlessly aggressive. Still, the discussion offers substance and displays subtlety. It counters each of Malcolm's four analogies with some striking points of disanalogy. I certainly felt, upon reading his essay, that he had succeeded in showing weaknesses in two of the analogies – the first and, to a greater degree, the fourth. I believe that the second analogy is somewhat stronger than Winch thinks. Much more significant, I think the third analogy can and should be defended from Winch's criticisms. I will endeavor to show this in what follows.

It must be admitted that arguments that rest on analogies or disanalogies are difficult to assess. There is no accepted procedure for weighing the strength of an analogy, or for deciding when points of analogy have been defeated by points of disanalogy (or vice versa). For these reasons, one does not readily feel that an assessment of the merits of an analogy can been completed in the way that, say, an assessment of the validity of a deductive argument can. Nonetheless, I cannot help thinking that had Malcolm had the opportunity to read and ponder Winch's remarks on his analogies, he would, at the very least, have accepted some of them and felt a need to alter his presentation to take them into account. I will discuss briefly some of Winch's more powerful observations about Malcolm's analogies – concentrating for now on the first, second, and fourth. In connection with the second analogy, I shall develop a modest rejoinder, one based upon independent textual evidence, to Winch's criticism. Finally, in the next section I will offer an extended defense of Malcolm's third analogy from Winch's criticisms. In so doing I will further develop Malcolm's root idea and provide much more in the way of support for it.

ii. Rebutting the First Analogy

Malcolm notes that both Wittgenstein's thoughts about religion and his late philosophical thoughts emphasize the importance, in some circumstances, of bringing the search for explanations to an end. This, he thinks, can be seen both in a religious attitude of acceptance and in Wittgenstein's own attitude toward language games. Malcolm claims that Wittgenstein thought that language games were beyond explanation and connects this claim to his further observation that Wittgenstein saw them in a way that bears a strong analogy to the religious attitude of acceptance.

Winch argues against Malcolm's strong claim that Wittgenstein regarded language games to be beyond any possible explanation. He suggests as an alternative, a view that emphasizes the *context* in which Wittgenstein criticizes and discourages the philosophical search for explanations of language games:

> His criticism did not terminate in pointing to the existence of something that happens to be beyond the reach of any explanation; the force of the criticism lay in his exposure of the confusions involved in the search itself and in the puzzlement that gives rise to it. ...The argument is not "You are trying to find an explanation for something which of its nature cannot be explained"; but rather: "Look at how you are arguing, don't you see that this way of thinking is not going to get you anywhere? You think you need an explanation, but your real difficulty is one that needs a quite different sort of treatment."[28]

I prefer Winch's reading to Malcolm's, in part because the latter represents a view that seems too implausible for Wittgenstein to have held.

Winch makes another point designed to help weaken the force of Malcolm's analogy. He insists that, for Wittgenstein, there is a multiplicity of very different contexts in which it is proper to abandon a search for explanations. He writes of Wittgenstein:

> He does not think that explanations come to an end with something that is intrinsically beyond further explanation. They come to an end for a variety of quite contingent and pragmatic reasons, perhaps because of a practical need for action, perhaps because the puzzlement which originally prompted the search for explanation has evaporated (for one reason or another).[29]

---

28 Ibid., p. 105.
29 Ibid., p. 104.

His emphasis on the claim that Wittgenstein saw important *differences* among the circumstances that warrant ending a search for explanations lays the ground for his main objection to Malcolm's analogy. In his words, the objection is:

> the practice associated with giving up the demand for explanation in philosophy bears little comparison with the giving up of the demand for explanation in religion, despite the similar words with which we may, in part at least, describe them.[30]

For Winch, Malcolm was too impressed by similarities and not sufficiently mindful of significant differences.

Winch does not simply state this. He cites passages from *Culture and Value* designed to show that Wittgenstein was explicitly mindful of fundamental differences between the philosophical and religious attitudes toward explanation that Malcolm compares. The passages are well chosen and Winch's interpretations of them – while not, I think, decisive – are both interesting and plausible. It is fair to say, on balance, that they contribute effectively to what is a well-conceived and forceful rebuttal to Malcolm's analogy. To effectively counter this rebuttal, I think, some direct textual evidence is needed that Wittgenstein himself would have endorsed Malcolm's analogy. I am unaware that any exists.

iii. Rebutting the Second Analogy

Malcolm's second analogy likens the religious sense of wonder at the existence of the world to a kind of wonder in Wittgenstein at the existence of the various language games and the forms of human life in which they are embedded. Winch's brief discussion of the analogy calls attention to Malcolm's own observation that wonder at the existence of the world is connected to seeing the world as a miracle, as the work of God. He then argues – citing passages from *Culture and Value* that touch on the subject of the miraculous – that "Wittgenstein's ... 'wonder' at what his investigations lay open to view, is an infinite distance from seeing the world, or human language-games, as the work of God."[31]

For Winch, the religious attitude of wonder at the existence of the world has, by its very nature, a quality that Wittgenstein's attitude of philosophical wonder lacks – specifically, a sense that its object is miraculous, is the work of God. While I don't think Winch establishes that Wittgenstein's attitude of philosophical wonder lacks a sense of the miraculous, I would agree with him that Malcolm's second analogy is not – as it stands – strong enough to bear the weight placed upon it. In the absence of even some slim additional textual evidence that Wittgenstein saw human language, or language games, as miraculous I would agree with Winch that Malcolm presents no independent evidence that Wittgenstein would have accepted the analogy which he puts forward.

In the case of the second analogy, however, *there is* evidence, some of it striking, that Wittgenstein was, at one time in his life, strongly inclined to think of human language itself in close connection with the miracle of existence. For this reason,

---

30 Ibid., p. 113.
31 Ibid., p. 118.

I am more inclined to accept Malcolm's second analogy than is Winch. I shall offer a brief defense of that analogy, citing two interesting – although certainly not conclusive – independent sources of textual support for it.

Let us first review in broad outline the controversy between Malcolm and Winch with respect to the second analogy. It is fair to say that Malcolm shows that Wittgenstein carried a sense of wonder at the existence of the world into his late philosophical period. He also shows, in painstaking detail, that Wittgenstein expressed a sense of wonder at human language games in his later philosophical writings, going so far as to urge it upon his readers. Winch, conceding all this, objects strongly that there is no reason to link the two, stating his sense that they are "infinitely far apart." In effect, he objects that the link between them that Malcolm contends for is much too weak, too much of a stretch, to have much credibility or to have appealed to Wittgenstein. Is this so? In "A Lecture on Ethics", Wittgenstein explicitly expresses his own tendency to connect his religious sense of wonder at the existence of the world and his sense of wonder over the existence of human language. Here are his words:

> I will now describe the experience of wondering at the existence of the world by saying: it is the experience of seeing the world as a miracle. Now I am tempted to say that the right expression in language for the miracle of the existence of the world, though it is not any proposition *in* language, is the existence of language itself.[32]

This last sentence is striking. Wittgenstein says – or, at least, indicates his strong temptation to say – that the right expression for the miracle of the existence of the world *is* the existence of language itself. This is certainly not self-explanatory, but it points in an interesting direction. Certainly, it provides evidence that Wittgenstein conceived a deep connection between the existence of the world as a miracle, and the existence of language itself. The precise nature of the connection is difficult to glean from this short passage, beyond saying that the latter is "the right expression for" the former. It is not clear just how Wittgenstein thinks that the existence of language itself, though not any proposition of language, somehow expresses a sense of the world as a miracle. This is an extraordinary conception – one that regards *the existence of language itself* as truly extraordinary. How else could the existence of language express "the miracle of the existence of the world"? Language itself, he intimates, expresses something – the miracle of existence – that no proposition in language can express.

"Lecture", as we saw in the last chapter, expresses Wittgenstein's sense that absolute values are *supernatural*. I will suggest, by way of interpretation, that the above passage, in context, suggests Wittgenstein's tendency to regard both the existence of the world and language itself as supernatural. For Wittgenstein, the existence of the world is supernatural insofar as it is miraculous. Further, he acknowledges an inclination to say that the very existence of language somehow expresses that miracle. This is noteworthy because, elsewhere in "Lecture", he indicates that the miracle itself cannot be expressed in ordinary propositions *of* language. As such,

---

32 Ludwig Wittgenstein, "A Lecture on Ethics", in James Klagge and Alfred Nordmann (eds), *Ludwig Wittgenstein – Philosophical Occasions 1912–1951*, p. 24.

language itself, for Wittgenstein, takes on a supernatural character: specifically, it appears to him as the vehicle by which an inexpressible miracle might find its "right expression".

Whether or not this interpretation is correct, the passage from "Lecture", far from regarding Wittgenstein's sense of the existence of the world and his sense of the existence of language as "infinitely far" from one another, explicitly links them. Thus, at least in 1929, Wittgenstein, far from regarding Malcolm's analogy as tortured or weak, would likely have endorsed it or something like it. This, to some extent, undermines an assertion upon which Winch's rebuttal of Malcolm's second analogy rests.

Had the passage above been written in 1939 or 1949, rather than 1929, it would, I think, provide a stronger vindication for Malcolm's second analogy. That Wittgenstein wrote it at all shows that he once held something very much like the attitude with which Malcolm thinks he approached the *Investigations*. Winch, or anyone else who would reject Malcolm's analogy, must argue that Wittgenstein, when he wrote the *Investigations*, had abandoned that attitude. I am not prepared to resolve this issue one way or another.

There is, however, a small measure of indirect evidence that Wittgenstein did carry this attitude into his later period. First, consider, the following passage:

> I want to say that the existence of language, and the development of the ability to speak..., is a miracle.[33]

Were this a quote from Wittgenstein, it would strongly disconfirm Winch's contention that Wittgenstein's sense of philosophical wonder "is an infinite distance from seeing the world, or human language-games, as the work of God." Wittgenstein, however, did not write the passage. It is found in *The Danger of Words*, a book written by Drury. Still, it does provide a further measure of vindication for the second analogy. It is the only book in which Drury endeavors exclusively to expound philosophical views of his own. He does so in five essays. He explains in the preface to the book that Wittgenstein powerfully influenced its most important ideas. He writes self-effacingly of the essays that are to follow:

> They are certainly not intended as in any sense a commentary on Wittgenstein's philosophy, but with the increasing importance that is now being given to his writings, they may possess a peripheral interest, as an illustration of his influence on one particular pupil.[34]

As such, the original passage could be taken as a measure of "peripheral" support for the view that Wittgenstein may also have regarded human language as miraculous. This is so because Drury's explicitly stated tendency to do so is, by his own account, stimulated by his discussions with Wittgenstein. Against this, Drury does offer the strong disclaimer that "I do not of course claim Wittgenstein's authority for a single idea expressed in these papers."[35]

---

33 M. O'C. Drury, *The Danger of Words* (New York, 1973), p. 76.
34 Ibid., p. xiv.
35 Ibid., p. viii.

Still, Drury is one of the few individuals with whom Wittgenstein discussed religion from both a philosophical and personal standpoint. It is significant that their discussions almost all took place well within Wittgenstein's later philosophical period. If Drury, in stating his sense that language is a miracle, is expressing an idea that was influenced by Wittgenstein, it was, given the chronology of their association, more than likely influenced by the *late* Wittgenstein. How much weight should we place on Drury's expression of exactly the attitude Malcolm ascribes to Wittgenstein in the second analogy? It is not clear. Still, it is significant that Drury is the single person with whom, as far as is known, the mature Wittgenstein most discussed religion, religious attitudes, and their relationship to his own work. It is at least interesting that Drury believed that the ethical and religious attitudes that Wittgenstein expressed in the *Tractatus* and in "Lecture" stayed with him for the rest of his life and influenced his later work. This too provides a measure of evidence that some of the religious attitudes Wittgenstein expressed in "Lecture" in 1929 continued to influence him as he wrote the *Investigations*.

iv. Rebutting the Fourth Analogy

I believe that Malcolm's fourth analogy is the least compelling. It sees, in Wittgenstein's philosophical insistence that our everyday concepts require a basis in action, an important similarity to St. James' insistence that faith, without works, is dead – a religious attitude Wittgenstein himself emphasized in conversations. This, he thinks, connects interestingly with Wittgenstein's repeated assertions that thought and reasoning cannot provide a basis for religious practice. In both the religious and the philosophical context, Malcolm thinks, Wittgenstein de-emphasizes thought and reasoning and emphasizes action. To this, Winch's most compelling criticism is that the religious attitude Malcolm cites in connection with the fourth analogy is mischaracterized. He makes his point this way:

> the relation between faith and works, as this is understood by St. James, is not simply a particular instance of the relation between thinking and acting, as this is discussed in, e.g., *Philosophical Investigations*. Faith, after all, has its expression in practices which St. James is surely *distinguishing* from "works": such as prayer, church attendance, religious observances and, in general, a language which is in its turn used in connection with certain kinds of activity in ways about which members of the community of believers are in broad agreement.[36]

The point here is that Malcolm mischaracterizes the analogy for which he contends. Whereas the philosophical tendency he ascribes to Wittgenstein emphasizes that our everyday concepts have a basis in action as opposed to thought and reasoning, the religious attitude he cites functions differently. It does not point to the importance of "works" in religious life as opposed to that of thought and reasoning, but rather, as Winch correctly observes, as opposed to certain activities – namely those conventionally associated with the specific religious practices of a community. The philosophical view seeks to redirect attention from thought and reasoning to action.

---

36 Norman Malcolm, *Wittgenstein – A Religious Point of View?*, p. 129.

The religious view seeks to redirect attention from one type of action to another. Malcolm believes his analogy to rest on a striking parallel; Winch, I think, succeeds in showing that the parallel breaks down.

I have accepted some of Winch's criticisms of Malcolm's first and fourth analogies, and raised one objection to his criticism of the second. I turn now to the third analogy, which, I believe, does not fall to Winch's criticisms. I seek to develop further Malcolm's root idea, which I regard as both insightful and, at bottom, correct.

VII. Defending Malcolm's Third Analogy

i. Winch's Criticism

Malcolm's third analogy is unique among the four analogies in that it identifies similarities, not in content, but rather in approach and attitude, between Wittgenstein's philosophical and religious thoughts. It stresses that Wittgenstein saw in both his own late philosophy and also in a religious approach to life's problems, a need to confront something strongly akin to a disease or an illness. In the case of his philosophy, it is a disease or illness of thought that he seeks to combat. In the case of religion, it is the problems of those who view themselves to be spiritually diseased or ill in some fundamental way that are confronted. In both, Wittgenstein thinks, the desired cure consists in a fundamental change in one's whole orientation toward the problems confronted. I think this is Malcolm's most insightful analogy. While Winch offers some relevant points of disanalogy, I believe he is too quick to dismiss the analogy as superficial. His main objection to the analogy parallels his main objection to the first analogy. He states it in one sentence:

> The senses in which one can speak of an "illness" in each of these contexts is far too heavily dependent on the extremely diverse contexts involved for any talk of an analogy to carry much weight.[37]

Why does Winch think Malcolm's analogy is so weak? What points of disanalogy come to the fore to support his sense that "extremely diverse contexts" are involved in talk of philosophical illness on one hand, and the sort of spiritual illness which religion seeks to remedy on the other? Winch certainly thinks that the disease of thought Wittgenstein combats in his later philosophy involves a milder, less urgent, more abstracted pathology than that disease of the soul, that wretchedness requiring "infinite help", that Wittgenstein reflects upon in *Culture and Value*. Malcolm, as noted in section III above, would concede this point. No doubt Malcolm would also agree with Winch that there are other differences to be uncovered – not only in the diseases treated, but in their treatments. There are, however, some good reasons to think that Wittgenstein himself would not have thought such points of disanalogy to be decisive in this regard. I will argue that there is good reason to suppose that he

---

37 Ibid., p. 118.

would have ascribed more weight to Malcolm's third analogy than to Winch's points of disanalogy.

In another context, Winch offers an objection to Malcolm's views that is readily applicable to Malcolm's third analogy. Specifically, he objects that he knows people who behave in ways that Malcolm characterizes as religious who would resist any characterization of their life stance as a religious one. Such an objection could be extended to the third analogy. I believe Winch *would have* so extended it. One might well question whether the attitude that Malcolm highlights in his third analogy is really a religious one. Does a willingness to regard oneself as spiritually ill combined with a whole-hearted commitment to combat that illness, count, *ipso facto*, as a religious attitude? Winch thinks not. He, of course, would concede that such an attitude could certainly be characterized as serious, honest, morally praiseworthy, decent, and humble. In context, it is clear enough that Winch admires people with such an attitude. His objection, however, is that an attitude can be all of these things without thereby being a religious attitude. This seems reasonable enough. I want to argue, however, that Wittgenstein's conception of a religious attitude was extremely unconventional, strikingly radical, and – even more interesting – that it was very close, if not identical, to the attitude Malcolm articulates in his third analogy. I turn now, to this very important matter.

ii. Engelmann on Wittgenstein's Early Religious Point of View

Paul Engelmann, in *Letters From Ludwig Wittgenstein with a Memoir*, gives interesting accounts of his interactions and conversations with Wittgenstein during a period of time that began shortly before World War I and continued through the war years, and well into the 1920s.[38] Some of these focus on what Engelmann calls spiritual or religious matters. More specifically, he writes of an attitude that, he asserts, Wittgenstein explicitly regarded as religious in nature. He explains that Wittgenstein deeply approved of this attitude and saw it in Engelmann himself:

> In me Wittgenstein unexpectedly met a person who ... suffered acutely under the discrepancy between the world as it is and as it ought to be according to his lights, but who tended also to seek the source of that discrepancy within, rather than outside, himself.[39]

Engelmann further describes this attitude and Wittgenstein's thoughts upon it, based upon their discussions:

> If I am unhappy and know that my unhappiness reflects a gross discrepancy between myself and life as it is, I have solved nothing; I shall be on the wrong track and shall never find a way out of the chaos ... so long as I have not achieved the supreme and crucial insight that that discrepancy is not the fault of life as it is, but myself as I am. ...The person who has achieved this insight and holds on to it, and who will at least try again and again throughout his life to develop it, is religious. He "has the faith", from which it does not follow by any means that he must use mythological concepts – self-created or handed

---

38 Paul Engelmann, *Letters from Ludwig Wittgenstein with a Memoir* (Oxford, 1967).
39 Ibid., p. 74.

down – to buttress and interpret his insight into the fundamental relationship between himself and human existence in general. If he depends on such concepts in order to stand by his faith, the reason may well lie in a weakness of that faith.[40]

These remarks are fascinating for a number of reasons. Clearly, they describe an attitude which is strikingly similar to the one Malcolm claims to be required of a person both on Wittgenstein's conception of a religious approach to life and on Wittgenstein's later conception of correct philosophical practice. The passages attribute to Wittgenstein a certain sincere attitude toward the important problems of life, those that can introduce unhappiness, chaos, and serious discrepancies. It is an attitude that readily recognizes the source of those problems in oneself and seeks relentlessly to change accordingly. It is an attitude that, on Wittgenstein's reckoning, was one of *faith* – a *religious* attitude. This is most surprising. On its face, this would appear to be much too broad a characterization of religiosity or faith. There are no qualifications about what kinds of problems one faces up to with the described attitude, except the clear indication that that they be serious ones, serious enough to threaten a discrepancy between oneself and the world. Even more strange, there is no requirement that this attitude connect with the practices or theological doctrines of any established religion. Yet, as I read the above passage, the absence of any such requirement is clearly not an oversight, but intended.

On Engelmann's account, Wittgenstein saw no need for such qualifications. His thought was that the attitude described in the passage is religious *whether or not* it is connected with conventional religious practices or dogmas. Indeed, he seemed to think that this attitude is *more purely* religious when it has no such connections. The remark in the passage above about "mythological concepts" that are "handed down" addresses the subject of the relationship between *conventional* religious thinking and the religious attitude described in the passage. It states that connections with particular mythologies or concepts are not necessary for genuine faith, and that when such connections function to reinforce faith, it can be a sign of weak faith. It is hard to know just why he regarded these as signs of weak faith. Here is one possibility that will be elaborated upon in the next chapter: these "mythological concepts" are useful when they motivate an individual to maintain the stance of genuine faith, but they also pose a danger in that an individual might become more attached to them than to the more important attitude of faith they serve. In any event, he appears to have thought that the attitude in question somehow *underlies* all genuinely religious life stances – whether adopted in connection with the conceptions and practices of an established religion or not. Needless to say, this is both an interesting and radical view. It would seem that Wittgenstein held that anyone for whom such a life stance is unshakable, *ipso facto*, has a religious attitude, one of faith, whether or not he or she accepts such a characterization. Certainly, on Engelmann's account, it was once Wittgenstein's view of what it is to have a religious point of view.

Indeed, Wittgenstein suggested to others the view that the mythologies associated with religion are not essential to, and can even threaten, true religion. One such remark offers some confirmation for Engelmann's account of his attitude. Drury describes

---

40 Ibid., pp. 76–7.

a conversation – one which occurred nearly a decade after Wittgenstein's talks with Engelmann – in which Wittgenstein recounted to him a morbid fear from which he had previously suffered. In Drury's account of the conversation, Wittgenstein appears again to be distinguishing between true genuine religion, genuine faith, and their common mythological accompaniments:

> [W]hen he was a student at Manchester he suffered at times from morbid fears. To get from his bedroom to his sitting room he had to cross over a landing, and sometimes he found himself dreading making the crossing. … [S]uddenly he stopped still and looked at me very seriously.
>
> WITTGENSTEIN: "You will think I have gone mad, when I tell you that only religious feelings are a cure for such fears."
>
> I replied that I didn't think he was crazy at all; that coming from Ireland I knew something about the power of religion. He seemed displeased with this answer as if I hadn't understood him.
>
> WITTGENSTEIN: "I am not talking about superstition but about real religious feeling."
>
> After this we walked on in silence for some time.[41]

To be sure, it is not certain just what Wittgenstein had in mind by the "superstition" that he distinguishes from "real religious feeling" in this passage. As we shall see in the next chapter, Wittgenstein believed that one source of religious superstition is a misreading of, and an overly literal attachment to, religious mythology that obscures the real function of mythology in a religious life. One can easily imagine that such a belief informed his remark to Drury. At any rate, this remark also connects interestingly with Malcolm's observation that, for Wittgenstein, a religious attitude requires that one willingly confront conditions in one's person that may be likened to an affliction or a sickness and, then, resolutely undertake to eradicate such conditions. Such a stance is exactly what Wittgenstein both described and recommended to Drury *as religious*.

Now, if both Engelmann's account is accurate and Wittgenstein did in fact carry the view it attributes to him, or something importantly like it, into his late period (as the remark to Drury may suggest), there are interesting consequences to be drawn. It would seem to follow that Malcolm's third analogy does indeed identify a very important parallel between philosophy as practiced by the late Wittgenstein and a religious approach to everyday life as described in *Culture and Value*. In both, as Malcolm notes, there is a kind of disease, a condition of self, that is the source of significant problems in one's life. As he also notes, there is, in both, the necessity of identifying the disease, and of eliminating it by altering one's own condition in a fundamental way. Finally, on Engelmann's account of Wittgenstein's view, the person who is resolutely and honestly committed to the latter task is *religious* and has *faith*, whatever the nature of the problems or the conditions of illness one seeks to rectify, so long as they undermine one's equilibrium in important ways. So, there is a very clear sense in which both Wittgenstein's later philosophy and a religious life as

---

41 M. O'C. Drury, "Conversations with Wittgenstein", pp. 115–16.

he describes it in *Culture and Value* proceed in accordance with an identifiable point of view that Wittgenstein thought of as religious – namely the one attributed to him by Engelmann. To the extent that Malcolm's third analogy highlights that viewpoint, and traces its operation in both realms, it seems to have touched on something of real significance.

Winch might well object to this line of defense of Malcolm's third analogy on conceptual grounds. Malcolm asserts that Wittgenstein's late approach to philosophy is analogous to a religious approach to the problems of life. My remarks above suggest a stronger connection between the two – namely that the former is not merely *analogous to* but is *an instance of* the latter. Winch, following his first argument against Malcolm's procedures, might conclude that this line could not, then, be used to defend Malcolm, who makes only the weaker claim.

This criticism can be resisted. It is important to review the details of Malcolm's third analogy while maintaining a broad view of its relation to his central question: In what way can Wittgenstein's later philosophy – which does not mention problems of God and religion or the central problems of human life – be said to represent a religious point of view? Malcolm's third analogy offers a partial answer to the question – specifically, that the approach Wittgenstein carried to his late philosophy is strikingly analogous or similar to what he took to be the religious approach to basic problems of human life. Winch specifically objects to this. He argues that the attitudes are not so similar after all. Against this, I have tried to show that they are similar enough to both qualify as "religious" in a sense once explicated in conversations with Engelmann by Wittgenstein himself! This consideration, at the very least, would provide evidence that Wittgenstein would have regarded the similarities identified by Malcolm to be more important than the dissimilarities noted by Winch. I would think that this constitutes a considerable vindication for Malcolm's third analogy.

Was the view described by Engelmann a mere passing enthusiasm or a remnant of some of Wittgenstein's early conceptions which he had long since abandoned once engaged in his late philosophical writings? I very much doubt it. I shall address this question and some of its ramifications in the next section. For now, I will note that, as late as 1937, Wittgenstein wrote this passage:

> The fact that life is problematic shows that the shape of your life does not fit into life's mould. So you must change the way you live and, once your life does fit into the mould, what is problematic will disappear.[42]

This passage puts forth an attitude towards life's problems that is strikingly similar to that described by Engelmann. While it does not characterize the attitude as religious, the passage clearly endorses the attitude, representing it as the correct stance with respect to life's problems. As such, there is some reason to think not only that Wittgenstein once viewed the attitude attributed to him by Engelmann as a religious attitude, but also that he himself carried something like that attitude into the late thirties, and so, well into his late philosophical period.

---

42 Ludwig Wittgenstein, *Culture and Value*, ed. G. H. Von Wright in collaboration with Heikki Nymnan (Oxford, 1980), p. 27e.

iii. Life's Problems and Philosophy's Problems: Wittgenstein's Approach to Philosophical Problems in the Investigations

It should be emphasized in this regard that Wittgenstein – perhaps more than any major contemporary philosopher – intimated important connections between the problems of philosophy and the problems of life. Malcolm, in his *Memoir*, quotes from a letter written to him by Wittgenstein:

> what is the use of studying philosophy if all it does for you is to enable you to talk with some plausibility about some abstruse problems of logic, etc., & if it does not improve your thinking about the important questions of everyday life. ...You see, I know that it is difficult to think well about "certainty", "probability", "perception" etc. But it is, if possible, still more difficult to think, or try to think, really honestly about your life & other peoples lives. And the trouble is that thinking about these things is not thrilling, but often downright nasty. And when it's nasty then it's most important.[43]

If Wittgenstein were as focused as Winch on the differences between the two, would he have emphasized so strongly the similarities between the obstacles to good philosophical thinking and those to good thinking about the important problems of everyday life? Clearly, he thought that both are extremely difficult, even "nasty", and that both require uncompromised honesty. Why? Wittgenstein's answer, or part of it, I think, would be that both require an individual to identify deeply entrenched and deceptive tendencies of thought, pathologies of thought, in his or her own nature, and, having done so, to confront and change those tendencies. The *Investigations* is replete with such suggestions. On Engelmann's account, Wittgenstein once believed that an earnest willingness to engage these sorts of tasks is *characteristic* of a religious attitude of faith. In connection with this, I would add that the *Investigations* also specifically refers to the need to overcome *temptations, seductions*, and *bewitchments* in order to achieve philosophical clarity. The uniqueness of this terminology in a philosophical context, and its suggestion of religious themes, is, for me, striking. For Wittgenstein, philosophical problems were *serious* ones and he famously treated them with a high sense of seriousness that impressed and even intimidated many of his fellow philosophers. His struggles with them were, for him, *personal* struggles of the highest importance. Far from acknowledging Winch's distinction between the problems of everyday life and those of philosophy, Wittgenstein would contest it, seeing no important distinction to be made.

One final point: Wittgenstein, in the *Investigations*, does not merely express his belief that philosophy requires confronting and curing one's diseases of thought, changing one's very nature. Far more interesting, he *enacts*, even *dramatizes*, in words the struggle to do so. As noted in Chapter 2, he frequently bifurcates his philosophical presentation into a confrontational dialogue between a wayward voice, which labors under and expresses prejudices, misconceptions, and other pathologies of thought, and a wiser voice, which attempts to combat these. This is a remarkable feature of his philosophical writing – one that runs very much against the far more

---

43 Norman Malcolm, *Ludwig Wittgenstein – A Memoir*, 2nd edn, with a biographical sketch by G. H. von Wright and Wittgenstein's letters to Malcolm (Oxford, 1984), pp. 93–4.

staid tendencies of the philosophical prose of his and subsequent times. If Malcolm is right, Wittgenstein saw the struggles he enacts as typical of what good philosophy requires and also, in very important ways, as typical of the struggles involved in confronting life's central problems religiously. On Engelmann's account, they would qualify as an instance, for Wittgenstein, of a religious approach to philosophy's problems.

I think Malcolm is correct to emphasize that Wittgenstein thought of his later philosophy as a confrontation with deeply flawed tendencies in his own thought – what he thought of as a disease of thought. He is also right to focus on Wittgenstein's conviction that only radical changes in one's habits of thought, changes that cannot be made without overcoming deep-seated tendencies, can eradicate these diseases of thought. Finally, I think he is right in suggesting that Wittgenstein would have seen this feature of his late philosophical writings as representative of a religious point of view. As such, I accept Malcolm's third analogy as a modest, partial solution to his book's central problem.

iv. Malcolm's Third Analogy and a Contrary Claim in Winch

Winch devotes almost his entire essay to criticisms of Malcolm's views. Only the last few pages are devoted to his own account of a religious viewpoint in Wittgenstein's late philosophy. What he offers there is of the nature of an elaborate sketch. Winch allows that his conclusions are not clear-cut. Indeed, he argues that there can be no clear-cut account of a religious viewpoint in Wittgenstein's late writings. Read in another way, his remarks can be taken to make a case – and a strong one – for the pessimistic view that no account at all is possible. Either way, I do not feel sufficiently in command of the many difficult points he addresses in his short discussion to give an account of his discussion or offer helpful comments. For these and other reasons, I offer no overview of the substance of these last few pages of Winch's essay. I want to continue to restrict myself to Malcolm's views and Winch's evaluation of them. Still, even given this restriction, there is one line of thought explored toward the end of Winch's essay that I ought to address.

In this section, I have been defending a modified version of Malcolm's third analogy. I have argued that none of Winch's specific contentions against the third analogy, none of the points of disanalogy he emphasizes, are powerful enough to undermine Malcolm's root idea. So, it is important to note that Winch offers further observations that run contrary to the third analogy in the final pages of his essay. These are interesting and provocative in their own right. As such, I want to take them up.

At one point in his essay, Winch seems to be on the verge of suggesting something along the lines of Malcolm's third analogy. He writes:

> I should like to say that ... we find in Wittgenstein's strictly philosophical works ... a spiritual dimension seldom met with in the works of "professional philosophers". It is difficult to

pin this down of course. It has partly to do with the passion to which Wittgenstein gives free rein in the dialogues between the various conflicting philosophical voices.[44]

It appears from this that Winch means to imply that there is a religious – or, at least, "spiritual" – viewpoint associated with the passions involved in Wittgenstein's struggle for philosophical clarity. This appearance is enhanced by Winch's insistence that, for Wittgenstein, religious feelings are passions. But Winch resists this conclusion. He has something more complicated in mind. He goes on to cite this passage from *Culture and Value*:

> My ideal is a certain coolness. A temple providing a setting for the passions.[45]

and then explains why he thinks the passage illuminates some of Wittgenstein's deeper purposes in the *Investigations*:

> *Philosophical Investigations* it seems to me can be described in just this way. In it Wittgenstein's own voice, speaking in its own person, is rarely heard; he provides the context within which the various conflicting voices that together make up philosophical bewilderment can confront each other in a way is otherwise usually impossible for them.[46]

His idea seems to be that Wittgenstein's viewpoint in the *Investigations* is not one that is caught up in the struggle for clarity or its attendant passions – which Winch himself characterizes as "spiritual", but rather, a "cool" point of view, a more removed perspective, which makes clarity possible in the face of passion. So, if I understand Winch correctly, the real viewpoint of the *Investigations* – and, thus, whatever *religious* viewpoint it represents – is not, in any important way, tied to that struggle or those passions, because it is not Wittgenstein's struggle and they are not Wittgenstein's passions. This is an interesting conclusion that rests on an equally interesting reading of the *Investigations*. I will state some of my misgivings regarding the latter and leave the matter there.

First, I have doubts as to whether the passage Winch cites from *Culture and Value*, the one that identifies his "ideal" as "a certain coolness", was intended by Wittgenstein as a characterization of his *philosophy*. There is nothing in the remark itself that suggests that he is writing about philosophy. Relative to this, I would note that the original passage is not accurately reproduced in Winch's response. The latter unaccountably changes the word "ideal" (translated straightforwardly from the German "*Ideal*" in the original) to the more philosophical word "idea". There is no acknowledgement of the change and no justification is offered. This could, of course, be a simple typographical error and the point, while worth noting, is surely not decisive. There are, however, more serious difficulties with the use Winch makes of this passage. For one thing, the passage was written in 1929 – probably too early to shed much light on the *Investigations*. It is also significant that the remarks in *Culture and Value* surrounding the passage in question do not discuss philosophy,

---

44 Norman Malcolm, *Wittgenstein – A Religious Point of View?*, p. 129.
45 Ludwig Wittgenstein, *Culture and Value*, p. 2e.
46 Norman Malcolm, *Wittgenstein – A Religious Point of View?*, p. 129.

but rather, music, musicians, and culture. In addition, the succeeding passage makes reference to what Wittgenstein calls his "cultural ideal". All this suggests that the passage in question refers not to a philosophical idea, but, more likely, to a cultural or musical ideal. It certainly does not go without saying that it relates to his philosophy or any philosophical idea.

Perhaps none of this much matters. Winch may not be supporting his reading of the *Investigations* with the passage from *Culture and Value*, but merely noting that the latter gives elegant expression to the former. Still, that reading puzzles me, specifically his contention in the passage above that "Wittgenstein's own voice, speaking in his own person" is virtually absent from the *Investigations*. Of course, I would not reject this out of hand, but I have grave doubts. A good deal of what I have written in this book urges a contrary reading of the *Investigations*. In addition, Winch's reading, at face value, seems implausible. Is Wittgenstein, as author of the *Investigations*, really as far removed from the philosophical disputes the work enacts as Winch suggests? Certainly, it would require more than a bare assertion to convince me of that.

Finally, beyond this, Winch's claim that Wittgenstein's voice "is rarely heard" in the *Investigations* is unnecessary, given the main contention of the interpretation he is urging. Roughly, Winch asserts that the viewpoint of the *Investigations* is not presented in Wittgenstein's voice, but rather in a dispassionate setting within which the underlying nature of the disputes between its "conflicting voices" is illuminated. Surely, however, the *Investigations* could do both. This is not only a coherent reading, but also one that represents the work as one of subtlety and depth. I am suggesting that Winch's latter claim may well be true, but that the "conflicting voices" he refers to are Wittgenstein's: sometimes wayward, sometimes wiser. Thus, the *Investigations* both re-enacts Wittgenstein's philosophical struggles, his arguments with himself, and also seeks to provide its reader with a cooler perspective, one which both affords a perspicuous representation of the true nature of the elusive underlying issues and points in the direction of a resolution.

Chapter 7

Was Wittgenstein a Spenglerian Atheist?

I. Wittgenstein as a Spenglerian Atheist – Clack's Position in Outline

In this final chapter I will discuss a bold claim made by Brian S. Clack in his noteworthy book, *An Introduction to Wittgenstein's Philosophy of Religion*. Clack's book is, in most respects, excellent. It provides a painstaking examination of Wittgenstein's view of religion – both in the early and later phases of his thought on the subject. He shows an impressive command not only of Wittgenstein's major works, but of the esoteric sources one must peruse in order to get a full picture of this daunting subject. The book fills a need in the secondary literature on Wittgenstein and I agree with many of its conclusions. In this discussion I will restrict myself for the most part to a striking claim made by Clack – one which, coming as it does, at the end of the book's final chapter, strikes one as its *denouement*. Boldly, Clack suggests that Wittgenstein had become, in the late stages of his life, a Spenglerian "apocalyptic atheist" who reluctantly accepted that the time in which one could live religiously had passed. This is certainly a most intriguing and original claim. At the very least, it takes seriously, as one should, Spengler's influence on Wittgenstein.

Clack begins his argument in his book's fifth and final chapter, "Aftermath", by re-examining his account of Wittgenstein's later view of religious language. This account is, I believe, accurate as far as it goes. Clack's focus, unlike mine in the previous chapter, is not so much on Wittgenstein's doubts about religious expressibility in his time, but rather upon Wittgenstein's view of the underlying nature of religious language. The difference in focus between us does not by itself manifest significant deeper differences, and I will try to show this in more detail below. Clack thinks it natural that an acceptance of Wittgenstein's view of religious language, at least for many people, would discourage religious belief. I will discuss this too at some length below. He suggests obliquely that it may have had such an effect on Wittgenstein – not, as it were, forcing him into atheism, but, perhaps, leading him in such a direction. Clack's final thought is that, whatever else might have tended to distance Wittgenstein from his earlier fascination and experiments with religious living, it was a Spenglerian cultural pessimism that offered the final and most powerful impetus that led him to his final alleged atheism.

Clack offers what he takes to be independent indications that Wittgenstein had become a non-believer, that his lifelong fascination with religion had given way to a rejection of it. I will have more to say about this below, as I do not think Clack supports this important and interesting claim nearly well enough. Convinced that Wittgenstein had reached a final resting place of unbelief, Clack seeks an explanation for it that goes beyond his view of religious language, which he saw as a partial explanation at most for what he took to be Wittgenstein's final stance of unbelief. It is in this context that he turns to Spengler and his influence upon Wittgenstein as the final and decisive impetus to that attitude.

Clack's claim takes very seriously the influence that Spengler had upon Wittgenstein. He sees that influence as an essential component to understanding Wittgenstein's late attitude toward religion. Certainly I agree with this strategy, and have employed it myself in the preceding chapters. I think, however, that Clack's conclusion, in the end, is not supportable and overlooks some details and subtleties in Spengler's writings and in the nature of Spengler's influence on Wittgenstein.

Clack claims, quite rightly, that in order to understand Wittgenstein's late religious attitude "we must pay ... attention to the thought of one of the greatest influences on Wittgenstein's philosophy: Oswald Spengler."[1] He adds, also entirely appropriately, "[o]ne is struck by the extent to which Wittgenstein's philosophical project meets the restrictions laid down by Spengler concerning what is and is not possible in an age of decline".[2] This, of course, is exactly what I tried to show a decade ago in my article, "Wittgenstein and Spengler", and also, with far more support and elaboration, in Chapter 2 of this book.[3] Clack proceeds to give a brief, but accurate, accounting of Spengler's conception of a culture:

> A culture is here envisaged as an organism, and it can be analysed in an analogous fashion to the way the life-cycle of a plant can be described. If we observe the life of the flower, we see it first as a little shoot springing from its mother soil; its bud appears, and it blossoms before withering away into death. Likewise, says Spengler, a culture emerges energetically, and brings forth great art, music, poetry, metaphysical systems, *and its own religion*, before all possibilities of artistic creation disappear as it wilts, as our Western culture has, into materialism and triviality. Although religion is a mark of the vibrancy of a culture, it has for Spengler no life independent of it, and hence its destiny is to die.[4]

He then adds the following:

> The possibility of belief is no longer open in an age such as ours, not even to those who mourn its passing. They must accept that the possibility for belief has vanished, for to do otherwise would be akin to the dying flower longing to bloom again.[5]

He supports this with a quotation from Spengler's *Decline*:

> The megalopolitan is irreligious, this is part of his being, a mark of his historical position. Bitterly as he may feel the inner emptiness and poverty, earnestly as he may long to be religious, it is out of his power to be so. All religiousness in the Megalopolis rests upon self-deception.[6]

---

1   Brian R. Clack, *An Introduction to Wittgenstein's Philosophy of Religion* (Edinburgh, 1999), p. 127.

2   Ibid., p. 129.

3   William James DeAngelis, "Wittgenstein and Spengler", *Dialogue*, vol. xxxiii, 1994.

4   Brian R. Clack, *An Introduction to Wittgenstein's Philosophy of Religion*, p. 128 (Clack's emphasis).

5   Ibid., pp. 128.

6   Ibid.

There is, I think a subtle, but illicit shift in Clack's use of the third passage to support the view expressed in the first two. I will discuss this too later in this chapter. For now I will focus on what Clack draws from this. Simply, he believes that Wittgenstein accepted Spengler's view of the inevitability of social decline and the inevitability of religious decline. For Clack's Spengler-influenced Wittgenstein, a high culture has ossified into a megalopolitan civilization in which there is no hope for religion. He sees Wittgenstein as one of those who came to "accept that the possibility for belief has vanished", while acknowledging that he was certainly also one of those who would certainly "mourn its passing". On the book's final page, Clack attributes to Wittgenstein "a despairing, apocalyptic atheism", essentially linked to his "frustrated and bitter recognition that the passionate beauty of the religious life is no longer open to us".[7] This is an interesting and powerful conclusion. I believe, however, that it can and should be resisted. I believe that Clack's evidence that the later Wittgenstein was an unbeliever is weak and subject to plausible contrary interpretations. Clack takes no note of Wittgenstein's departures from, and criticisms of, Spengler's views (which I have emphasized in Chapters 1 and 2) – an omission that weakens his case. In this way, and others upon which I will identify, Clack has misassessed and overestimated Spengler's influence of Wittgenstein. Perhaps most important, I don't think Clack has been sufficiently careful to distinguish Spengler's claims about the prototypical forms that social decline takes in *any culture* from the specific claims he makes about *his own culture* – specifically, he has not attended sufficiently to Spengler's proclamations about how far his own civilization was into its own decline. There is ample evidence, indeed an overabundance of textual evidence, that Spengler himself did not believe that a megalopolitan age in which religion is no longer possible was at hand in the West. On the contrary, Spengler clearly thought that such a time would take several centuries to take hold. This is, I think, the strongest point to be made against Clack's view. First, however, I will turn to a fuller analysis of some features of Clack's interesting case and indicate some of my doubts regarding them.

II. A Critique of Clack's Position

i. Clack on Wittgenstein's View of Religious Language and Religion

In his book's final chapter, Clack takes seriously Wittgenstein's extremely unconventional views of what it is to be religious and to have faith. In doing so, he revisits a careful, painstaking analysis of these in his book's previous, penultimate chapter. Clack explains correctly how Wittgenstein's later view of religious language implied a radical view of religious belief. That view would have as a consequence, for example, that it should not be relevant to a committed Christian whether the Bible or conventional Christian theology is literally true. Religious belief on that view, properly understood, is not grounded in and does not require a belief that the sacred writings of one's religion or those of its theologians are literally true. On Wittgenstein's view, religious language functions to describe neither

---

7   Ibid., p. 129.

transcendent nor natural realities, but rather, at bottom, to establish in the believer a commitment to a certain uncompromisingly moral way of life. Roughly, religious language, which seems on its surface to function descriptively, in fact, is primarily motivational in nature, functioning more in the manner of an exhortation than in that of a description.

For Clack's Wittgenstein then, religious language as it is used within a religious community, in sacred texts, and in religious rituals and ceremonies, functions primarily to impose and reinforce a wholehearted commitment to a certain moral life stance. Further, on this view, the "surface grammar" of religious language imposes a wrong picture of its real grammar, its real function, thus, deceiving the believer about the true nature of what is believed. Clack's synoptic expression of the view:

> In tune with [Wittgenstein's] remark that although religious belief, "is really a way of living", the contention seems to be that a religion is only apparently (only in its surface grammar) a set of quasi-theoretical statements (concerning God, the destiny of the individual, the meaning and end of history, and so on). For it is, in fact, an aid to conduct, a collection of pictures which serve to reinforce a distinctive morality, "rules of life ... dressed up in pictures."[8]

So, for Clack's Wittgenstein, religion is a wholehearted commitment to a remarkable moral life stance, one that is aided by religious discourse and the reading of sacred texts. This is, of course, strikingly similar to the attitude of "faith" that Engelmann ascribed to Wittgenstein, described in the previous chapter. I shall return to this shortly. On Wittgenstein's conception as described here, one could be religious without taking sacred texts, or theologies based upon them, to be literally true. Indeed, as Clack notes – I believe quite correctly – Wittgenstein saw such literalism as a deep mistake. The mistake, for Wittgenstein, lies in being deceived by the "surface grammar" of religious language and missing its deeper function – that of imposing rules of life, not describing transcendent, metaphysical realities.

Clack explains that, for Wittgenstein, false literalism deceives the religious into conceiving of God as an existent being who causally influences events in the world. On this false conception, miracles occur when this being intercedes in the world, prayer functions mainly as a request to this being to intercede, and the belief in immortality is a confused conviction that some non-biological component of a person in fact survives biological death.

The view Clack correctly attributes to Wittgenstein may seem an implausible and even an arrogant one. Many intelligent people who consider themselves religious believers would assert that their belief is just what Wittgenstein claims religious belief is not. Millions of them would say their belief in God includes the conviction that He *is* an existing being, that He *does* intercede in worldly events (sometimes in response to prayer), that He *does* reward and punish people for their actions, and that most of these rewards and punishments are meted out in an afterlife that stretches temporally beyond biological death. Are such individuals wrong about what they believe? Wittgenstein's answer seems to be that they are, that the *underlying character* of religious belief, *stripped of superstition and correctly understood*, is as

---

8   Ibid., p. 124.

he describes it. Clack appears to be uneasy with such a view and, as we shall see, indicates, in various ways, doubts about such a view of religion.

Having established this much, Clack moves on to pose an interesting problem. He wonders whether religious belief might in fact be easier to maintain on what Wittgenstein thinks of as the false interpretation of religious language and of religion that its surface grammar imposes on most of us. Clack is intrigued by the possibility that, psychologically, religious belief is easier to maintain on what Wittgenstein thought of as the mistaken, literalistic view than on the view he held. Clack's tendency is to think that a self-reflective acceptance of Wittgenstein's later view of religious language and religion would tend to alienate one from religion. With respect to Christianity, he says this:

> Once ... one had come to [a] recognition that Christianity is a set of admonishing pictures tied into a particular way of living, and once the fountainhead of religion is located in ... [a] way of reacting to the world, could one's faith in God feasibly remain intact? In other words, though Wittgenstein's attention to ... religious discourse may well have revealed its true nature, does not a person's own belief depend for its continued life on an acceptance of the surface grammar of religion? Do not believers have to think there is a God, that there will be an afterlife, that there have been miraculous occurrences, and so on, in order to engage in the religious life? ... Our question is whether atheism is the inevitable consequence of an acceptance of Wittgenstein's approach to religious belief, and what kind of atheism that would be.[9]

Clack asks this question because he appears to think that atheism is a natural, though perhaps not inevitable, response to such a conception of religion. Further, Clack never says so, but, as we shall see, in a number of passages he seems to doubt that Wittgenstein's view is a correct one. Specifically, he says:

> It would ... be somewhat perplexing were someone to accept all that Wittgenstein has to say about religion in his later period and yet still be able to continue in his or her faith, or that a person might be converted to Christianity having understood it in Wittgenstein's terms.[10]

Clack, as his view develops, is not fully convinced that the final stance of unbelief that he attributes to Wittgenstein was influenced by such a response. He appears to think, however, that his view of religious language may have been a contributing factor to his presumed atheism. Clack's perspective on Wittgenstein's presumed final atheism seems to be that his later view of religious language possibly played some role in leading him away from religion. Still, Clack thinks that there was more to Wittgenstein's alleged rejection of religion. The deeper explanation that he poses insists "that it was something about the character of 'this age' which constrained his religious impulses."[11]

I am not persuaded that Wittgenstein's later views on religion played any role at all in alienating him from religion. Indeed, Wittgenstein's views on religious language,

---

9   Ibid., p. 125.
10 Ibid.
11 Ibid.

from the mysticism-influenced *Tractatus* right through to the end of his life, retain a common conviction. He never abandoned the conviction that religious language, talk of God, immortality, and miracles is of a singular type whose function is not descriptive. He never thought that belief *in* God is the belief *that* some transcendent being exists, can be described, and influences the world in ways that can themselves be observed and described (sometimes in response to supplicant prayer). His later view of religious language, *in this respect at least*, is not so different from his early view. On both views, religious literalism and traditional theology rest on a mistaken view of the functioning of language. His later view of language rejected much in the earlier – but both views had the consequence that there is no conflict between science and religion. If the early version of this view did not discourage him from a religious stance, it is difficult to see why the later version of the view would have done so. Indeed, Wittgenstein insisted for his entire adult life that religious belief does not consist in accepting that certain religious propositions are true, as traditionalists and theologians assume it does. As I see it, Wittgenstein never wavered from this stance. If anything discouraged him from living religiously late in his life, it was not this conviction. His attitude toward the traditional view, as we have seen, seems at times to border on one of contempt.

Indeed, we saw in the preceding chapter, in connection with Engelmann's explication of Wittgenstein's view of faith, that far from requiring the literalistic beliefs Clack enumerates above, Wittgenstein appeared to think that faith, *in its purest form*, could, and ideally should, exist without them. It is worth repeating that Wittgenstein, in his conversations with Engelmann, emphasized that true faith did not require "mythological concepts", and that if one's faith "depends on such concepts … the reason may well lie in a weakness of that faith". Against this, Clack holds that that the rejection of such beliefs would naturally tend to undermine religion in most believers. This is plausible. In raising the possibility that such a rejection may have had such an effect on Wittgenstein, however, I think Clack badly misses the mark. In so doing, Clack misreads Wittgenstein. As a check against Clack's general claim, it is worth noting too that millions of Buddhists who are undeniably religious do not embrace any such beliefs.

There is scant reason to believe that Wittgenstein's view of religious language dissuaded him from a religious stance – *as he conceived of such a stance* – nor should it have. Beyond this, we shall see, there is little reason to believe that Wittgenstein accepted what Clack characterizes as a Spenglerian "apocalyptic atheism". First, there is insufficient evidence to establish that Wittgenstein had become a non-believer. Second, and much more important relative to Clack's position, it is not difficult to show that the best evidence strongly indicates that *neither Wittgenstein nor Spengler* believed that Western civilization had reached an endpoint in which religious living is no longer an option. Accordingly, I will be arguing, in what follows, that Clack's case for his view of Wittgenstein's supposed atheism, while bold and original, will not survive careful scrutiny.

ii. Did Wittgenstein Reject Religion Per Se?

Clack suggests – but never claims directly – that Wittgenstein's view of religious language may have alienated him from religion. While his tendency is to think that a Wittgensteinian view of religious language might well alienate many, or even most, from religious belief, he does not explicitly attribute such a tendency to Wittgenstein. Clack acknowledges Wittgenstein's early fascination with, and inclination toward, religious belief, and comments, "this inclination is of a somewhat idiosyncratic order, and appears to arise from traits of Wittgenstein's own distinctive character, rather than ... describing a faith which others might plausibly decide to embrace."[12] This is an appropriate caveat: Wittgenstein's belief, such as it was, seemed indeed to be of a different character – distinctive in nature from that of most believers of his time. Thus, he would not have been dissuaded from belief, as other believers might have been, merely as a consequence of accepting his equally distinctive view of religion and religious discourse. Clack hints that Wittgenstein may have been so dissuaded, but never claims that he was. As such, Clack realizes that if he is to make the bold claim that Wittgenstein embraced atheism he had better support it with a good deal in the way of independent and direct evidence. To his credit, he attempts to do so. He addresses a number of passages and remarks of Wittgenstein which he thinks constitute evidence that Wittgenstein had, in the last years of his life, abandoned religion.

In Chapter 6, I discussed at length a most intriguing, but puzzling remark of Wittgenstein – that in which he said to Drury, "I am not a religious man, but I cannot help seeing every problem from a religious point of view."[13] My discussion focused, for the most part, on whether Wittgenstein meant to include philosophical problems among those that he saw "from a religious point of view". The remark is problematic in other ways as well. How can one not be a religious man while at the same time employing a religious point of view? What "religious point of view" did he employ? What did Wittgenstein mean in saying that he was not a religious man? Had he rejected religion *as he conceived of it*, or was it more a matter of refusing to affiliate with any existing religious group or engage in its practices and ceremonies? If it was the former, then he was certainly an unbeliever; if the latter, then perhaps he did harbor within himself, and against the tendencies of his time, something that he, if not others, thought of as a religious point of view.

Clack, without support or further discussion of what Wittgenstein might have meant, calls this remark "the most significant of his expressions of unbelief".[14] This reading – as Clack undoubtedly knows, but never acknowledges – is in stark contrast to that of Drury, Malcolm, and Winch.[15] Those three all interpreted the remark as a qualified acceptance of a religious point of view. The remark is certainly not self-

---

12   Ibid., p. 126.

13   M. O'C. Drury, "Notes on Conversations with Wittgenstein", in Rush Rhees (ed.), *Ludwig Wittgenstein – Personal Recollections* (Totowa, NJ, 1981), p. 94.

14   Brian R. Clack, *An Introduction to Wittgenstein's Philosophy of Religion*, p. 126.

15   Norman Malcolm, *Wittgenstein – A Religious Point of View?*; see especially pp. *vii–viii*, Chapter 1, and p. 132.

explanatory: Something is denied; something is asserted. There is an ironic tension between them. In emphasizing what is denied, as Clack does, one might reasonably take it as an expression of unbelief. But why not emphasize what is asserted as Drury, Malcolm, and Winch do? As we have seen in the preceding chapter, Malcolm, in effect, devoted a whole book, *Ludwig Wittgenstein – A Religious Point of View?*, to justify that reading of that remark. Clack, in contrast, appears to take it as just obvious that the remark is an expression of unbelief.

But it is not obvious. If this remark is to be taken as an "expression of unbelief", a fuller interpretation of just what it meant and a rationale for emphasizing what it asserts over what it denies is called for. The remark might have been an expression of unbelief, but could also have been an expression of an acceptance of an *underlying* religious viewpoint combined with a rejection of *conventional* religiosity. It is fair to say that the vagaries of context make it difficult, if not impossible, to find a fully satisfying interpretation. It is clear, however, that whatever interpretation one offers, one should support it. It certainly does not go without saying that Wittgenstein's puzzling remark, which, as we have already seen, has been interpreted in many ways, is a statement of unbelief. By itself, the remark raises more questions than it answers and cannot bear the weight Clack places upon it.

Another source of Clack's conviction that Wittgenstein had become an unbeliever emerges from his reading of striking passages from *Culture and Value*. In them, Wittgenstein offers truncated suggestions about Christianity and his temptation to believe as a Christian, a temptation that he evidently rejected. Clack notes a passage in *Culture and Value* in which Wittgenstein reveals that he is unable to call Jesus "Lord", and adds, by way of elaboration, "[b]ecause I do not believe that he will come to judge me; because that says nothing to me."[16] Clack notes too, a passage in which Wittgenstein expresses an attitude toward prayer:

> I cannot kneel to pray because it is as though my knees were stiff. I am afraid of dissolution (of my own dissolution), should I become too soft.[17]

These are striking passages. Let us first consider the latter. It is certainly not self-explanatory. Was it an expression of a passing mood or a more settled attitude? Was he rejecting prayer in general, or, perhaps, a specific ritualized form of prayer involving kneeling and addressing God inwardly as Christians often do? Is it possible that the remark uses prayer as a synecdoche to express a more complicated sentiment about religion? Even if he was expressing a settled attitude to supplicant prayer in general (which is far from clear), one might still reasonably wonder whether Wittgenstein might have embraced some underlying form of religion that did not involve praying on one's knees. These passages are interesting, but, again, the vagaries of context raise questions that are difficult to answer. Many, indeed the majority of those people in the world who consider themselves religious, do not call Jesus "Lord". Many of them do not pray on their knees, believe in a final judgment, or call Jesus "Lord". Think of Buddhists, for example. These passages show only that Wittgenstein twice

---

16   Ludwig Wittgenstein, *Culture and Value*, ed. G. H. von Wright in collaboration with Heikki Nymnan (Oxford, 1980), p. 33e (Wittgenstein's emphasis).

17   Ibid., p. 56e.

expressed a rejection of some of the striking *particulars* of Christianity. This is not the same as rejecting religion *per se*.

On the view of religious language and religion that Clack correctly ascribes to the later Wittgenstein, it is not very hard to see how someone might be religious without calling Jesus "Lord" and without getting on one's knees to pray. Was the "dissolution" of which Wittgenstein wrote in connection with prayer linked to a fear that a genuinely religious lifestance (in his sense) would lead to dissolution? Or, might he have had something else in mind: that engaging in one of the trappings of ritualized Christianity might lead to others that would ultimately undermine his cherished independence of thought and, thus, lead to the sort of dissolution he feared most? At the least, it is difficult to decide, but here, I would suggest, without insisting on it, that the latter is more likely.

It is important to remember that Wittgenstein, in conversation with Drury, expressed his hopes for a "religion of the future ... without any priests or ministers", a religion that is "extremely ascetic; and by that I don't mean just going without food and drink".[18] He went on to say, "There is a sense in which you and I are both Christians."[19] These remarks certainly raise as many questions as they answer. Nonetheless, several observations might be offered. First, Wittgenstein, in making these remarks, expressed his belief that some religious stance might suit the needs of his time. Second, in describing it as a religion "without any priests or ministers", Wittgenstein appears to be suggesting that institutionalized religions, with their priests and ministers, are somehow wanting and in need of replacement. Further, in describing his religious ideal as "extremely ascetic", he is suggesting a practice to which one directs one's entire being in an austere and demanding manner that goes beyond even the usual sense of "ascetic". Finally, his remarkable assertion that he and Drury were both "in a sense" Christians, while puzzling, suggests an interesting possibility. In whatever way Wittgenstein took himself to be "in a sense" a Christian, it was surely not a matter of calling Jesus "Lord", praying on his knees, or a literalistic belief in Christian dogma or theology. This is significant in that it shows that Wittgenstein, at least at one point in his life, believed himself to be "in a sense" a religious man, even a Christian, without engaging in the formalized practices of Christianity or any other religion. I am suggesting that there is reason to think that Wittgenstein – while unable to call Jesus "Lord", pray on his knees, accept divine intervention in worldly affairs or a personal afterlife, or embrace the traditional theologian's metaphysical God – nonetheless, might have taken himself to be in some deeper, underlying sense, religious. This is not such a strange suggestion, being, as it is, about a man whose ideal of faith was an unshakable attitude toward life and the world, which, in its strongest form, requires no myths or doctrines to sustain it. I would suggest that it may well have been such a stance that he confided to Engelmann. Further, such a stance may well have motivated his admonishment to Drury not to become "too familiar with holy things".[20]

---

18   M. O'C. Drury, "Conversations with Wittgenstein", in Rush Rhees (ed.), *Ludwig Wittgenstein – Personal Recollections* (Totowa, NJ, 1981), p. 129.

19   Ibid.

20   Ibid., p. 136.

Beyond this, I believe that it is plausible that Wittgenstein, very late in his life, may well have been engaged in an experiment with the sort of asceticism he described to Drury. Remember, Wittgenstein, very much as a matter of choice, lived much of his later life in nearly complete isolation in a remote location in coastal Ireland. (It is worth remembering too that this is not the only time in his life he isolated himself in such a manner.) He avoided cities, eschewed material possessions beyond absolute necessities, and abandoned his many learned acquaintances, restricting himself to the occasional company of simple folk and natural surroundings. It is no stretch to call such a life an ascetic one. It is reasonable to suggest, though, of course, hardly possible to prove, that Wittgenstein's asceticism of this period (and of others in which he lived in extreme isolation) could have been an experiment in just the kind of religion he had tried to describe to Drury. At any rate – to anticipate a point I will pursue at greater length in what follows – it is certainly true, that Wittgenstein, during this period, had consciously chosen an austere and limiting environment. This choice afforded him both an ascetic set of surroundings, and, it should also be noted, surroundings more characteristic of a life lived in the early epoch of a culture than one lived in a civilized megalopolis.

iii. Did Wittgenstein Accept Spenglerian Atheism?

In *i* and *ii* above, I have rebutted some of Clack's reasons for viewing Wittgenstein as a non-believer. I have tried to show that those remarks of Wittgenstein that Clack takes to be good evidence of unbelief *per se* can be reasonably interpreted differently. I have tried to provide a context for showing that those remarks are consistent with religious belief, at least as Wittgenstein conceived of it.

My main objection to Clack's interpretation is, I think, much more important and more compelling. It is simply that Clack portrays Wittgenstein as far more blankly accepting of Spengler's picture of cultural and religious decline in the West than he in fact was. Beyond this, he does not adequately attend to Spengler's own assessment of how far the Western world was into its own period of decline as he wrote. In fact, there is much in Spengler that Wittgenstein rejected and much of it is directly relevant to Clack's interpretation. Beyond this, while Spengler did believe that irreligiousness was inevitable in a culture that is in a state of complete decline, an ossified megalopolitan civilization, his considered opinion was that the West had not yet reached the final stage of decline. Indeed, there is abundant evidence that he believed that Western decline was only beginning, that it was still far from an advanced stage. It is to these very important matters that I now turn.

In Chapter 1, it was shown that Wittgenstein forcefully rejected Spengler's doctrine of the historical inevitability of cultural decline. He and Drury agreed that Spengler was wrong to try to put historical facts "into a mould". Most important, Wittgenstein rejected Spengler's doctrine of historical inevitability as a conceptual confusion – one that conflated his "prototype", his blueprint for cultural development and decline, and the historical facts it was meant to illuminate. He indicated to Drury that Spengler, presumably for this reason, cannot be "trusted with details". Given all this – especially Wittgenstein's explicit rejection of Spengler's doctrine of historical necessity – Wittgenstein certainly did not accept Spengler's conviction that civilized times are, *as a matter of historical necessity*, irreligious times. If Wittgenstein believed that the time for religion had passed, it was not because he had fully embraced Spengler's view – because he plainly did not embrace it. The question of whether Wittgenstein believed that religion was possible in his time must, then, be answered on independent grounds.

I think it is more likely that Wittgenstein regarded religion in his time as an endangered, but not extinct form of life. He surely felt that the character of his time added greatly to the already formidable obstacles to living religiously – a point emphasized in the previous two chapters. Against this, it must be noted that he often encouraged those of his friends, like Drury, Malcolm, Engelmann, and Bouwsma, who were believers. He discussed with all of them the character and requirements of a religious life. One ought not to forget that Wittgenstein was able to hope that his civilization might produce a culture and some form of religion, however austere and ascetic, that might suit the needs of those living in his time of decline. Such hopes show that he did not share Spengler's necessitarian cultural pessimism. Finally, and, I think, most significant, even in those dramatic passages from *Culture and Value* cited by Clack in which Wittgenstein ponders the forces that prevented him from adopting the Christian faith, he writes only of *conditions within himself*. He never so much as mentions cultural impediments in this regard. In respectful opposition to Clack, I would offer this: If Wittgenstein *had* determined to embrace religion in any form, then the irreligiousness of his time, far from weakening his resolve, would, more likely, have strengthened it. This is a man who was capable of saying of himself, "I manufacture my own atmosphere."[21] It is worth noting too that Drury describes this exchange with Wittgenstein:

> DRURY: "I think I could be happy working as a priest among people whom I felt shared the same beliefs as I have."
>
> WITTGENSTEIN: "Oh, don't depend on circumstances. Make sure that your religion is a matter between you and God only."[22]

The attitude expressed by Wittgenstein here is hardly that of a man who felt that a collapse of religion around him would be a good reason to give up religion. On the contrary, he seems to be saying that a genuinely religious attitude *need not and should not* depend "on externals", and, so, could be maintained even in an irreligious setting. This conversation took place in 1930, when Wittgenstein took Spenglerian concerns most seriously. As such, I believe it likely that Wittgenstein's admonishment to Drury was motivated in part by his recognition that Drury, whom he regarded as singularly serious and honest about religion, might not find many similarly serious persons with whom to practice – a circumstance which, I have shown, he saw as characteristic of "the darkness of this time". Seen in this way, Wittgenstein's remarks were an admonishment to Drury – a warning that if one aspires to live religiously, one had better be prepared to go it alone. Such an admonishment connects interestingly

---

21   Ibid., p. 136.
22   Ibid., p. 117.

with Wittgenstein's suggestions (also made to Drury and discussed at some length in the previous subsection) about a future religion without priests and ministers.

Far more damaging to Clack's case, however, it can be seriously questioned whether even Spengler himself believed that Western civilization had declined to the point where religion must, of necessity, give way to an "apocalyptic atheism". We have seen that Wittgenstein, in rejecting Spengler's view of historical necessity, states that Spengler confuses "prototype" with "object" – that is, he does not clearly enough distinguish his archetype for cultural development and decline, a conceptual construct, from the facts of cultural history it is meant to illuminate. Here is the passage in which Wittgenstein characterizes the mistake he ascribes to Spengler:

> ... willy-nilly we shall ascribe the properties of the prototype to the object we are viewing in its light; and claim "*it must always be ...*" This is because we want to give the prototype's characteristics a purchase on our way of representing things. But since we confuse prototype and object we find ourselves dogmatically conferring on the object properties which only the prototype necessarily possesses.[23]

I suspect that Clack has made this very mistake in concluding that Spengler believed that religion, in his own time, was an impossibility. Let us reexamine the quote from Spengler that Clack cites:

> The megalopolitan is irreligious, this is part of his being, a mark of his historical position. Bitterly as he may feel the inner emptiness and poverty, earnestly as he may long to be religious, it is out of his power to be so. All religiousness in the Megalopolis rests upon self-deception.

It is crucial to recognize that Spengler in this passage is not writing specifically about the Western civilization in which he stood. The quotation is meant to describe *an important feature of the final stage of any civilization that has undergone full decline from a living culture*. In this passage, Spengler is writing about his *prototype* – his own conception of the natural endpoint of any civilization. He is not writing specifically about his own civilization. Clack ought not to conclude that Spengler, in writing this passage, meant it as a description also of his own time in the absence of clear evidence that he also believed that his own time was one of *final decline*. In fact, it will be shown that Spengler most certainly did not see his time in such terms.

We need to ask: did *Spengler himself* believe that Western civilization had reached its final stage and, with it, a state of complete irreligiousness? His bombastic prose and small inconsistencies notwithstanding, it remains clear enough that Spengler thought that Western culture was only in the beginning stages of its decline into civilization. He does not address this subject in a unified manner – rather, one must sort through observations made throughout his *Decline of the West*. Those remarks collectively express a sense that the West is entering, or has entered, the *early stage* of a decline that would not culminate into a final decline for centuries. With respect to religion, his remarks, for the most part, suggest that Western religion has begun

---

23 Ludwig Wittgenstein, *Culture and Value*, p. 14e.

to decline, but, again, that the decline is not yet complete. As we shall see, in one interesting passage, he allows that, while features of a generalized religious decline could be observed in the Europe of his day, pockets of living religion still exist even there. His view appears close to the one I have attributed to Wittgenstein: religion in the civilization of the twentieth-century West is endangered, but not extinct. Let us focus on some of Spengler's clearer and more detailed expressions on these subjects.

Certainly, those of Spengler's characterizations of Western culture being in its *early* winter (and sometimes, inconsistently, in its late autumn) that we have already considered generally suggest the beginning, not the endpoint, of the decline of the West. I referred, in Chapter 1, to the appendices in Spengler's *Decline* in which he summarizes his historical overview in graphic fold-out sheets. These outline the supposed prototypical sequences of cultural development in a column and, in parallel columns, outline the developmental sequences of actual cultures as they run through the prototypical sequences. The resulting graphic purports to show how world cultures have actually developed along the lines of the Spenglerian prototype. Thus, the stages of the development, ripening, and decline of Western culture may be seen to be in accord with the prototype and also compared to analogous stages of different cultures of the past.

Significantly, here, as well as in the body of *Decline*, Spengler indicates specifically that the civilization of any culture, according to his prototype, may be divided into three stages. In the appendix he describes three distinct stages through which a civilization runs: 1) a "transformational" stage; 2) an "end of form-development" stage; 3) a final, "fixed form" stage.[24] The specific details here need not, for our purposes, concern us. What is important is that Spengler's appendix shows Western civilization to be only in the first of the three stages of its civilization. It indicates that certain Western trends, most notably, impressionism in art, the music of Liszt and Wagner, and American architecture, are indications that this first stage has begun. In contrast, the appendix clearly indicates Spengler's view that *the second and third stages of Western civilization have not yet begun*. Instead, it indicates only that the second stage will commence "[f]rom 2000" and, so, that the third lies even further in the future. Spengler's appendix further reveals that past civilizations have taken roughly three hundred years from the onset of civilization to the endpoint of complete decline. Given his explicit claims that some features of stage 1) are observable in the late nineteenth and early twentieth centuries and also that the full development of a civilization takes three hundred years, it can be concluded that Spengler did not believe that the final phase of Western civilization was remotely near. He envisioned just the second of its three phases to be a century away, and its third phase, it seems, he anticipated in the late twenty-second or early twenty-third century.

Elsewhere in *Decline* there is corroboration for this estimate. In comparing the decline of Classical culture with that of the West he states:

---

24   Oswald Spengler, *The Decline of the West* (New York, 1965), vol. II, appendix immediately following p. 428.

... the finality that awaits every living culture – is the purport of all the historic "declines", amongst them that decline of the Classical which we know so well and fully, and another decline, entirely comparable to it in course and duration, which will occupy the first centuries of the coming millennium but is heralded already and sensible in and around us to-day – the Decline of the West.[25]

Again, we see a clear indication that the decline of the West, for Spengler, has only begun, that its fuller development lies in the next millennium and will take centuries to play itself out. Spengler's appendices indicate clearly that the Classical decline, as well of those of the Egyptian, Indian, and Arabian cultures, occupied roughly three centuries. Fully convinced that his "morphological" analysis of history was correct, he expected the civilization of the West to decline over a similar period. Such confidence may appear bold or misplaced, but there is no doubt that Spengler had every confidence both that he had uncovered the natural scheme for the development and decline of all cultures and that they, as a matter of historical necessity, took place in set sequences each of which occupied nearly exactly similar time frames. His statement of this confidence is expressed with a flourish and, for emphasis, printed in his own italics:

Every Culture, every adolescence and maturing and decay of a culture, every one of its intrinsically necessary stages and periods, has a definite duration, always the same, always recurring...[26]

There seems little doubt that Spengler fully expected the worst of the decline of the West to take place in the twenty-first and subsequent centuries. Western decline was only beginning.

Further corroboration that Spengler did not believe that the West was well into its decline may be observed in a fascinating passage in which he discusses the work of the playwrights, Henrik Ibsen and George Bernard Shaw. He sees in Ibsen and Shaw, a kind of proto-feminism that devalues traditional women's roles and, in Spengler's view, presages the attitudes of a new megalopolitan woman and of a time that makes a "case against children". The details of his literary analysis of Ibsen and Shaw here are not what are most significant. What is significant is a full-blown claim about what these beginnings foreshadow – a tendency, he claims, of every civilization:

...all Civilizations enter upon a stage, which lasts for centuries, of appalling depopulation. The whole pyramid of Cultural man vanishes. It crumbles from the summit.[27]

Such an "appalling depopulation", Spengler states, is the destiny of every civilization and will, in time, be upon the West. Surely, however, Spengler knew that his time, far from being one of depopulation, was still one of population growth, even within Western civilization. The depopulation, of which he felt certain, would occur in the future. Once it occurred, it would last for centuries. Such a time would be characteristic of a civilization that is into its full decline. So, once again, we see

---

25 Ibid., vol. I, pp. 106–7.
26 Oswald Spengler, *Decline of the West*, vol. I, pp. 109–10.
27 Ibid., vol. I, p. 105.

a strong indication of Spengler's sense that the worst of Western decline, while foreshadowed by his own time, would take place in centuries yet to come.

There is another clear indication that, for Spengler, the West is not far along its inevitable path to decline. It is especially noteworthy because it explicitly addresses the subject of religious decline in the West. He states that in the early stages of any civilization there are still traces of the religion of the culture that spawned that civilization, but that what passes for religion in an early civilization has little connection with the true religions of its cultural past. His clear indication is that the civilization of the West is in such a phase.

> We have in the European-American world of to-day the occultist and theosophist fraud, the American Christian Science, the untrue Buddhism of drawing-rooms, the religious arts-and-crafts business (brisker in Germany than even England) that caters for groups and cults …

> Everywhere it is just a toying with myths that no one really believes, a tasting of cults that it is hoped might fill the inner void. The real belief is always in atoms and numbers, but it requires this highbrow hocus-pocus to make it bearable in the long run. Materialism is shallow and honest, mock-religion shallow and dishonest.[28]

As damning as this passage reads, it is elsewhere moderated with descriptions of ongoing and more authentic forms of religion:

> To this day in southern France, southern Italy, and northern Spain tangible relics of it endure. In these countries the popular Catholicism is tinged from beneath with the late Classical coloring, that sets it off quite distinctly from the Church of Catholicism of the West-European layer above it. South Italian Church-festivals disclose Classical (and even pre-Classical) cults, and generally in this field there are to be found deities (saints) in whose worship the Classical constitution is visible behind the Catholic names.[29]

It seems, for Spengler, pockets of religion that retain features of the genuine religion of a high culture still exist in European civilization. These remarks, taken collectively, certainly bode ill for the future of religion in the West but do not evidence a strong belief that anything like the complete decline of religion he predicted was yet upon the civilization of his time.

There is more explicit material in Spengler that supports the assessment that the decline of the West is only in its beginning stages. The passages above strongly suggest that true religion is on the wane. Spengler, however, sees the downfall of religion to involve phases and processes that, he explicitly states, the West has not even begun.

Most notable, Spengler claims that, as the authentic religion of a culture begins to disappear and lose its hold on the individuals of a civilized time, every civilization goes through a period he refers to as its "second religiousness". He mentions this "second religiousness" a number of times. Interestingly, one of his most vivid descriptions of this "second religiousness" occurs in a paragraph immediately succeeding the one cited above in which he described some of the preliminary signs

---

28 Ibid., vol. II, p. 310.
29 Ibid., vol. I, p. 110.

of religious decline in his own time of early civilization. In the former he mentions "theosophist fraud", "the American Christian Science", and "the untrue Buddhism of drawing rooms". In the latter, he mentions what appears to be a more significant feature of every civilization, one that he thinks will constitute the next phase of religious decline in the civilization of the West:

> This next phase I call the Second Religiousness. It appears in all civilizations as soon as they have fully formed themselves as such and are beginning to pass slowly and imperceptively ... (So far as Western Civilization is concerned, therefore, we are still many generations short of that point.) ... The material of the Second Religiousness is simply that of the first, genuine young religiousness – only otherwise experienced and expressed. It starts with Rationalism's fading out in helplessness, then the forms of the Springtime become visible, and finally the whole world of primitive religion, which had receded..., returns to the foreground, powerful, in the guise of the popular syncretism that is to be found in every culture at this phase.[30]

There is much in here that is not self-explanatory, but some important features stand out. First, Spengler is explicit both that a civilization's "Second Religiousness" is reached when a civilization becomes "fully formed" and that this point, for the West, lies "still many generations" into the future. Thus, we have more strong and explicit evidence that Spengler saw the civilized decline of the West as a phenomenon that was only beginning in his time and that would not finalize until a considerable time had passed. Second, he does not think that anything like a Second Religiousness is yet visible in the West, because the West has not nearly reached such a point in its civilization:

> The Second Religiousness is the necessary counterpart of Caesarism, which is the final political constitution of Late Civilizations; it becomes visible, therefore, in the Augustan Age of the Classical and about the time of Shi-hwang-ti's time in China. In both phenomena the creative young strength of the early Culture is lacking.[31]

Spengler, as noted in Chapter 1, often states that the West has not yet seen its analogue to Caesar, that this lies well into the future and so, it follows, the period he describes also lies well into the future.

What is equally interesting in connection with the notion of a "second religiousness" is that Spengler appears to anticipate something of a religious awakening before the endpoint of any civilization – including that of the West. Admittedly, he sees this renewed focus on religion to lack the vibrancy, authenticity, and spontaneity of religion in times of high culture. These are serious caveats. Still, the passages we have examined collectively suggest a very different attitude toward the fate of religion in the West than that attributed to Spengler by Clack. It is certainly not one in which religion is extinct. It is one in which religion is on the wane, but with pockets of genuine religiousness still evident. It is not one in which religion will never again appear, but rather, one in which a final religious phase, albeit lacking the power of religion in a time of culture, but linked to it, still lies in the future.

---

30 Ibid., vol. II, pp. 310–11.
31 Ibid., p. 310.

In summary, even if one grants Clack's dubious assumption that Wittgenstein came to accept Spengler's necessitarian view of both cultural decline and religious decline, one should, nonetheless, resist Clack's final conclusion. We have seen that *Spengler himself* did not accept the overly simplified "Spenglerian" position that Clack attributes to Wittgenstein!

iv. Did Wittgenstein Accept Spengler's Ideal of Religion?

There is an important and noteworthy way in which Wittgenstein's conception of religion differed from Spengler's. As we have seen, Spengler specifically stated that there were locations in the West in which religion was still practiced during his time, and practiced in ways that retained important connections to its origins in previous times of high culture. Spengler, however, specifically cites as signs that religion is still alive in these areas the focus on what Wittgenstein certainly thought of as the "mythological" aspects of religion. These include a still living belief in the myths of cults, in icons, the worship of saints to whom festivals are offered in the hope that they might intercede benevolently in the world, and, in general a focus on those "holy things" with which Wittgenstein warned Drury not to become "too familiar".[32] It is apparent that Spengler regarded a robust religion as being, at its core, connected to things of this sort, especially mythological constructs. It is clear too, that he thought that the rise of science and technology in civilized times plays an important role in undermining religion. On his view, when people come to believe "in atoms and numbers", when the accepted paradigm for knowledge becomes the scientific method which, he thinks, leads to a shallow materialism, then the mythologies of cultish religion will inevitably be undercut and religious belief will wither away. The evident presupposition in all this is that scientific truth and the core of what a religion regards as truth will inevitably conflict.

I have argued that Wittgenstein never held this view. Certainly his conception of religious language and of religion itself underwent significant changes. Still, in both his early and later periods it is clear enough that he believed that, whatever religious language may or may not express, it does not at bottom function descriptively or empirically. What remains constant through the significant changes in his views on the subject is the conviction that religious language asserts no facts with which the discoveries of science can conflict. We have seen that this is clearly true of Wittgenstein's later view. It held that it is only a false literalistic interpretation of religious language, a misleading preoccupation with surface grammar, which suggests any such thing. So, Wittgenstein never believed that religious discourse, on a proper understanding of its primary function, states anything that *could possibly* conflict with science. Although Wittgenstein concurred with Spengler that religion was in decline during their time, their agreement was in an important way, superficial and masked a deeper underlying disagreement about the nature of religion. For Spengler, the decline of a religion manifests itself in the rejection of its cult mythology in favor of scientific truth which comes to supersede it. For Wittgenstein, mythologies are only accompaniments to an attitude of genuine religious faith, which he insists on

---

32   M. O'C. Drury, "Conversations with Wittgenstein", p. 136.

a number of occasions, can exist without them. As we saw in the previous chapter, he even suggests that an attitude of genuine faith might *better* exist without them. We would do well to revisit Drury's account of a conversation in which Wittgenstein recounted to him a morbid fear from which he had previously suffered. Significantly, according to Drury, this conversation took place in 1929 or 1930, when Wittgenstein was in the initial stages of his fascination with Spengler:

> [W]hen he was a student at Manchester he suffered at times from morbid fears. To get from his bedroom to his sitting room he had to cross over a landing, and sometimes he found himself dreading making the crossing. ...[S]uddenly he stopped still and looked at me very seriously.
>
> WITTGENSTEIN: "You will think I have gone mad, when I tell you that only religious feelings are a cure for such fears."
>
> I replied that I didn't think he was crazy at all; that coming from Ireland I knew something about the power of religion. He seemed displeased with this answer as if I hadn't understood him.
>
> WITTGENSTEIN: "I am not talking about superstition but about real religious feeling."
>
> After this we walked on in silence for some time.[33]

Wittgenstein's conception of the decline of religion is the decline of a certain attitude toward life, an attitude of faith. This is reflected not in a belief in the literal truth of religious myths, or that saints intervene in the world, or that holy icons have special causal properties, but rather in an uncompromised moral lifestance that the great religious figures of the past embraced and were capable of imparting to others. It is this moral attitude that, he thought, is barely observable in the civilized world. Religion declines for Wittgenstein not because a literal belief in its mythology disappears, but because a shared moral perspective, a commitment to a restrained, strongly moral way of life disappears. Indeed, Wittgenstein would very likely have taken no satisfaction in the practices Spengler cited as evidence of a still living religion in the south of France, Italy, and the north of Spain. More likely he would have viewed them as evidence that an inessential part of a once living religion had survived into his time, leaving open the question of whether the more essential underlying attitude of faith had survived along with it.

v. Why the Term "Atheist"?

Finally, I want to express not so much a criticism as a sense of puzzlement as to why Clack, in characterizing Wittgenstein's final attitude toward religion, used the term "atheist". The characterization is provocative and bold, but I think, all things considered, the term is misleading and does not do justice to Clack's interesting final conclusion. Clack would have done better to avoid it. I can understand and, to some extent, even sympathize with his employment of the term; but, in the end, I want to combat his characterization. Clack's view of Wittgenstein as an "atheist"

---

33 Ibid., pp. 115–16.

is motivated, in large measure, by the importance he places on the influence of Spengler's cultural and religious pessimism on Wittgenstein. I have already raised and supported three sorts of objections to this. First, Clack overestimates Spengler's influence on Wittgenstein, ignoring a number of sharp criticisms of some of Spengler's central claims made by Wittgenstein. Second, Clack tends to confuse the true claim that Spengler believed that cultures, *prototypically* decline into profoundly irreligious civilizations with the very different and demonstrably false claim that Spengler believed that Western civilization had reached such a stage and become profoundly irreligious. Finally, I have argued that, far from making the latter claim, Spengler believed that the West had not yet reached, and would not for centuries reach, its own final descent into complete irreligiousness. So, there is ample reason to doubt Clack's claims. In this section, I want to put all of that aside and ask whether – even if Clack were right in holding that Spengler and Wittgenstein both believed that the West had already reached its irreligious endpoint – his characterization of Wittgenstein as an atheist would be appropriate.

What is an atheist? Traditionally in the philosophy of theology atheism is an epistemic attitude with respect to the proposition, "God exists". Theists accept the proposition as true; atheists reject it as false; agnostics withhold judgment. So, traditionally, atheism would be a view held by anyone who rejects as false the proposition, "God exists".

It is notable that the Wittgenstein of the *Tractatus* was neither a theist nor an atheist in this sense. This is so on something of a technicality, but, still, it will prove helpful to examine the reasons for saying so. First, it cannot be said that Wittgenstein accepted as true or rejected as false the proposition, "God exists", or even that he withheld judgment as to its truth or falsity. Rather, in the *Tractatus*, Wittgenstein holds that the purported proposition is a pseudo-proposition that lacks sense. It is neither true nor false. So, the early Wittgenstein, as such, cannot be said to be an atheist in the traditional sense. The later Wittgenstein, holding as he did that religious belief was a passionate commitment to a way of life and rejecting any notion that religious belief is primarily an epistemic stance, would similarly not qualify as an atheist in the traditional sense. Unlike the early view that held that "God exists" and most other theological propositions are senseless, the later view took traditional philosophy of religion to be predicated on a radical misreading of such propositions – one overly influenced by the deceptive surface grammar of such language and lacking in a perspicuous view of its underlying function. What the two views share is hostility to the traditional way of thinking of theism, atheism, and agnosticism as epistemic attitudes toward a proposition, "God exists", which purportedly states a metaphysical truth. Even the late Wittgenstein was no atheist in the traditional theological sense of that word because he would reject the presuppositions upon which traditional theology rested.

But, surely more must be said. I do not merely want to deny that Wittgenstein was an atheist on a technicality. Interestingly, it could equally be said about the logical positivists of the Vienna Circle that they were not, in the above sense, atheists. They too held that theological propositions were meaningless and, so, would not reject "God exists" as false. The Positivists, however, might be thought to have been atheists – at least in an acceptable, extended sense of the word. For the

Positivists did not merely reject religious discourse as meaningless, *they rejected religion*. They thought of religious belief as confused and nonsensical. Religion, in effect, has nothing to offer the human species. As we have seen in Chapter 3, their unofficial leader, Moritz Schlick, thought of religion as a kind of childhood phase in the intellectual development of humankind, a phase that will wither and become obsolete as scientific ways of knowing become the accepted paradigm. To this extent, one can say that Schlick's attitude and that of most of his fellow Positivists was atheistic. It is highly significant that the early Wittgenstein could not be said to be an atheist even in this extended sense. Indeed, in conversations with Schlick, Wittgenstein continued to emphasize, as he had in the *Tractatus* and the "Lecture", that religion is not on the same plane as science because is not concerned with facts, and so, is not in any way in competition with science.[34] In those conversations he held, as he indicated in "Lecture", that religious language, while senseless, "points to something" very important. For Clack, of course, the later Wittgenstein's position differed significantly. For Clack, the later Wittgenstein still admired religious ways of living, regretted the passing of religion as an irreligious civilization emerged, but, nonetheless, reluctantly came to believe that the time in which religious living was possible lay in the past. Even granting this (which, it should be clear by now, I do not), I doubt that it is helpful to characterize someone with such a view as an "atheist", however qualified the use of that term. That term, suggesting, as it does, a personal rejection of religion, does not seem to fit the case, even as described by Clack. I believe that Clack's use of the term carries too many in the way of pre-existing contrary connotations to serve effectively as a label for the interesting view he attributes to Wittgenstein. Clack, without intending to, summarizes a cluster of excellent reasons for not applying the term "atheist" to Wittgenstein in an explanation of what he did not mean by the term:

> This is not an atheism based on denying the existence of super-empirical realities…, nor is it the rebellious atheism of an Ivan Karamazov, nor yet the positivistic atheism of denying sense to religious propositions.[35]

This quotation contains an exhaustive enumeration of the ways in which most people who understand the concept think of atheism! What other conception remains? Clack speaks of an "intuition that religion is not possible in this time, which gives [Wittgenstein's] account a distinctly atheistic character."[36] But, *is this* atheistic? Let us consider an analogical situation. Suppose someone who accepts the principles of socialism, who in the past had sought to establish a socialist society through political action, and who believes that an ideal society would be guided by socialist principles, comes to believe also that socialism is no longer possible. Perhaps this individual comes to believe that a capitalist based economy has taken hold irrevocably in the world. Is that person, *ipso facto*, no longer a socialist? Is that person an anti-socialist? I think that an honest response to these questions would recognize that a simple "yes" or "no" answer would be misleading. Suppose one were to insist, in

---

34 Friedrich Waismann, *Wittgenstein and the Vienna Circle* (Oxford, 1979), pp. 115–17.
35 Brian R. Clack, *An Introduction to Wittgenstein's Philosophy of Religion*, p. 129.
36 Ibid.

parallel with Clack, that such a person's intuitions have "a distinctly anti-socialist character", explaining:

> This is not an anti-socialism based on denying socialist principles, nor the rebellious anti-socialism of an Ayn Rand, nor yet the positivistic rejection of socialism that depends on denying literal sense to propositions that purport to express social values.

This, however, would have something of a hollow ring. It would insist on applying the term "anti-socialist" to an individual who is so far from being paradigmatically "anti-socialist" that such an insistence would seem misleading and arbitrary. For parallel reasons, I think that it is, at best, unclear whether Clack's Wittgenstein – even granting Clack much that I most emphatically do not grant – should be called an atheist. It is a very strange sense of "atheism" that conflicts with all the straightforward ones that Clack enumerates in the above quote. Such an employment, I want to say, threatens to stretch the commonly accepted use of the term "atheism" beyond the point of recognition. On balance, I believe Clack would have done far better to clearly and completely describe Wittgenstein's view as he saw it and let it go at that. The term "atheist" is one whose use generally suggests a wholesale rejection of religion, a sense that religious attitudes are false, unsupportable, muddled, or nonsensical – none of which can be said even of Clack's Wittgenstein. It is noteworthy that Clack qualifies his attribution of atheism to Wittgenstein with such terms as "reluctant" and "apocalyptic" – but these qualifications do not remove the difficulty. What is gained by characterizing a man who is still capable of saying "I cannot help seeing every problem from a religious point of view", and still very much impressed with "the passionate beauty of the religious life" (Clack's own words), an atheist?

There are, I think, other motives that led Clack to characterize Wittgenstein as an atheist for which I have some sympathy. Clack devotes a chapter of his book to the work of a number of authors who have collectively tended to defend a cluster of views on religion that, for better or worse, have been referred to as "Wittgensteinian Fideism". This view rests on a quite viable reading of Wittgenstein's later thoughts on religion. The chief progenitor of this view, and the one whose views Clack focuses on, is D. Z. Phillips. Phillips has articulated roughly the views that Clack and I have ascribed to Wittgenstein and has painstakingly attempted to develop them into a coherent, if unconventional, philosophy of religion. According to Clack, Phillips attributes to Wittgenstein and accepts all of the following:

1) Religious discourse is primarily exhortational, not descriptive of ultimate realities.
2) "God" does not refer to an entity.
3) The religious belief in immortality, properly understood, is not the belief that a non-physical self survives biological death.
4) Prayer – properly exercised, properly understood, and stripped of superstition – is not a request to God that one's deepest desires be granted and has no causal efficacy.
5) Religious belief does not conflict with scientific belief.

6) Belief in God is not a belief that some remarkable or supernatural being exists, but rather, a passionate commitment to a certain sort of self-disciplined and demanding moral point of view.

7) The ways in which one criticizes factual or theoretical beliefs cannot normally be used to criticize religious belief.

8) The ways in which one proves or justifies factual or theoretical beliefs cannot and need not be used to justify religious belief.[37]

I think that Clack's characterization of Phillips' interpretation of Wittgenstein's view is, for the most part, accurate.[38] Beyond this, it should be clear, given what I have written in the preceding two chapters, that I think that his version of Phillips' interpretation of Wittgenstein is, in most of its particulars, correct as an expression of Wittgenstein's thoughts. Something about this view does not sit well with Clack. He thinks that Phillips' view, and the view commonly understood as "Wittgensteinian Fideism", have a number of highly interesting and controversial consequences. Such a view sees much of traditional philosophy of religion as pointless. First, reasoned attempts to prove the existence of God (or to infer God's "attributes") and understanding "God" to refer to a maximally perfect being, involve a deep mistake. The traditional attempts to prove God's existence, so understood, presuppose a wrong view of what it is to believe in God. As such, they are misdirected. They are a product of a misunderstanding of the grammar of religious language. Beyond this, it would follow too that traditional attempts to discredit the belief in God are also misdirected, since they presuppose a mistaken view of what it is to believe in God. Finally, since religious belief, on such a view, is not at bottom a factual belief, or a set of factual beliefs, but rather a deep commitment to a certain lifestance, it would appear that no possible scientific discovery could conflict with religious belief. A believer, convinced of such a "fideistic" stance, might understandably conclude that none of the criticisms of religious belief offered in traditional philosophy of religion constitutes anything like a reason to abandon his or her religious way of life. "Wittgensteinian Fideism" offers nearly complete protection for religious belief from the criticisms encountered in standard works in the philosophy of religion.

Clack finds this unconvincing. For one thing, he sees nothing like a determinate philosophy of religion, even a radical one, in the later Wittgenstein's scattered remarks on religion and religious language. Before even discussing Phillips and other "Wittgensteinian Fideists", he offers a preliminary caution:

---

37   Ibid. Chapter 4 elaborates upon each of the numbered propositions.

38   Of course, any such attempt to reduce the thoughts of a philosopher to a few numbered propositions carries with it the risk of oversimplification and distortion. Phillips' contributions on these problems span many decades and have evolved. The following, for me, are especially helpful and clear: D. Z. Phillips, *Religion and Friendly Fire: Examining Assumptions in Contemporary Philosophy of Religion* (Aldershot, 2004); D. Z. Phillips (ed.), *Wittgenstein and Religion* (Basingstoke, 1994); D. Z. Phillips, *Belief, Change and Forms of Life* (Library of Philosophy and Religion) (New York, 1986); D. Z. Phillips, *Religion and Understanding* (Oxford, 1967).

Those looking for a systematic treatment of religion in the later writings of Wittgenstein will be disappointed. There is no comprehensive philosophy of religion here. What we have is rather what Iris Murdoch has fittingly called "exasperating hints" a collection of observations and reminders about the character of religious belief and its role in the lives of the faithful. ...This will not have produced a fully coherent account of religion, but we do none the less find a unifying theme... [T]he theme is that the temptation to construe religious beliefs as hypotheses, theories about metaphysical entities, the workings of the world, the ultimate destiny of history and of the individual, and so on, is fundamentally in error.[39]

There would appear to be two further problems – more important ones – for Clack. Both concern whether Wittgenstein's later remarks on religion and religious language, taken in their totality, provide the sort of protection for religious belief for which Phillips and others have contended. First, Clack is not comfortable with one of the consequences of a view that Phillips (and, for the most part, he himself) attributes to Wittgenstein about the true nature of religious belief. We have seen that Clack suggests that an acceptance of Wittgenstein's radical view of religious language might undermine, for many, religious belief. In addition, Clack himself, against Phillips, seems never to be convinced that the radical view is correct. With respect to Phillips' more elaborated and systematic position and the consequence that traditionalist views of God, prayer, miracles, and immortality are superstitions, Clack raises similar concerns in strong terms:

...if Phillips means by a superstition anything intended to influence the natural order of things then the unfortunate consequence is that practically everything which has formerly gone by the name of religion is in fact a "trust in non-existent, quasi-causal connections", for people really did fear the fires of hell, believed that miracles occurred, that prayer could be effective, and so on. One may well react harshly to the claim that all of that is superstitious.

Moreover, some may even find the concerns placed at the heart of Phillips' account of deep religion distasteful and certainly less valuable than he himself believes.[40]

Clack seems in sympathy with such distaste. With respect to Phillips' account of immortality, he says flatly that it "just does not go without saying that such sentiments are not pathological".[41] Clearly, Clack's concerns go beyond his stated observation that such a view of religion could undermine religious belief. Indeed, Clack makes it clear enough that he rejects the view itself. More important, and more to the point here, he appears worried that such a view of religion does away with what most people would see as essential to religion – so much so that reflective, conventional theists might well be tempted to brand it atheistic.

Independent of such concerns, Clack appears unconvinced that Wittgenstein himself would have wanted his views on religion to be used to legitimize religion as it was practiced in his time. Clack was well aware that Wittgenstein opposed

---

39 Brian R. Clack, *An Introduction to Wittgenstein's Philosophy of Religion*, p. 75.
40 Ibid., p. 104.
41 Ibid., p. 103.

much, if not all, of what passed for religion in his time. Something in this dissuades Clack from viewing Wittgenstein as a fideistic defender of religion – at least as it is practiced during his own time. Clack recognizes that Wittgenstein was serious about religion. He takes seriously Wittgenstein's pointed reminders about the terribly serious nature of religious belief and its requirements, how deep and pervasive a commitment they impose, how relentlessly the true believer must strive to remain true to that commitment, and how easily one can stumble into a self-deceived counterfeit of religion. Indeed, he saw the religious practices of his time as shallow and self-deceived in just such a way.

But, there is more. Beyond all this, Clack was convinced that Wittgenstein's presumed Spenglerian pessimism had persuaded him that such a commitment was no longer possible in his civilized time. Presumably, Clack was looking for a dramatic way of both expressing his strong reservations about any notion that Wittgenstein could be viewed simply as a fideist and also emphasizing what he saw as Wittgenstein's *opposition to* religion in a time during which it was no longer possible to live religiously. Evidently, he came to the conclusion that a description of Wittgenstein as a reluctant, apocalyptic atheist would serve these needs. Clack, in effect, is trying to shock those who would use Wittgenstein's later views to justify a continued engagement in the idle ceremonies, the lifeless vestiges of a once living religious spirit whose time has come and gone, into a realization of a serious error. He wants to instill a recognition that Wittgenstein would not have approved of attempts to use his work to support the pervasive counterfeit of genuine religion he saw all around him. In this, at least, I think, Clack is right, and I commend his intention, if not the details of his execution.

In the previous chapter, I emphasized that one must make an important distinction in coming to grips with Wittgenstein's later view of religion. The work on the grammar of religious language, the source of the fideistic interpretation, was meant to describe religious language when it is functioning properly. In contrast, Wittgenstein did not believe that religious language often functioned properly during his time. What he was describing in his work on religious language was an idealization – an account of how religious language functions during a time of culture, when the background against which such expressions get their meaning is in place. Against this, his pessimistic Spenglerian remarks question whether his dedicating the *Remarks* "to the glory of God", or other sincere expressions of religious sentiments, can even be understood "in these times". They question the legitimacy of what passed for religion in his time, and, more specifically, as an attempt to explain why religious language may no longer, or at least not often, function in what he took to be its proper manner. They suggest that, in various ways, the background against which religious expression derives its meaning has all but disappeared in "the darkness of this time". I am convinced that this is the only way to reconcile two apparently contrary tendencies of thought, both of which can be gleaned from Wittgenstein's later remarks on religion. One can discern a clear distinction between 1) his grammatical analysis of religious expression when it functions properly and 2) his Spenglerian cautions that religious expression was being undermined by the civilized tendencies of his time. An appreciation of this distinction provides the best perspective from which to see that Wittgenstein was not an eager proponent of religion in his time. If this is correct, an understanding of Wittgenstein's Spenglerian pessimism about the future of religion offers one key to a fuller understanding of Wittgenstein's late thoughts about religion. It places Phillips' interpretation in a more perspicuous context. Rather than brand Wittgenstein as an atheist, Clack might have done better to accept Phillips' interpretation of Wittgenstein's later remarks about religion – but with an important caveat. It is far from clear that Wittgenstein – who, after all, shared many of Spengler's doubts about religion in his time – would have wanted to see his view of religion and religious language used to serve as a defense for most of what passed for religion in his time.

If this is so, it is significant. It shows that there is one significant area in which an appreciation of the cultural point of view of Wittgenstein's later thought does lead to a deeper understanding of the content of his thought. Indeed, if I am right, such an appreciation is indispensable to a perspicuous understanding of his thoughts on religion and the grammar of religious language.

Afterword

In the preface of this book, I characterize what is to follow as "a modest breakthrough". I am in a better position now to explain more fully this assessment. I think this work does represent a breakthrough in a number of ways. It deals with a neglected aspect of Wittgenstein's later thought and does so more completely and systematically than any prior work on Wittgenstein. I think I have shown successfully that Wittgenstein was concerned with the civilization of his time, more specifically with cultural decline. I have made a case that he sought, in his philosophical works, to address, albeit latently, what he described in the *Philosophical Investigations* as "the darkness of this time". I think that I have shown too, that Wittgenstein's cultural concerns were influenced by and, in some important respects, were similar to those expressed by Spengler in his *The Decline of the West.* Beyond this, I have shown that the shape and content of Wittgenstein's straightforwardly philosophical thoughts were almost certainly influenced by Spengler. Making these cases was essentially a scholarly effort – sorting through and identifying bits and pieces of evidence for these claims from disparate, sometimes esoteric, sources.

Following Cavell, I have sought to show how Wittgenstein's *Investigations* may be viewed as a latent "philosophy of culture" with "a Spenglerian valence". I am not fully confident that Cavell's attempt to construct and support such a view, which, for the most part, I endorse, or that my own attempt to supplement it, are successful. I do think that both are plausible, being mindful of the necessary restrictions that must apply to any such account and, at least, point in the right direction. All of this, I think, constitutes a useful contribution to Wittgenstein scholarship.

I ended Chapter 7 with an observation about Wittgenstein's later thoughts about religion and religious language. That claim was that, within this circumscribed area of Wittgenstein's later thought, an appreciation of his cultural point of view does indeed lead to a deeper understanding of the philosophy itself. This observation is important for another reason. As I have presented the material in this book, it is an exception to my overall tendency. I have not argued that, as a general principle, an understanding of Wittgenstein's cultural point of view is required in order to understand the direct content of his work. I would not know how to justify such a claim. It is for this reason that I rest content to characterize this work as a modest breakthrough.

There is what might be called an "*and also*" component in much of what I have written in the preceding chapters. I have claimed that Wittgenstein *both* seeks to show how philosophers misuse words *and also* characterizes these misuses in ways that are meant to evoke an image of cultural decline. I have claimed that the *Investigations*' well-known thought experiment involving Wittgenstein's imaginary builders seeks to illuminate *both* how the meanings of words connect importantly with their usage in a life setting *and also* uses that thought experiment to intimate a shortcoming characteristic of cultural decline. I have claimed that Wittgenstein, in the *Investigations*, seeks to *both* identify and correct the pathologies of thought that lead to philosophical confusion *and also*, in so doing, to invoke a latent religious point of view – one that he thought was antithetical to the tendencies of his time. On my understanding of how the cultural component of Wittgenstein's work stands in relation to its philosophical and grammatical component, one can master the philosophical content with little or no appreciation of the cultural intimations. So, while proud to have identified a latent cultural component of Wittgenstein's late thought, one that he deemed important, I am not prepared to claim that an understanding of that component is a requirement for understanding the explicit content of that work – the philosophical, grammatical investigations that are its centerpiece.

I may be wrong about this. In the case of Wittgenstein's remarks about the grammar of religious language, I have argued that an appreciation of his cultural viewpoint is necessary to clarify the import of those remarks. Might there be equally good arguments that such an appreciation is *generally* necessary in order to understand Wittgenstein? Wittgenstein may have thought that an appreciation of his opposition to the civilization of his time was somehow *a* requisite for a full understanding of all, or even many, of the grammatical observations he employed as palliatives to wayward philosophical tendencies. If so, I have not shown that. In any event, I see no reason to think that he did. I will conclude with this observation: were someone else to make that case convincingly, I would regard that as a *major* breakthrough in the interpretation of Wittgenstein's philosophy.

Bibliography

Bouwsma, O. K., *Wittgenstein – Conversations 1949–1951* (Indianapolis: Hackett, 1986).

Canfield, John V., *Wittgenstein, Language and World* (Amherst: University of Massachusetts Press, 1981).

Cavell, Stanley, "Declining Decline: Wittgenstein as a Philosopher of Culture", *Inquiry*, 31, 3 (September 1988): 253–64.

Cavell, Stanley, "Declining Decline", in Stephen Mulhall (ed.), *The Cavell Reader* (Oxford: Blackwell, 1996).

Cavell, Stanley, *This New Yet Unapproachable America: Lectures After Emerson After Wittgenstein* (Albuquerque, NM: Living Batch Press/University of Chicago Press, 1989).

Clack, Brian S., *An Introduction to Wittgenstein's Philosophy of Religion* (Edinburgh: University of Edinburgh Press, 1999).

DeAngelis, William James, "Ludwig Wittgenstein – A Religious Point of View?: Thoughts on Norman Malcolm's Last Philosophical Project", *Dialogue*, xxxvi (1997): 819.

DeAngelis, William James, "Wittgenstein and Spengler", *Dialogue*, xxxiii (1994): 41–61.

Drury, M. O'C., *The Danger of Words* (New York: Humanities Press, 1973).

Engelmann, Paul, *Letters from Ludwig Wittgenstein with a Memoir* (Oxford: Blackwell, 1967).

Gardiner, Patrick (ed.), *Theories of History* (London: Collier Macmillan, 1959).

Garver, Newton, *This Complicated Form of Life* (Chicago: Open Court Publishing Company, 1994).

Grayling, A. C., *Wittgenstein* (Oxford: Oxford University Press, 1988).

Haller, Rudolf, *Questions on Wittgenstein* (Lincoln: University of Nebraska Press, 1988).

Klagge, James C., "Wittgenstein in Exile" in D. Z. Phillips and Mario von der Ruhr (eds), *Religion and Wittgenstein's Legacy* (Aldershot: Ashgate, 2004).

Kripke, Saul, *Wittgenstein on Rules and Private Language: An Elementary Exposition* (reprint edition, Cambridge, MA: Harvard University Press, 2004).

Malcolm, Norman, *Ludwig Wittgenstein – A Memoir*, 2nd edn, with a biographical sketch by G. H. Von Wright and Wittgenstein's letters to Malcolm (Oxford: Oxford University Press, 1984).

Malcolm, Norman, "Language Game (2)", in Georg Henrik Von Wright (ed.), *Wittgensteinian Themes – Essays 1978–1989* (Ithaca, NY: Cornell University Press, 1985).

Malcolm, Norman, *Nothing is Hidden* (reprint edition, London: Blackwell, 1989).

Malcolm, Norman, *Wittgenstein – A Religious Point of View?* (Ithaca, NY: Cornell University Press, 1992), edited with a response from Peter Winch.

McGinn, Marie, *Routledge Philosophy Guidebook to Wittgenstein and the Philosophical Investigations* (London: Routledge, 1997).

McGuinness, Brian (ed.), *Wittgenstein in His Times* (Chicago: University of Chicago Press, 1982).

McGuinness, Brian, *Wittgenstein: A Life; Young Ludwig – 1889–1921* (Berkeley: University of California Press, 1987).

Monk, Ray, *Ludwig Wittgenstein: The Duty of Genius* (New York: Free Press, 1990).

Monk, Ray, *Reading Wittgenstein* (London: Granta Books, 2005).

Mulhall, Stephen (ed.), *The Cavell Reader* (Oxford: Blackwell, 1996).

Niele, Russell, *Wittgenstein: From Mysticism to Ordinary Language* (Albany: State University of New York Press, 1987).

Peterman, James F., *Philosophy as Therapy* (Albany: State University of New York Press, 1992).

Phillips, D. Z., *Religion and Understanding* (Oxford: Blackwell, 1967).

Phillips, D. Z., *Belief, Change and Forms of Life* (Library of Philosophy and Religion, New York: Humanities Press, 1986).

Phillips, D. Z. (ed.), *Wittgenstein and Religion* (Basingstoke: Palgrave Macmillan, 1994).

Phillips, D. Z., *Religion and Friendly Fire: Examining Assumptions in Contemporary Philosophy of Religion* (Aldershot: Ashgate, 2004a).

Phillips, D. Z., "Voices in Discussion" in D.Z Phillips and Mario von der Ruhr (eds), *Religion and Wittgenstein's Legacy* (Aldershot: Ashgate, 2004b).

Rhees, Rush (ed.), *Discussions of Wittgenstein* (London: Routledge & Kegan Paul, 1970).

Rhees, Rush (ed.), *Ludwig Wittgenstein – Personal Recollections*, (Totowa, NJ: Rowman & Littlefield, 1981).

Schilpp, Paul Arthur (ed.), *The Philosophy of Rudolf Carnap* (Library of Living Philosophers, LaSalle, IL: Open Court, 1963).

Spengler, Oswald, *The Decline of the West*, vols I and II (New York: Modern Library, 1965).

Waismann, Freidrich, "Intellectual Autobiography", in Paul Arthur Schilpp (ed.), *The Philosophy of Rudolf Carnap* (Library of Living Philosophers, LaSalle, IL: Open Court, 1963).

Waismann, Friedrich, *Wittgenstein and the Vienna Circle* (Oxford: Blackwell, 1979).

Wittgenstein, Ludwig, *Philosophical Investigations*, trans. G. E. M. Anscombe (New York: Macmillan, 1953).

Wittgenstein, Ludwig, *The Brown Book* (Oxford: Blackwell, 1958).

Wittgenstein, Ludwig, *Philosophical Remarks*, ed. R. Rhees, trans. R. Hargreaves and R. White (Oxford: Blackwell, 1964).

Wittgenstein, Ludwig, *Lectures and Conversations on Aesthetics, Psychology and Religious Belief* (Berkeley: University of California Press, 1967).

Wittgenstein, Ludwig, *Zettel*, ed. G. E. M. Anscombe and G. H. Von Wright, trans. G. E. M. Anscombe (Oxford: Blackwell, 1967).

Wittgenstein, Ludwig, *Remarks on Frazer's "Golden Bough"*, ed. Rush Rhees (Retford: Brynmill, 1979).

Wittgenstein, Ludwig, *Culture and Value*, ed. G. H. Von Wright in collaboration with Heikki Nymnan (Oxford: Blackwell, 1980).

Wittgenstein, Ludwig, *Philosophical Occasions 1912–1951*, (eds) James Klagge and Alfred Nordmann (Indianapolis and Cambridge: Hackett, 1993).

Wittgenstein, Ludwig, "A Lecture on Ethics", in James Klagge and Alfred Nordmann (eds), *Ludwig Wittgenstein Philosophical Occasions 1912 1951* (Indianapolis and Cambridge: Hackett, 1993).

Wittgenstein, Ludwig, *Tractatus Logico-Philosophicus* (London: Routledge & Kegan Paul, 2002).

Wright, Georg Henrik Von (ed.), *Wittgensteinian Themes – Essays 1978–1989* (Ithaca, NY: Cornell University Press, 1985).

Index

(Ludwig Wittgenstein is referred to as LW in
the index, except for his own main entry.)